KANJI

PICT·O·GRAPHIX

To Hyang
I'll never forget

KANJI
PICT·O·GRAPHIX

Over 1,000 Japanese Kanji and Kana Mnemonics
Michael Rowley

Stone Bridge Press
Berkeley, California

■ ACKNOWLEDGMENTS

My wife, Kang Hyang Kil, has helped me with every facet of this book for the past three years; giving insights into meaning of characters, critiquing my drawings and page designs, and constructing layouts on the computer. I dedicate this book to her for all her sacrifices and inspiration. I'd also like to thank my brother Chris Rowley for helping put the manuscript on disk, my parents for their help and encouragement, and my publisher, Peter Goodman, for his patience and skill.—M.R.

Kanji definitions are taken from *A Guide to Remembering Japanese Characters* by Kenneth G. Henshall (Tokyo, Japan, and Rutland, Vermont: Charles E. Tuttle Co., Inc., 1988) with permission of the publisher.

This book was produced on an Apple Macintosh II computer. Illustrations were drawn by hand, scanned into the computer, and redrawn using Adobe Illustrator, Streamline, and Photoshop. The pages, including the text and illustrations, were laid out in Adobe Illustrator and then imported into QuarkXPress. QuarkXPress was also used for the front- and backmatter. Macrons and underlines for the Roman characters were made with Altsys Fontographer. The kanji were set on a Toshiba Dynabook laptop computer and output on a Compugraphic phototypesetter in Tokyo, and were placed both electronically in QuarkXPress and by hand. Final output was done on a Linotronic 330.

Book design by Michael Rowley, Eye Cue Design.

Copyright © 1992 Michael Rowley.

All rights reserved.

2nd Printing January 2024

No part of this book may be reproduced in any form without written permission from the publisher.

Published by Stone Bridge Press, P.O. Box 8208, Berkeley, CA 94707.

Printed in Japan by Shinano Publishing Press, Inc.

Library of Congress Cataloging-in-Publication Data
Rowley, Michael.
  Kanji pict-o-graphix: over 1,000 Japanese kanji and kana mnemonics / Michael Rowley.
      p.   cm.
  Includes index.
  ISBN 978-0-9628137-0-2
  1. Chinese characters—Japan—Glossaries, vocabularies, etc. 2. Japanese language—Glossaries, vocabularies, etc. I. Title.
PL677.6.R69   1991
495.6'82421—dc20   91-23153
                                     CIP

Contents

INTRODUCTION 7

KANA 11

CHAPTER 1: WORLD 17
The Sun 18
The Moon 19
The Day 20
Time 22
Wind, Rain, & Clouds 24
Water 26
Wash 28
Fire 30
Ice 31
Soil 32
Metal 33
Bamboo & Grass 34
Trees 36
Timber 40
Mountains & Valleys 42
Stones 44
Cave 46

CHAPTER 2: FOOD 47
Field & Plant 48
Rice 50
Eat 52
Wine 54
Tray 55
Meat 56

CHAPTER 3: ANIMALS 57
Cow, Pig, & Sheep 58

Horse 60
Bugs 62
Snakes & Birds 63
Plumage 64
Heron 66
Dog 67
Forest Animals 68
Sea Creatures 70

CHAPTER 4: PEOPLE 71
People 72
Person 76
Populace 77
People's Burdens 78
Woman & Man 80
Marriage 82
Family 84
Self 86

CHAPTER 5: BODY 87
Body 88
Flesh & Bone 90
Skin 92
Tooth, Fang, & Claw 93
Heart 94
Love 96
Hate 97
Head, Neck, & Hair 98
Eye 100
Ear 101
Mouth 102
Hand 104
Hold 107

CONTENTS

Reach 108
Give 109
Leg 110
Stand 112

CHAPTER 6: SPIRIT **113**
Spirit 114
Pain 116
Dead Bodies 118
Past 120
Temple 122
Shrine 123
Religion 124

CHAPTER 7: POWER **125**
Money 126
Wealth 128
Master 130
King 131
Power 132
Soldier 133
(Never Budge an) Inch 134
Enclosed 136
Attack 138
Strike with a Stick 140
Bow & Arrow 142

CHAPTER 8: LEARN **143**
Learn 144
Speak 146
Read 148
The Arts 150
Measure 152
Numbers 154
Sizes 156
Colors 158
Positions 160

Oppose 162

CHAPTER 9: TOOLS **163**
Thread 164
Baskets 168
Needles 169
Cloth 170
Knife 172
Equipment 174
Brooms 175
Build 176
Ax 178

CHAPTER 10: PLACES **179**
Places 180
Village 182
Hill 183
Gate 184
Door 186
Building & Roof 188
Shelter 190

CHAPTER 11: JOURNEY **191**
Move 192
Escape 194
Boat 196
Cart 197
Road 198
Crash! 199
Stop 200
… & Start Again 201
Come 202

NOTES **203**

INDEX **207**

Introduction

How do you study the written Japanese characters known as kanji? If you are a child in a Japanese school, you write each kanji hundreds of times at your desk. After a while, by sheer persistence, it sticks in your memory. If you are not a Japanese schoolchild, you probably do what I did. You stare at each kanji and make up a story in your head that you can mentally "attach" to the kanji to help you recall its meaning when you meet it again in the future. This kind of mental memory aid is called a "mnemonic" device. In this book I provide mnemonic devices in the form of text and pictures for over 1,000 kanji, or about half of all the kanji in general use in Japanese newspapers and other printed material.

Kanji developed from pictures used by the Chinese several thousand years ago to represent the world around them. Some types of kanji have retained their pictographic forms and look very much like the objects they represent. The group of kanji called **pictographs** are stylized representations of actual physical objects:

川 *river 55*   山 *mountain 167*   門 *gate 1101*

Symbols use logical designs to indicate more abstract notions:

上 *over 942*   下 *under 943*   中 *middle 950*

Ideographs put two pictographs or symbols together to create a related idea:

日 *sun 1* + 月 *moon 14* = 明 *bright 8*

The above three types of kanji are fairly easy to remember. The group of kanji called **phono-ideographs**, however, are more challenging. These kanji combine an element that gives a clue to pronunciation with an element that hints at the "subject matter" of the kanji. Most kanji—perhaps 80%—fall into this category. The theme element, called a radical, may itself be a stand-alone kanji or some graphic variant of one. TREE 126, for example, is a character by itself. Used as a radical it usually indicates something made of wood or relating to trees:

木 *tree 126*   柳 *willow 128*   材 *timber 152*

The right-hand elements here give a clue to pronunciation. The problem is that they may have little or nothing to do with the character's meaning. This makes creating a mnemonic for them much more difficult. But even pictographic forms have often been simplified and stylized over the centuries. The kanji STOP 1205, for instance, has changed greatly from its original depiction of a footprint:

■ HOW TO USE THIS BOOK

The organization of this book differs from that used in most kanji-learning books for Westerners, where characters appear in order of frequency or in the order used in Japanese schools. Since the whole point of mnemonics is to create associations, I have grouped my kanji thematically with their cousins and near cousins in sound, meaning, or appearance. There is no formal pedagogical basis for my organization. My goal was simply to discover graphic and mnemonic affinities, thus bringing kanji together that are normally very distant from each other in dictionaries as well as people's minds.

My kanji selections do include several that are not on the list of kanji approved for general use by the Japanese Ministry of Education. They are here because they were visually interesting to me. By the same token, several common kanji have been excluded because frankly I couldn't come up with a satisfactory visual or textual mnemonic. For a comprehensive, graduated course in kanji, see Kenneth G. Henshall's very fine book, *A Guide to Remembering Japanese Characters* (Charles E. Tuttle, 1988). I have relied heavily on Henshall's book, which was especially useful for its kanji definitions and its descriptions of kanji elements and origins. For simplicity and economy of space, I have occasionally made modifications to Mr. Henshall's listings.

You may find it easier to learn the complex kanji if you begin with the stand-alone characters and the other elements used as radicals. Many of these basic kanji and kanji elements are presented here alongside the large-format illustrations. Flip through the book and concentrate on these characters first.

The smaller entries on each two-page spread often incorporate the basic elements presented in the large-format illustrations. A few character entries appear without an illustration. Illustrations of the elements that appear in these characters can be found using the schematics and cross-reference numbers at the bottom of each entry.

INTRODUCTION

■ GUIDE TO THE ENTRIES

The standard kanji entries in this book include the following information:

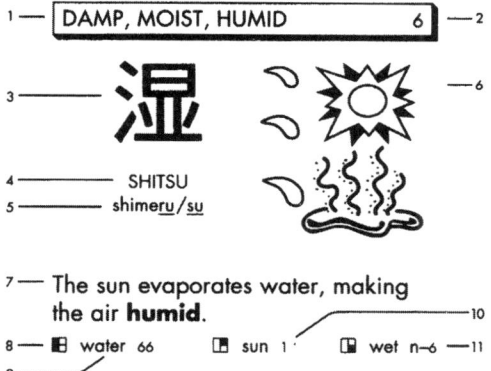

1. **Meaning in English.** For the most part the kanji definitions are drawn from Henshall's book. Definitions that treat the whole kanji as a semantic form are somewhat misleading and imprecise, however. The meaning of any kanji is best gleaned from the many words it is used to represent. When the entry kanji is used in Japanese only as an element within other kanji, the definition is enclosed in quotation marks.

2. **Reference number.** A sequence number used in the index and in kanji cross-references.

3. **Kanji character.** A plain typeset form was selected for each entry character to make the association with the visual mnemonic more clear. This form is commonly encountered in printed materials. (Kanji written by hand sometimes look very different from their typographic forms.)

4. ***On* (borrowed Chinese) reading.** Always in upper case. These pronunciations (*on-yomi*) derive from those used in China when the kanji was first brought to Japan. The Japanese adapted the Chinese sounds to their own speech. The same character may have been imported several times each time with a different reading, thus producing the multiple readings in use today.

5. ***Kun* (Japanese) reading.** Always in lower case. These pronunciations (*kun-yomi*) represent native Japanese words "fitted" to the imported kanji. Most Japanese verbs and adjectives are *kun* readings. Underlined letters represent verbal or adjectival inflections that are not a part of the kanji's actual reading.

6. **Visual mnemonic.** I have taken many liberties in creating the pictures that go with the kanji. Sometimes I have tried to preserve the historical etymology of the character; elsewhere I have abandoned it in favor of something that, to my eyes, made more sense. I usually used the identical drawing to represent the same kanji element in different visual mnemonics, but not always. I have,

for example, taken creative license with the element MOUTH 566 (also used to express "opening," or "enclosed"), drawing it instead as a tomato in CULTIVATE 246 and a box in DOUBLE 631. I have also

willfully visually "confused" certain elements that Japanese teachers are always insisting must *never* be confused. One example: the interchanging of SOIL 101 and WARRIOR 753. The schematic of elements (see number 8, below) identifies the correct form.

7. Text mnemonic. Keyed to the visual mnemonic. The keywords are in boldface type.

8. Schematic of elements. Each box indicates the position of one of the main elements in the kanji. The element may be a radical, or it may be another kanji (if it is another kanji, its shape as an element may be compressed or slightly altered). The schematic boxes are not used when the entry kanji is a stand-alone kanji or is a radical or element with no other use except as a combining form. And again, sometimes I have had to concoct and interpret elements when none, according to Henshall

and others, may actually exist. While the schematic of elements is a helpful reference aid, keep in mind that it is a guideline only.

9. Element meaning. Refers to the first definition given for the kanji or radical used as an element in the entry kanji. I have tried to use the meaning of the element in the visual and text mnemonics.

10. Cross-reference number. Refers to the sequential reference number of the element used in the entry kanji.

11. Notes reference number. Some characters have elements whose meanings are archaic or that correspond to no stand-alone character or radical in Japanese, such as the right side of PLACE 28. Other characters, like COCOON 307, are too complex graphically to describe with a simple schematic:

Comments on such complex elements appear in a numbered Notes section at the back of the book. These comments are referenced by "n–000" instead of a cross-reference number. Again, much of the information here derives from Henshall's book, which describes the kanji elements in detail.

THE SYLLABARIES

In addition to kanji, Japanese uses two phonetic syllabaries, hiragana and katakana. Each syllabary of forty-six characters represents the same sounds. The cursive hiragana are used to write words not normally written in kanji and for verb endings and parts of speech. The angular katakana are used for emphasis and to write words and names not of Japanese or Chinese origin.

GOODBYE	MCDONALD'S
さ sa	マ ma
よ yo	ク ku
う (u)	ド do
な na	ナ na
ら ra	ル ru
	ド do
(hiragana)	*(katakana)*

KANA

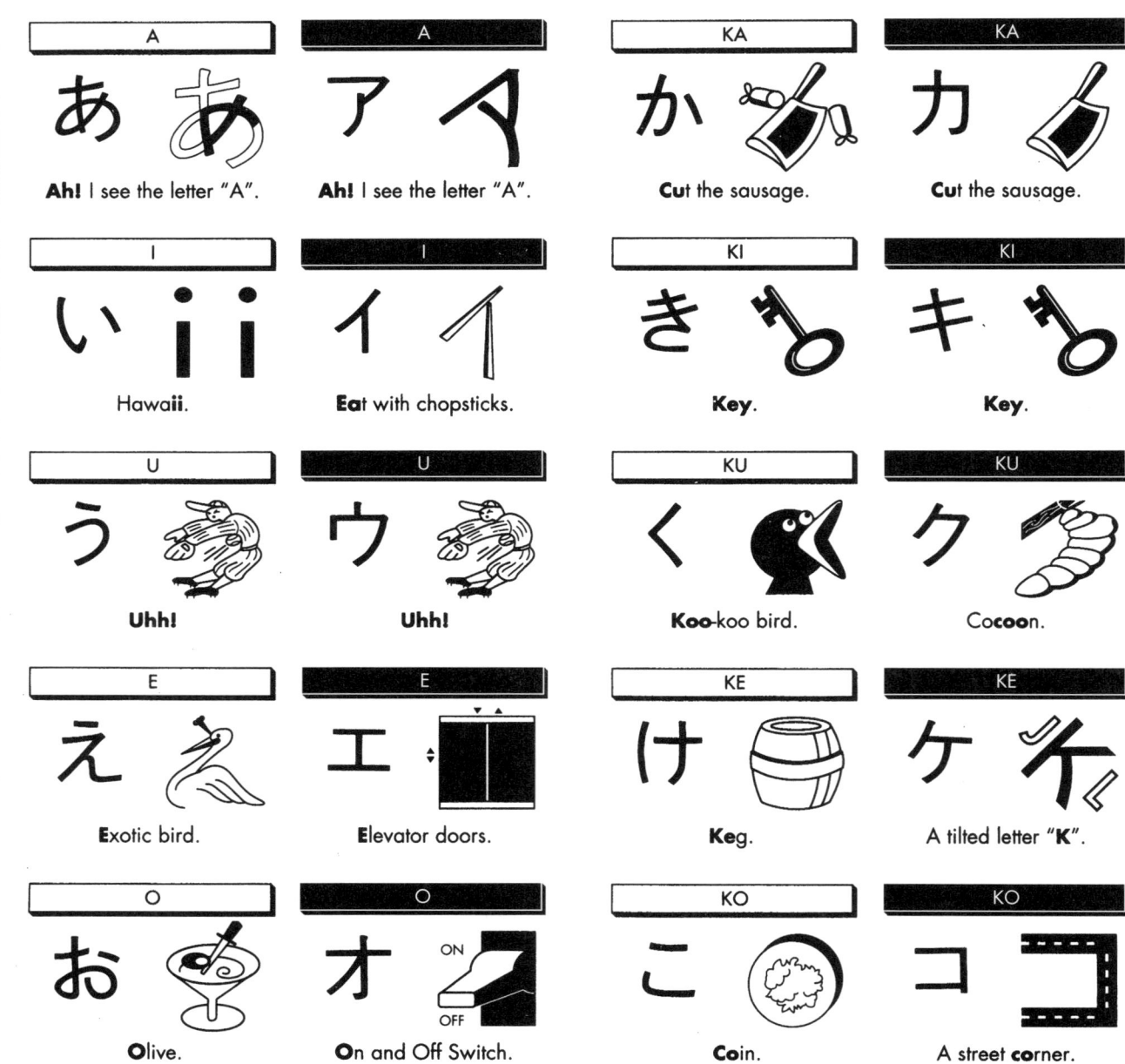

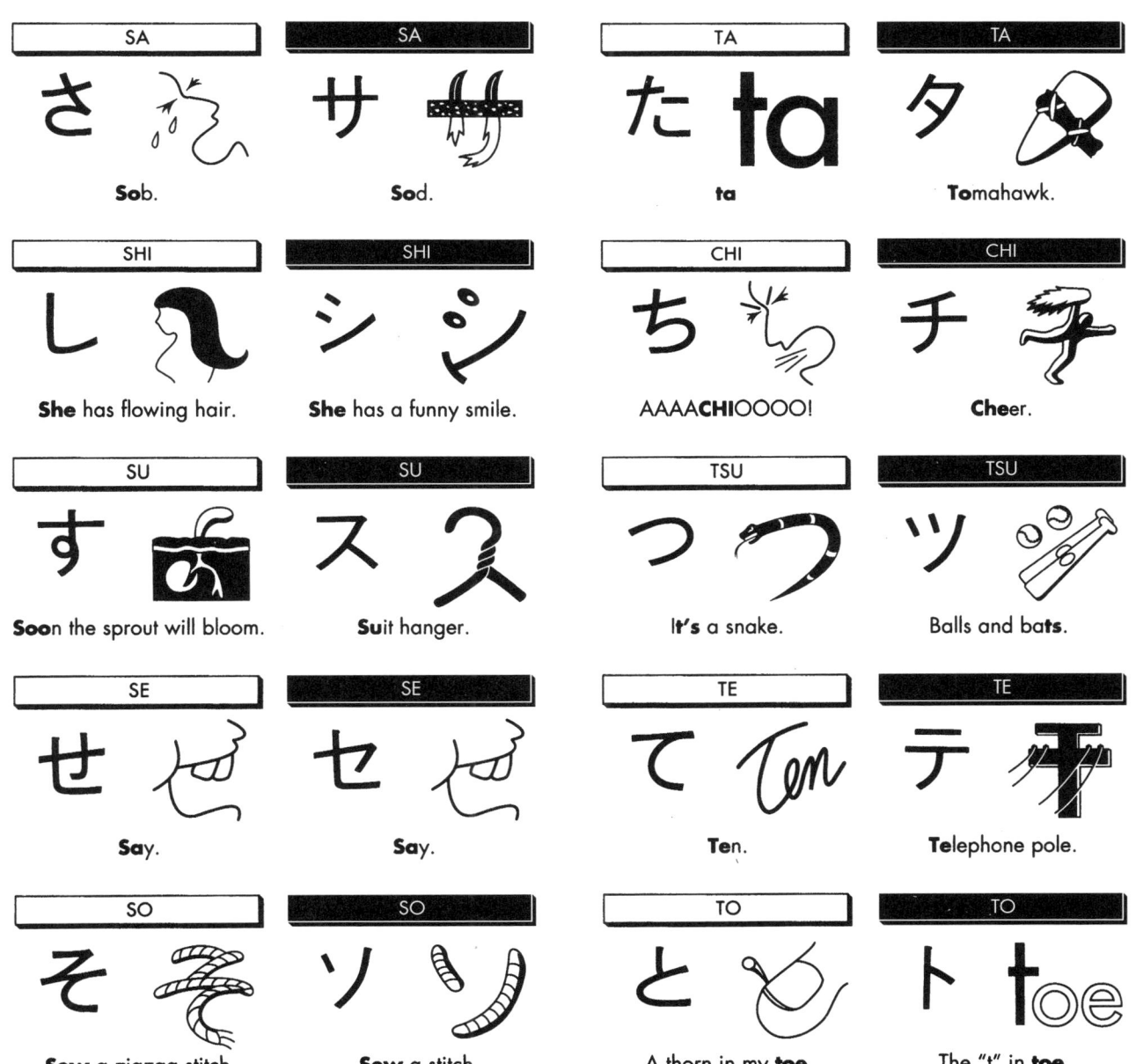

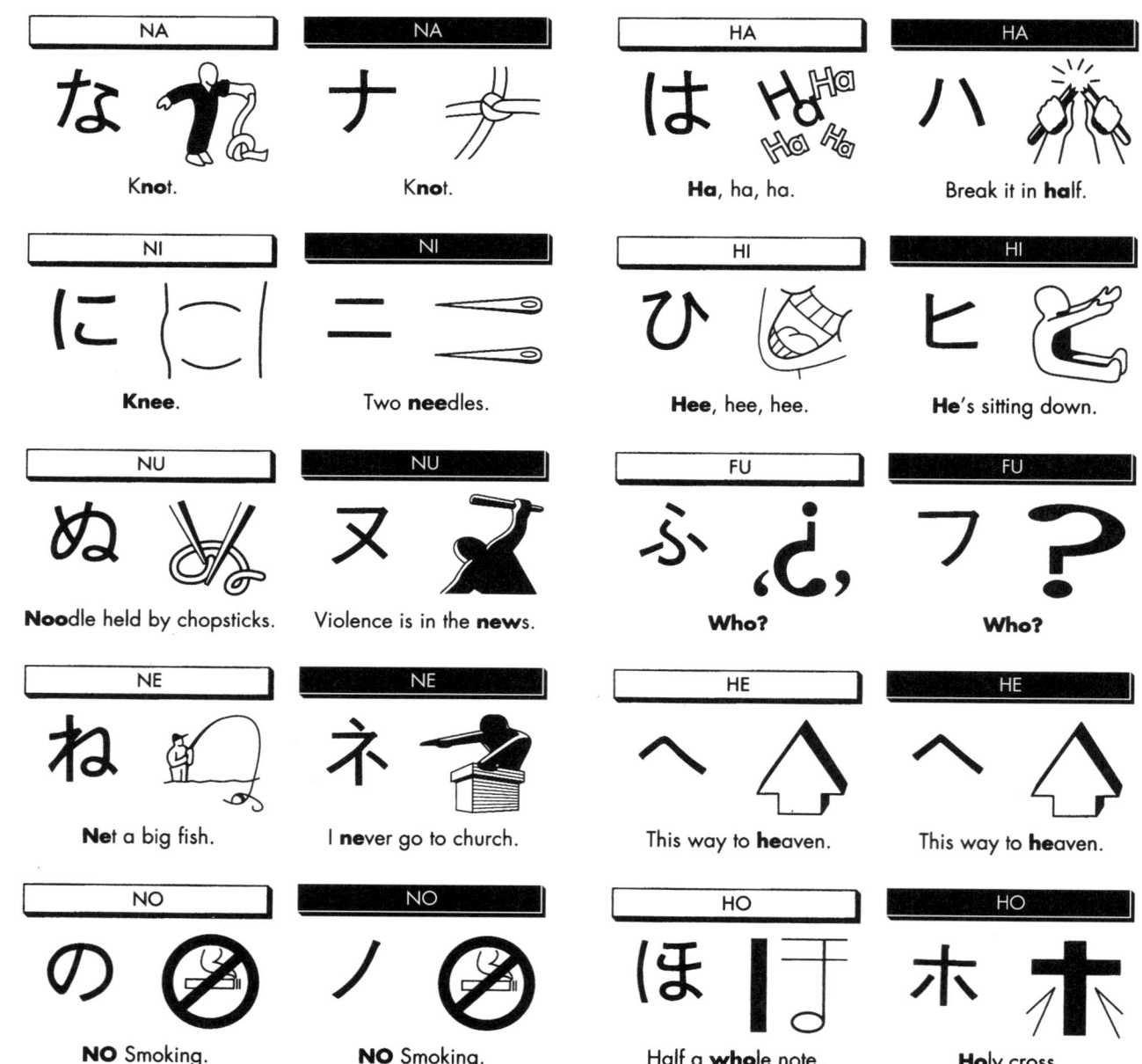

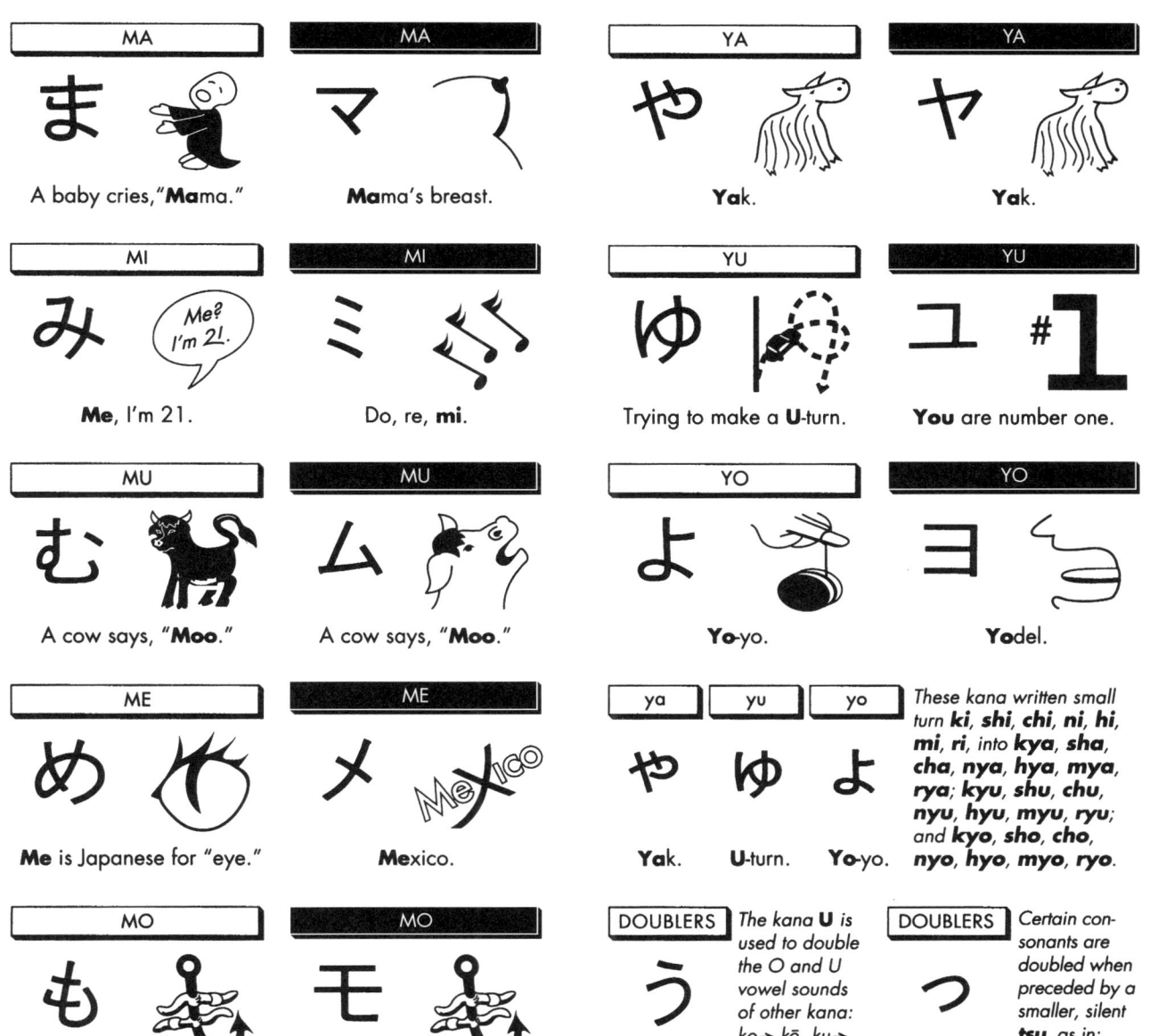

HIRAGANA KATAKANA

RA	RA	WA	WA
ら 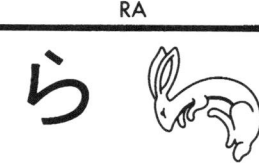	ラ 	わ 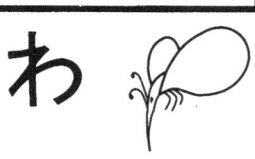	ワ 
Roger the rabbit.	**Ro**cket.	**Wa**sp.	**Wo**w, his head's knocked off!

RI	RI	(W)O	(W)O
り	リ	を 	ヲ 
Reeds.	**Ree**ds.	The cowboy said, "**Whoa**."	An arr**ow** head.

RU	RU	N	N
る	ル	ん	ン 
Three **ru**bies.	Leg and tail of kanga**roo**.	The sound of "n".	**N**icks and cuts.

RE	RE	NONVOICED SOUNDS	
れ 	レ 	ぱ 	*This mark changes the pronunciations of ha, hi, fu, he, and ho to popping sounds: pa, pi, pu, pe, and po.*
Rain and lightning.	**Rai**n shoe.	(Soda) **p**op sound.	

RO	RO	VOICED SOUNDS	
ろ	ロ 	ば 	*This mark changes the pronunciations of all the kana in the series beginning ka, sa, ta, and ha to vibrating sounds: ga, za, da, and ba.*
Three rubies **ro**lled away.	**Ro**tate a nut.	Vocal cord vi**b**rations.	

KANJI COMPOUNDS

Each kanji has meaning by itself. Kanji also can be combined in kanji compounds, or *jukugo*, to form new meanings, much as root words, prefixes, and suffixes are combined in English. The compound meaning "world," shown at right, is composed of **SE** 1081, meaning WORLD, and **KAI** 203, meaning BOUNDARY. Other combinations include:

JAPAN	FEBRUARY
日本	二月
NI **HON**	**NI** **GATSU**
sun 1 origin 125	two 898 month 14

FOREIGNER	EXIT
外人	出口
GAI **JIN**	**de** **guchi**
outside 13 person 363	emerge 955 opening 566

STUDENT	LETTER
学生	手紙
GAKU **SEI**	**te** **gami**
study 839 gain 214	hand 579 paper 974

世界

1 — WORLD

The Sun

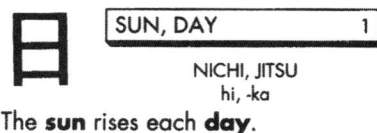

SUN, DAY	1
NICHI, JITSU hi, -ka	

The **sun** rises each **day**.

PROSPEROUS, GOOD, CLEAR — 2

昌 SHŌ

As **clear** as a day with two suns.

🔲 sun 1   🔲 sun 1

CRYSTAL, CLEAR, BRIGHT — 3

晶 SHŌ

As **bright** as a day with three suns.

🔲 sun 1   🔲 sun 1   🔲 sun 1

CLEAR, BRIGHT — 4

晃 KŌ

The sun and a candle shine **clear** and **bright** light.

🔲 sun 1   🔲 shine 869

REFLECT, SHINE — 5

映 EI utsuru/su, haeru

The sun **shines** outward from its center.

🔲 sun 1   🔲 center 955

DAMP, MOIST, HUMID — 6

湿 SHITSU shimeru/su

The sun evaporates water, making the air **humid**.

🔲 water 66   🔲 sun 1   🔲 wet n-6

WARM — 7

温 ON atatakai/meru

The sun **warms** water in a tray.

🔲 water 66   🔲 sun 1   🔲 dish 265

THE SUN / THE MOON

| CLEAR, BRIGHT | 8 |

MEI, MYŌ
aka<u>rui</u>, a<u>keru</u>

As **bright** as the sun and moon together.

sun 1   moon 14

| MORNING, COURT | 9 |

朝

CHŌ
asa

The **morning** is shared by the sun and the moon.

rise n–9   moon 14

| DARK, GLOOMY | 10 |

暗

AN
ku<u>rai</u>

Gloomy people see the **dark** shadow instead of the sun.

sun 1   stand 627   sun 1

| EVENING | 11 |

SEKI
yū

In the **evening**, the moon rises ...

| NIGHT | 12 |

夜

YA
yo, yoru

... making a nice view at **night**.

shelter 1147   person 362   evening 11

| OUTSIDE, OTHER, UNDO | 13 |

外

GAI, GE
soto, hoka, hazu<u>su</u>

He went **outside** and **undid** his pants when nature called.

evening 11   crack n–13

The Moon

月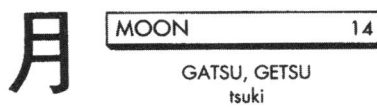

GATSU, GETSU
tsuki

A crescent **moon** in the clouds.

The Day

MORNING, DAWN — 15
旦 TAN

From **dawn** ...

- sun 1
- one 897

NOON, DAYTIME — 16
昼 CHŪ / hiru

... til **noon**, we measure the land.

- measure 884
- dawn 15

DAY OF THE WEEK — 18
曜 YŌ

The **days of the week** fly by.

- sun 1
- winged bird n–18

EVENING, LATE — 17
晚 BAN

We can only escape the sun's heat in **late evening**.

- sun 1
- escape 1167

EARLY, PROMPT, FAST — 19
早 SŌ / hayai

The sun rises through the grass **early** in the morning.

- sun 1
- grass n–19

DAWN, LIGHT, EVENT — 20
暁 GYŌ / akatsuki

Three stars were seen at **dawn**.

- sun 1
- clear n–20

THE DAY

OLD, PAST — 21
旧 KYŪ

One day is **past** …

- high n–21
- sun 1

CHILD — 22
児 JI, NI / ko

… and one more **child** is born.

- past 21
- kneeling n–22

EASY, CHANGE, DIVINATION — 23
易 EKI, I / yasui, yasashii

Life is **easy** in the sunshine.

- sun 1
- big-eyed lizard n–23

BRIGHT, LIGHT — 24
昭 SHŌ

The **bright light** of the sun glints off the sword.

- sun 1
- sword 1023
- opening 566

ILLUMINATE, SHINE — 25
照 SHŌ / teru/rasu

The sword is **illuminated** by the sun above and fire below.

- bright 24
- fire 82

RAISE, FRY — 26
揚 YŌ / ageru/garu

Raise your hand in the **frying** hot sun.

- hand 000
- sun 1
- rays n–26

SUNNY, MALE, POSITIVE — 27
陽 YŌ / hi

On the **sunny** side of the hill …

- hill 1094
- sun 1
- rays n–26

PLACE — 28
場 JŌ / ba

… is a **place** in the soil …

- soil 102
- sun 1
- rays n–26

HOT WATER, HOT SPRING — 29
湯 TŌ / yu

… where **hot water springs** up.

- water 66
- sun 1
- rays n–26

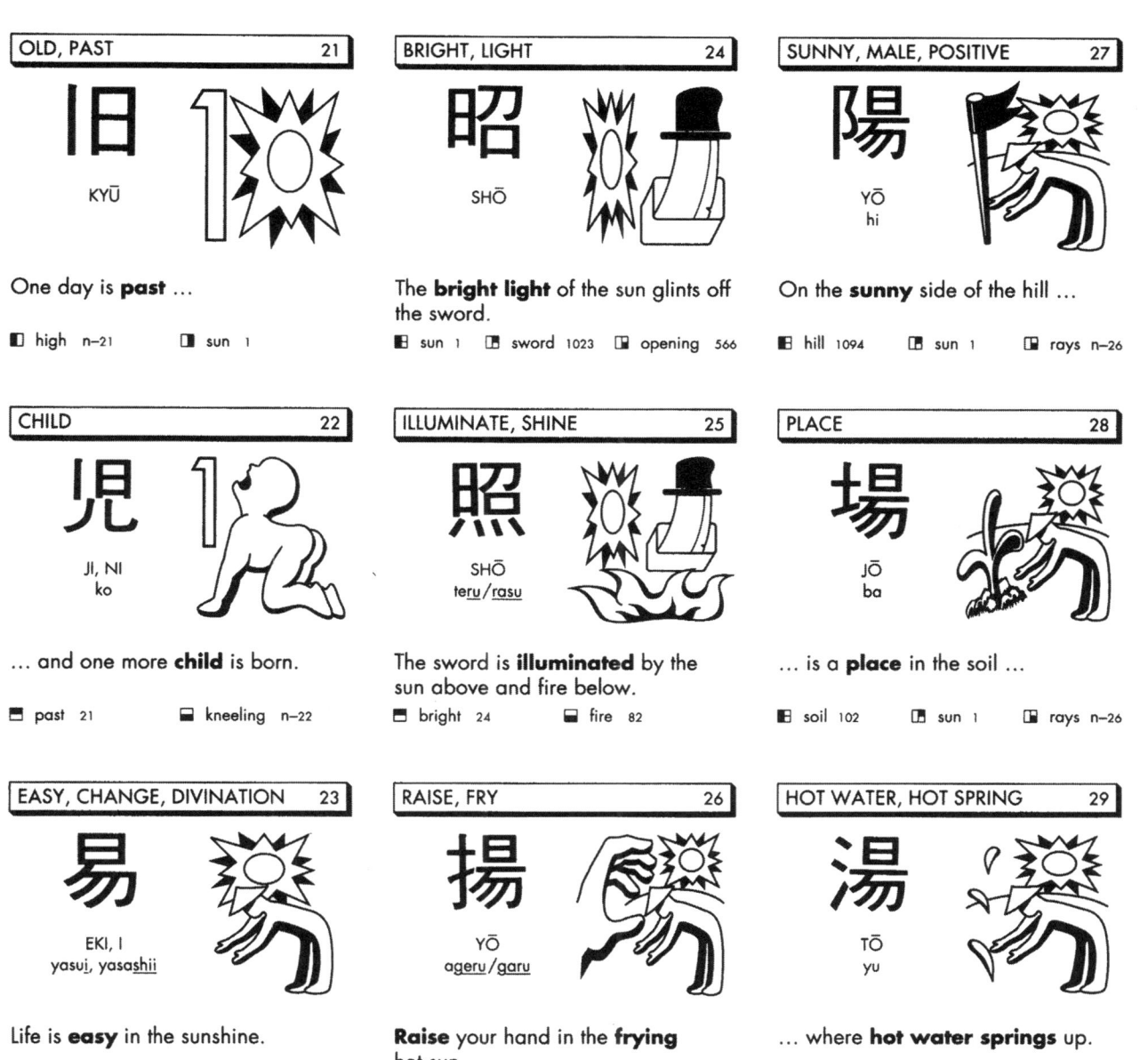

Time

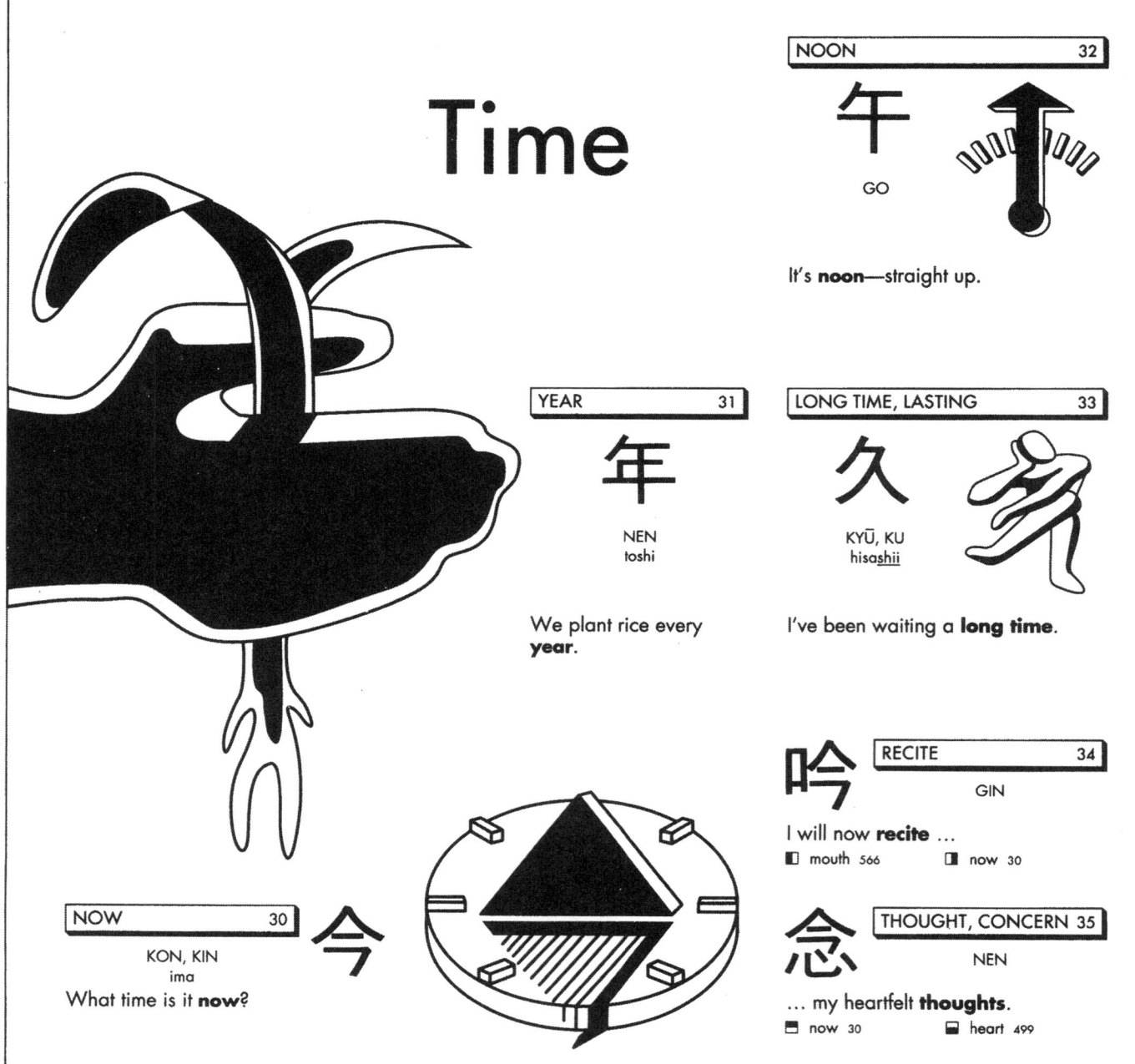

| NOON | 32 |

午 GO

It's **noon**—straight up.

| YEAR | 31 |

年

NEN
toshi

We plant rice every **year**.

| LONG TIME, LASTING | 33 |

久

KYŪ, KU
hisa*shii*

I've been waiting a **long time**.

| RECITE | 34 |

吟 GIN

I will now **recite** …
▫ mouth 566   ▫ now 30

| THOUGHT, CONCERN | 35 |

念 NEN

… my heartfelt **thoughts**.
▫ now 30   ▫ heart 499

| NOW | 30 |

今

KON, KIN
ima

What time is it **now**?

TIME

SEASON, YOUNG — 36
季
KI

A child as **young** and green as a new **season's** rice plants.

- rice plant 231
- child 447

TEN-DAY PERIOD — 37
旬 
JUN

Ten days of sunshine in June.

- wrap 949
- sun 1

PERMIT, FORGIVE — 38
許
KYO
yuru<u>su</u>, moto

Permit me to speak at noon.

- speak 840
- noon 37

GRIEF, SADNESS — 39
愁
SHŪ
urei/<u>eru</u>

I've got the autumn **blues**.

- autumn 41
- heart 499

SUMMER — 40
夏
KA, GE
natsu

Inescapable **summer** heat.

- mask n–40
- slow progress 1218

AUTUMN — 41
秋
SHŪ
aki

Rice stalks turn the fiery colors of **autumn**.

- rice plant 231
- fire 83

WINTER — 42
冬
TŌ
fuyu

Winter snow and ice impede my progress.

- slow progress 1218
- ice 94

SPRING — 43
春
SHUN
haru

Cherry trees bloom in the **spring** sun.

- branches n–43
- sun 1

Wind, Rain, & Clouds

WIND, STYLE 44
風
FŪ
kaze

A boat is tossed by the **wind**.

RAIN 45
雨
U
ame, ama–

Drops of **rain** come …

CLOUD 46
雲
UN
kumo

… and **clouds** swirl …

rain 45   cloud 54

WIND, RAIN, & CLOUDS

| CLOUD, DIM, MAR | 47 |

DON
kumo*ru*

... and **dim** the light of day.

🌧 sun 1   ☁ cloud 46

| THUNDER, LIGHTNING | 48 |

RAI
kaminari

Lightning flashes and **thunder** echoes in the field.

🌧 rain 45   ☐ field 201

| ELECTRICITY | 49 |

DEN

An **electrical** field travels down the wire.

🌧 rain 45   ☐ lightning n–49

| SHAKE, TREMBLE | 50 |

SHIN
furu*u*/*eru*

I **shake** and **tremble** at the foot of a cliff.

🌧 rain 45   ☐ tremble n–50

| DEW, REVEAL, SMALL, RUSSIA | 51 |

RO, RŌ
tsuyu

Dew is on the **Russian** road.

🌧 rain 45   ☐ road 1214

| CONVEY, TRANSMIT | 52 |

DEN
tsuta*eru*/*waru*

People **transmit** clouds of contagious diseases.

☐ person 362   ☐ cloud 54

| ATMOSPHERE | 53 |

FUN

Rain is part of the **atmosphere**.

🌧 rain 45   ☐ divide n–53

| "CLOUD" | 54 |

As an element this means **cloud**. *Alone, it is a rarely used character meaning "speak." See 840.*

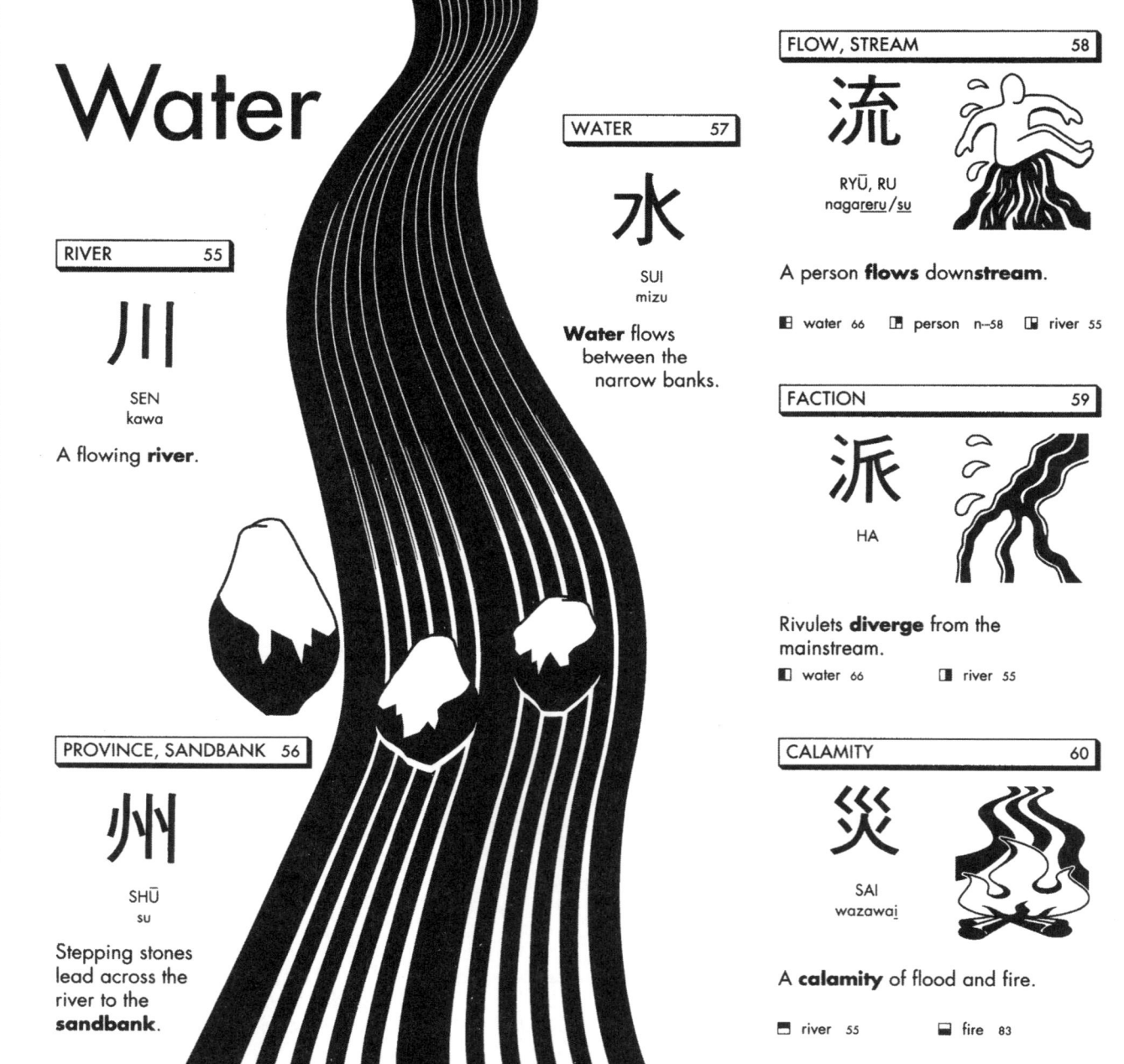

WATER

OPEN SEA, SOAR — 61
CHŪ / oki

A ship in the middle of the **open sea**.
- water 66
- middle 954

DEEP WATER, ABYSS — 62
EN / fuchi

Deep water engulfs the trees.
- water 66
- planks n–62

CAVE, PENETRATE — 63
DŌ / hora

Water **penetrates** the **cave**.
- water 66
- same 889

HARBOR, PORT — 64
KŌ / minato

Together, two people come to the **harbor** to see their reflection.
- water 66
- together 388
- self 450

"WATER" — 66

This is the radical for **water**.

BAY, GULF — 65
WAN

Sittin' on the dock of the **bay**.
- water 66
- red n–65
- pull 817

SEA — 67
KAI / umi

The **sea** is the mother of life.
- water 66
- person 363
- mother 446

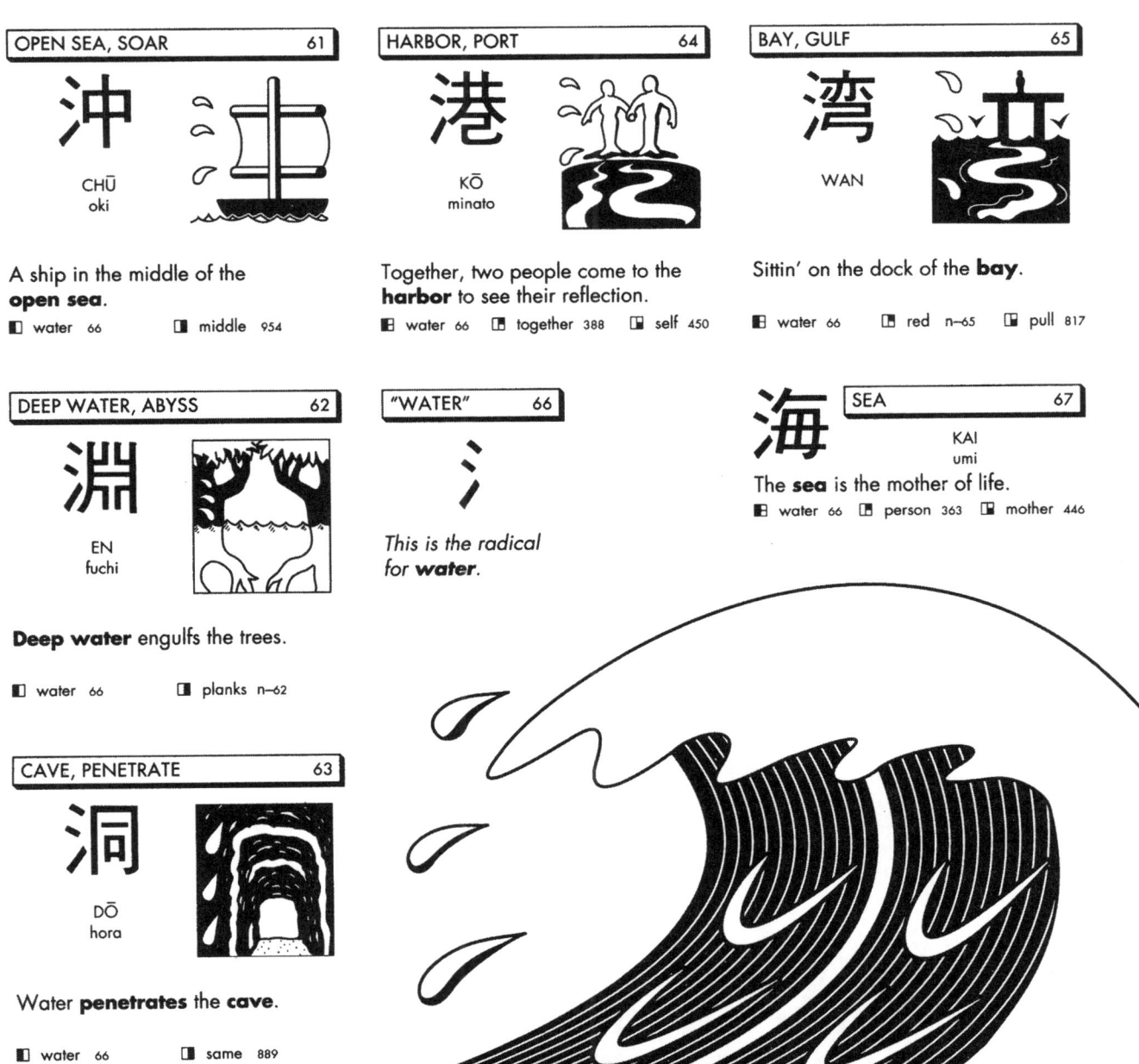

Wash

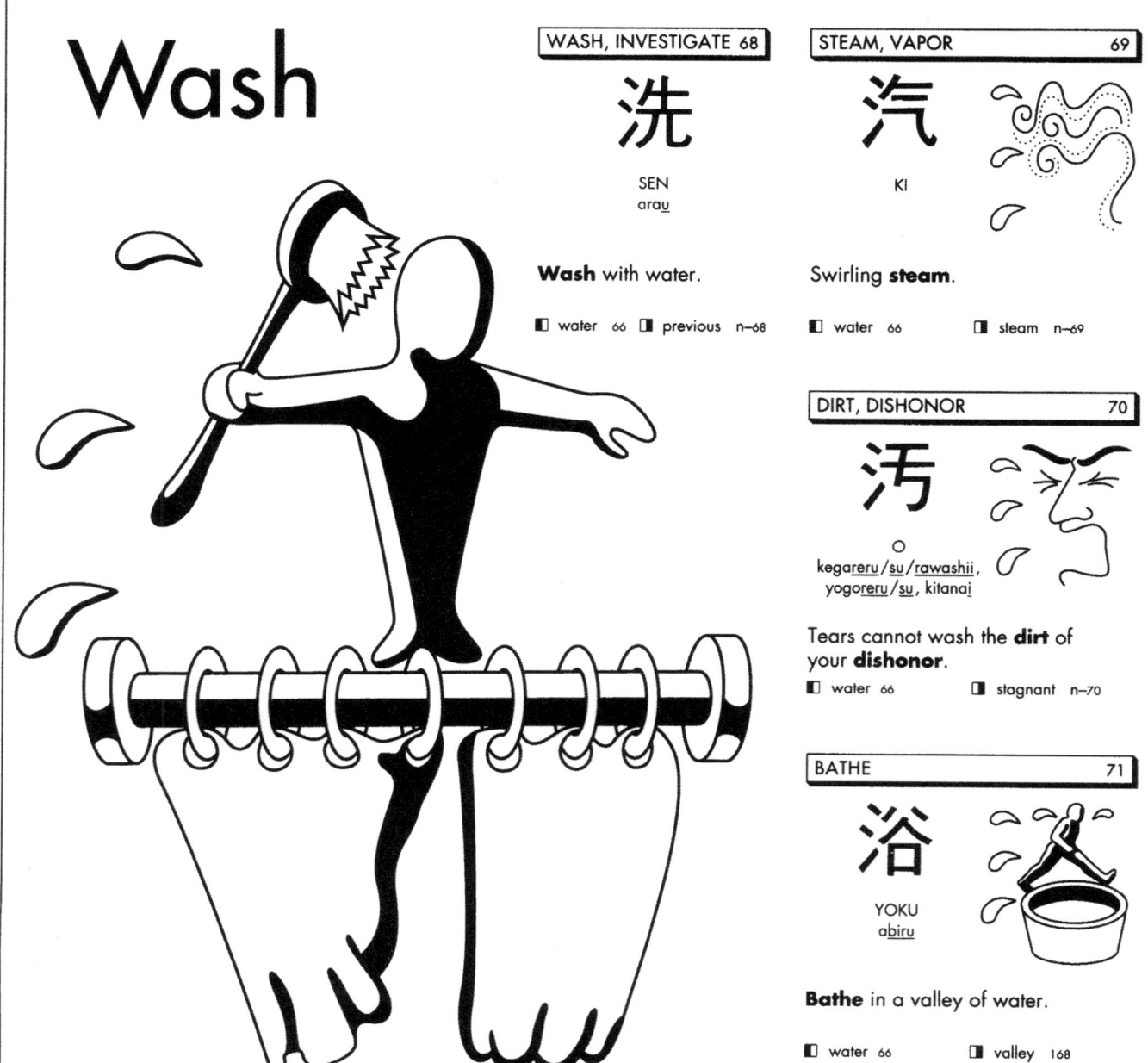

WASH, INVESTIGATE 68

洗

SEN
ara*u*

Wash with water.

▪ water 66   ▫ previous n–68

STEAM, VAPOR 69

汽

KI

Swirling **steam**.

▪ water 66   ▫ steam n–69

DIRT, DISHONOR 70

汚

o
kega*reru*/*su*/*rawashii*,
yogo*reru*/*su*, kitana*i*

Tears cannot wash the **dirt** of your **dishonor**.

▪ water 66   ▫ stagnant n–70

BATHE 71

浴

YOKU
a*biru*

Bathe in a valley of water.

▪ water 66   ▫ valley 168

WASH

SHALLOW, LIGHT 72

浅

SEN
asa<u>i</u>

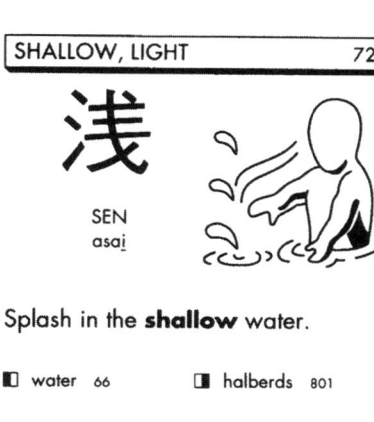

Splash in the **shallow** water.

- water 66
- halberds 801

FLOAT, FLEETING 75

浮

FU
u<u>ku</u>/<u>kabu</u>/<u>kaberu</u>

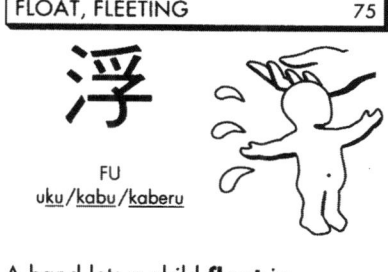

A hand lets a child **float** in the water.

- water 66
- hand 611
- child 447

BOIL, GUSH 78

沸

FUTSU
wa<u>ku</u>/<u>kasu</u>

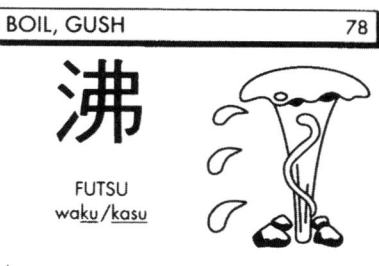

A **gushing** fountain of **boiling** water.

- water 66
- emerge n–78

DRY, DEFENSE 73

干

KAN
ho<u>ru</u>, hi<u>ru</u>

Clothes **dry** on the line.

DEPEND ON, DUE TO, REASON 76

由

YU, YŪ
yoshi

Depending on where you place the drill in the field …

SOURCE, ORIGIN 79

源

GEN
minamoto

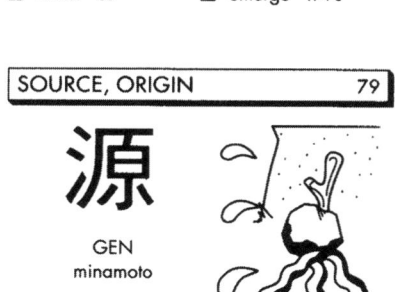

The spring is our **source** of water.

- water 66
- origin 81

SWEAT 74

汗

KAN
ase, ase<u>bamu</u>

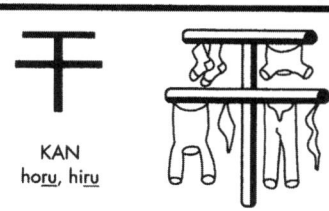

This sweater makes me **sweat**.

- water 66
- dry 72

OIL 77

油

YU
abura

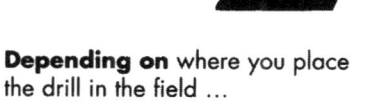

… you may have gushing **oil**.

- water 66
- depend on 76

泉

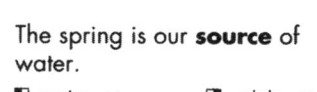

SPRING 80

SEN
izumi

A **spring** …

- white 45
- water 57

原

PLAIN, ORIGIN 81

GEN
hara

… **originates** from the **plain**.

- cliff n–81
- spring 80

29

Fire

| "FIRE" | 82 |

 This is a radical for **fire**.

| FIRE | 83 |

火

KA
hi

A camp **fire**.

| LIGHT, LAMP | 84 |

灯

TŌ
hi

Light the **lamp** with fire.

- fire 83
- exact 1089

| BURN, ROAST | 85 |

焼

SHŌ
ya<u>ku</u>/<u>keru</u>

Roast barbeque.

- fire 83
- high n–20

| FLAME | 86 |

炎

EN
honō

The **flames** of two fires …

- fire 83
- fire 83

| PALE, LIGHT, FAINT | 87 |

淡

TAN
awa<u>i</u>

… become **faint** because of the rain.

- water 66
- flame 86

| THREATEN, MENACE | 88 |

嚇

KAKU
odo<u>su</u>/<u>kasu</u>

Two samurai screamed when **threatened** by **menacing** flames.

- mouth 566
- red (x2) n–65

| VIOLENCE, EXPOSE | 89 |

暴

BŌ, BAKU
aba<u>reru</u>/<u>ku</u>

Exposed to the **violent** heat of the sun …

- sun 1
- offer n–89

| BURST, EXPLODE | 90 |

爆

BAKU

… a firecracker **explodes** in a **burst** of fire.

- fire 83
- violence 89

FIRE / ICE

EAST 91
東
TŌ
higashi

The sun rises through the trees in the **east**.

- tree 126
- sun 1

FREEZE 92
凍
TŌ
kō*ru*, kogo*eru*

It's **freezing** in the east.

- ice 94
- east 91

COLD 93
寒
KAN
samu*i*

When it's **cold**, the shrubs have no leaves.

- roof 1144
- plants n–93
- ice 94

Ice

ICE 94
氷
HYŌ
kōri

A penguin looks through cracks in the **ice**.

- water 66
- crack n–94

SNOW 96
雪
SETSU
yuki

Snow: rain you can hold in your hand.

- rain 45
- hand n–597

"ICE" 95
冫
*This element means **ice**.*

FROST 97
霜
SŌ
shimo

I can see the **frost** forming on the tree.

- rain 45
- tree 126
- eye 538

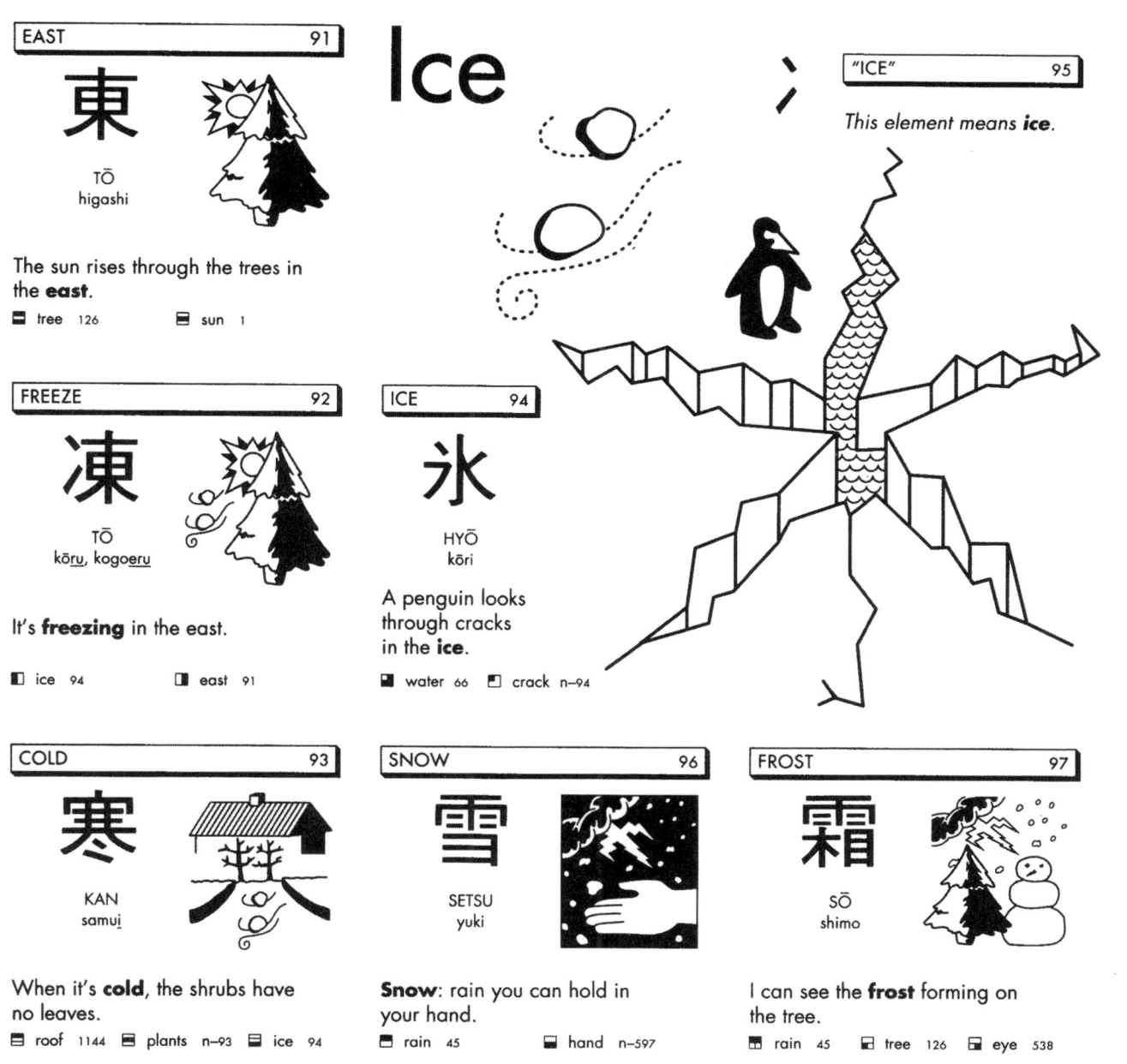

WORLD

AREA, LIMITS 98

域

IKI

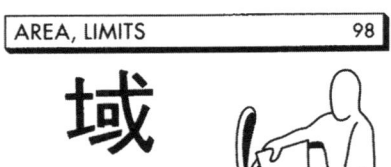

Hal draws up the **area's** boundaries.

- soil 101
- halberd 801

SLOPE 99

坂

HAN
saka

A man puts his hand against the **sloping** cliff.

- soil 101
- against 957

EMBANKMENT 100

堤

TEI
tsutsumi

The sun shines on the **embankment** of soil.

- soil 101
- sun 1
- leg 617

Soil

土

EARTH, SOIL, GROUND 101

DO, TO
tsuchi

A plant grows in the **soil**.

GROUND, LAND 102

地

CHI, JI

Creatures live in the **ground**.

- soil 101
- creature n–102

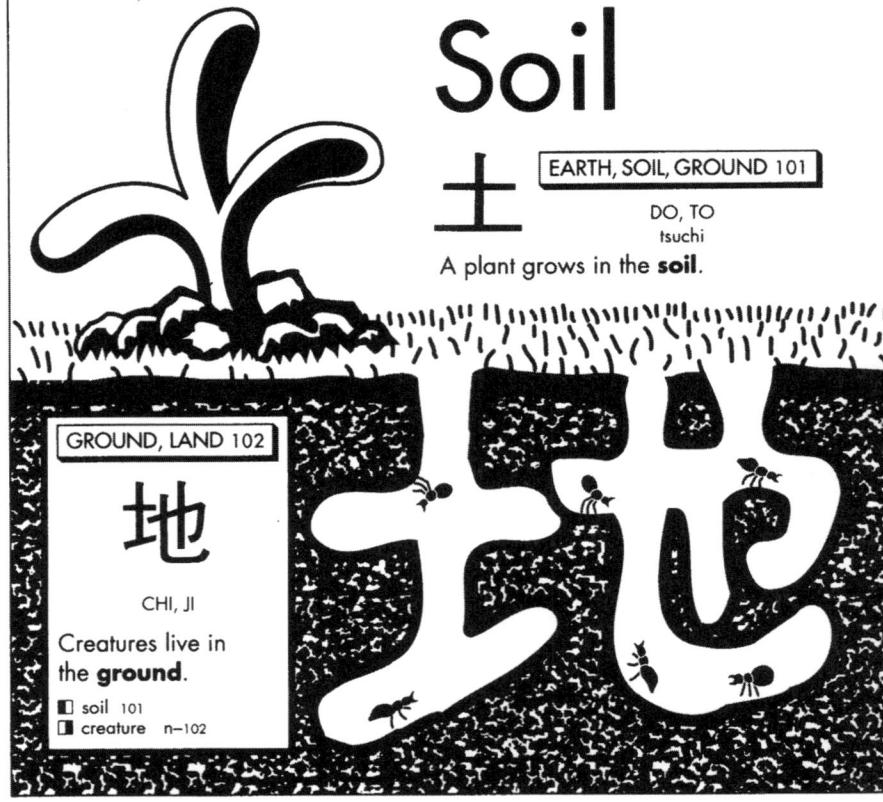

MINE, PIT, HOLE 103

坑

KŌ

Miners work in a **hole** deep in the earth.

- soil 101
- shelter 1147
- desk 157

RESIST, OPPOSE 104

抗

KŌ

The hands **oppose** management.

- hand 660
- shelter 1147
- desk 157

Metal

GOLD, MONEY, METAL 105
金 KIN, KON
kane, kana

Two **gold** nuggets in the soil.

FISH, LURE, CHANGE 108
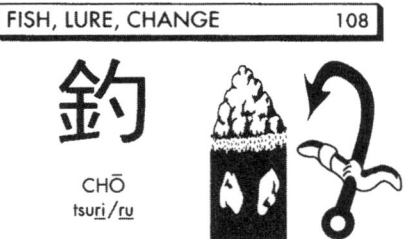
釣
CHŌ
tsu<u>ri</u>/<u>ru</u>

A metal **fish lure**.

 metal 105    ladle 265

NEEDLE, POINTER 109
針
SHIN
hari

The metal **needle points** ten degrees north.

metal 105   ten 906

MIRROR 106
鏡
KYŌ
kagami

He stands in front of the metal **mirror**.

 metal 105 stand 627  scene n–106

CHAIN, LINK 107
鎖
SA
kusari

A little metal **chain**.

 metal 105    little 926   money 708

COIN 110
銭
SEN
zeni

Hal flips a metal **coin**.

 metal 105    halberd 801

| TURF, LAWN 111 |

芝

SHI
shiba

A path winds through the **lawn**.

▢ grass 126   ▢ path n–111

| STALK, STEM 112 |

茎

KEI
kuki

A hand cuts the grassy **stalks** from the soil.

▢ grass 124   ▢ hand 600   ▢ soil 101

| CHRYSANTHEMUM 113 |

菊

KIKU

A **chrysanthemum** in the grass, with rice-colored petals.

▢ grass 124   ▢ rice 217

| WORK, DUTIES 114 |

勤

KIN
tsuto<u>meru</u>

My **duty** is to **work** in the garden.

▢ grass 124   ▢ flower 119   ▢ power 745

| GROW THICKLY 115 |

茂

MO
shige<u>ru</u>

Hal makes the grass **grow thickly**.

▢ grass 124   ▢ halberd 801

| FLOWER 116 |

花

KA
hana

The plants change into **flowers**.

▢ grass 124   ▢ change 374

| ART, SKILL, PLANT 117 |

芸

GEI

Planting is a **skill** and an **art**.

▢ grass 124   ▢ speak n–117

| FLOWER, SHOWY, CHINA 118 |

華

KA, GE
hana

A **Chinese flower** grows among the grass.

▢ grass 124   ▢ flower n–118

| FRAGRANT, SWEET SMELL 119 |

芳

HŌ
kanba<u>shii</u>

This person takes in the **sweet smell** of the grass.

▢ grass 124   ▢ person 386

Bamboo & Grass

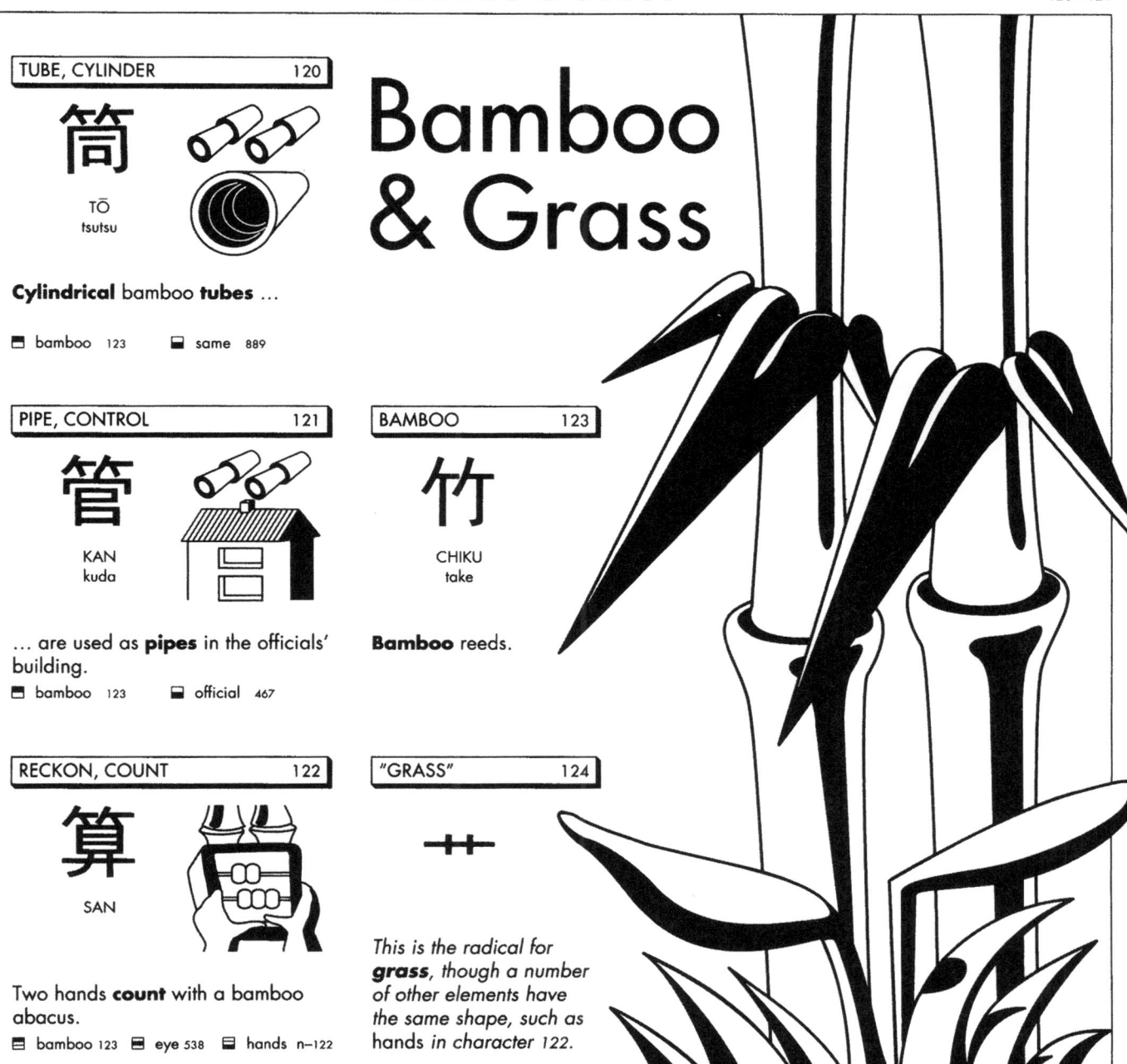

TUBE, CYLINDER — 120
筒
TŌ
tsutsu

Cylindrical bamboo **tubes** …

- bamboo 123
- same 889

PIPE, CONTROL — 121
管
KAN
kuda

… are used as **pipes** in the officials' building.

- bamboo 123
- official 467

RECKON, COUNT — 122
算
SAN

Two hands **count** with a bamboo abacus.

- bamboo 123
- eye 538
- hands n–122

BAMBOO — 123
竹
CHIKU
take

Bamboo reeds.

"GRASS" — 124
艹

This is the radical for **grass**, though a number of other elements have the same shape, such as hands in character 122.

Trees

ROOT, ORIGIN, BOOK 125
本 HON moto

The **roots** of a tree are cylindrical.
- tree 126
- roots n–125

*Character 125 is also used after numbers to indicated that the things being counted are **cylindrical**.*

TREE, WOOD 126

木 BOKU, MOKU, ki, ko-

A **tree** with spreading branches.

GLORY, FLOURISH, SHINE 127

栄 EI sakaeru, haeru

Blossoms **flourish** on the tree.
- shine n–127
- tree 126

WILLOW, WILLOWY 128

柳 RYŪ yanagi

A **willow** tree.
- tree 126
- flow n–128

GATHER 129

集 SHŪ atsumeru/maru

Birds **gather** in a tree.
- bird 319
- tree 126

NEST 130

巣 SŌ su

Three birds **nest** in a fruit tree.
- basket n–130
- fruit 126

BALANCE 131

権 KEN, GON

A heron **balances** in a tree.
- tree 126
- heron 331

TREES

TAKE, GATHER 132

采
SAI
to*ru*

Hands **take** acorns from the tree.

- hand 580
- hand 611
- tree 126

EXTREME, POLE 133

極 
KYOKU, GOKU
kiwa*meru*

Magnetic **poles** are at the **extreme** ends of earth.

- tree 126
- extreme n-133

BODY 134

体
TAI, TEI
karada

The **body** is the "root" of a person.

- person 362
- root 125

LEAF 135

葉
YŌ
ha

Plants and trees generate **leaves**.

- grass 124
- generation 100
- tree 126

PLANTING 136

栽
SAI

Hal **plants** a tree in the soil.

- soil 101
- tree 126
- halberd 801

REST 138

休
KYŪ
yasu*mu*

A vacationer **rests** by a tree.

- person 362
- tree 126

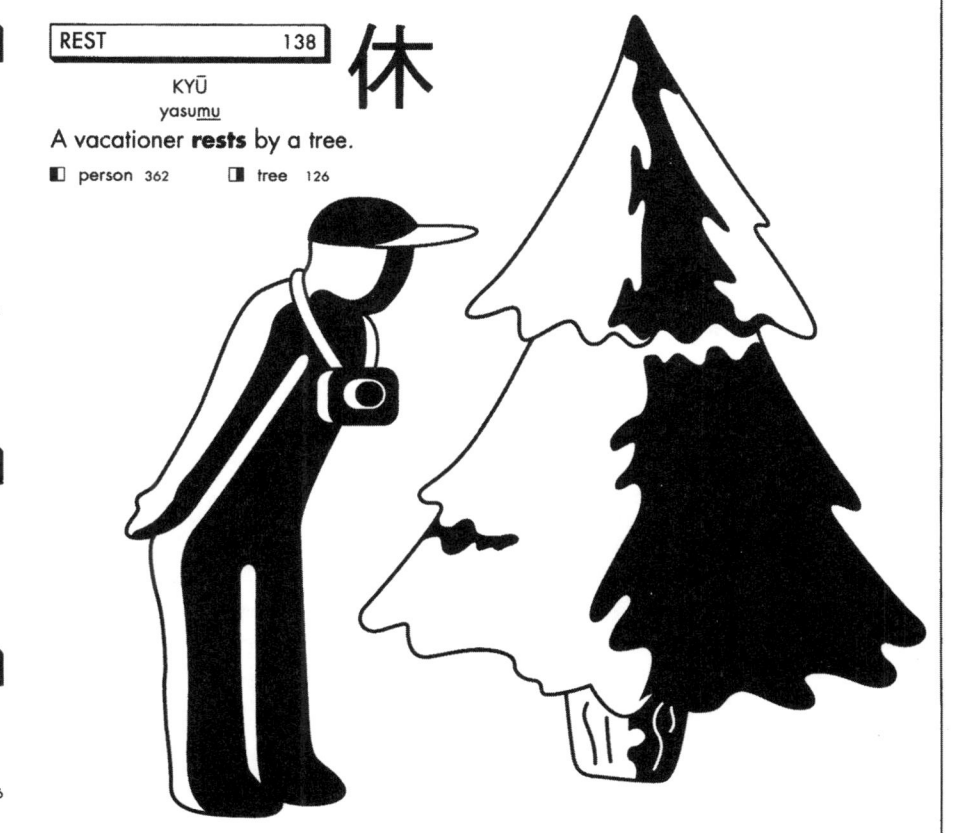

PLANT 137

植
SHOKU
u*eru*

Plant a tree in the soil.

- tree 126
- upright n-137

DIVIDE, ANALYZE 139
析
SEKI

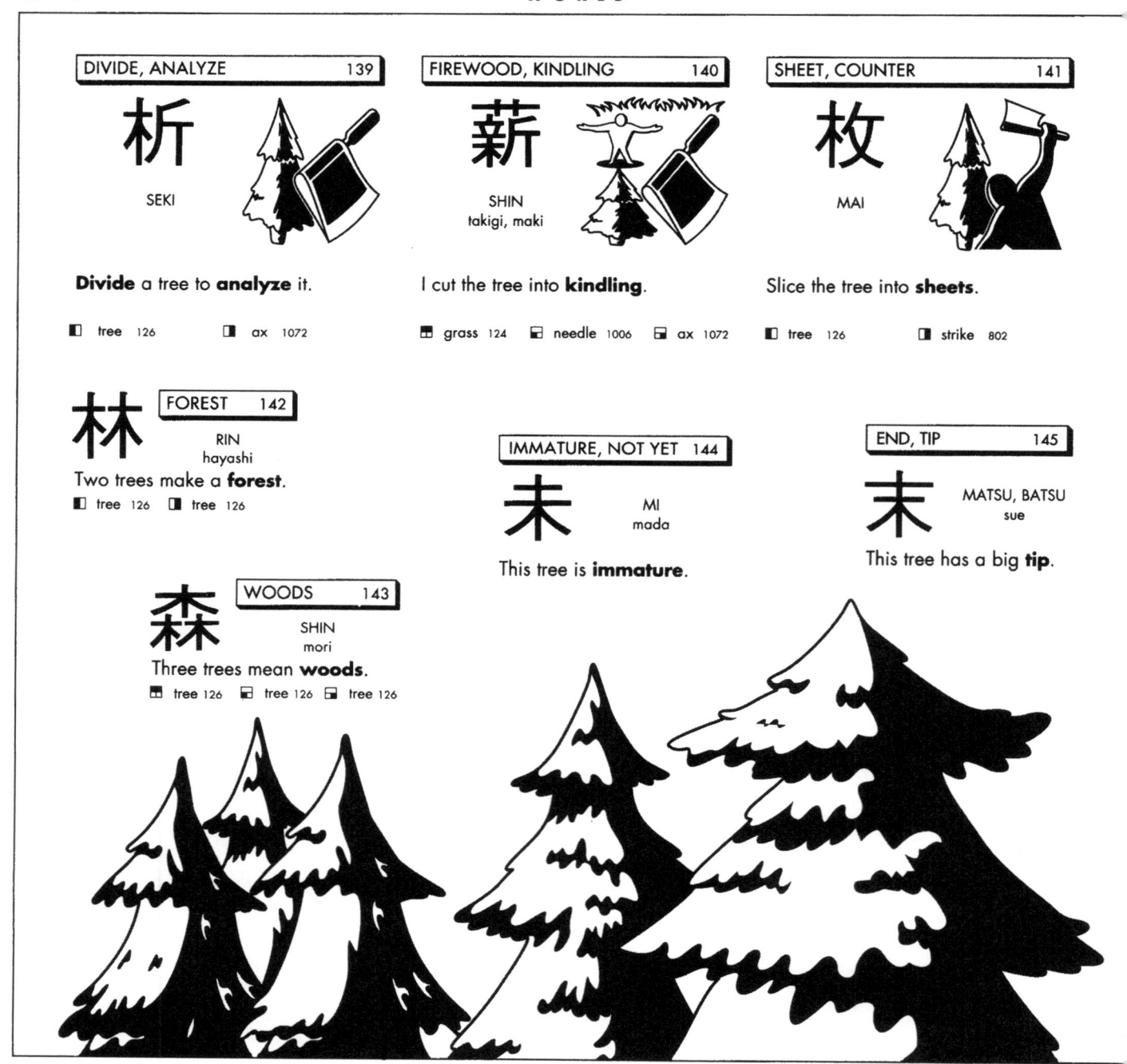

Divide a tree to **analyze** it.

- tree 126
- ax 1072

FIREWOOD, KINDLING 140
薪
SHIN
takigi, maki

I cut the tree into **kindling**.

- grass 124
- needle 1006
- ax 1072

SHEET, COUNTER 141
枚
MAI

Slice the tree into **sheets**.

- tree 126
- strike 802

FOREST 142
林
RIN
hayashi

Two trees make a **forest**.
- tree 126
- tree 126

IMMATURE, NOT YET 144
未
MI
mada

This tree is **immature**.

END, TIP 145
末
MATSU, BATSU
sue

This tree has a big **tip**.

WOODS 143
森
SHIN
mori

Three trees mean **woods**.
- tree 126
- tree 126
- tree 126

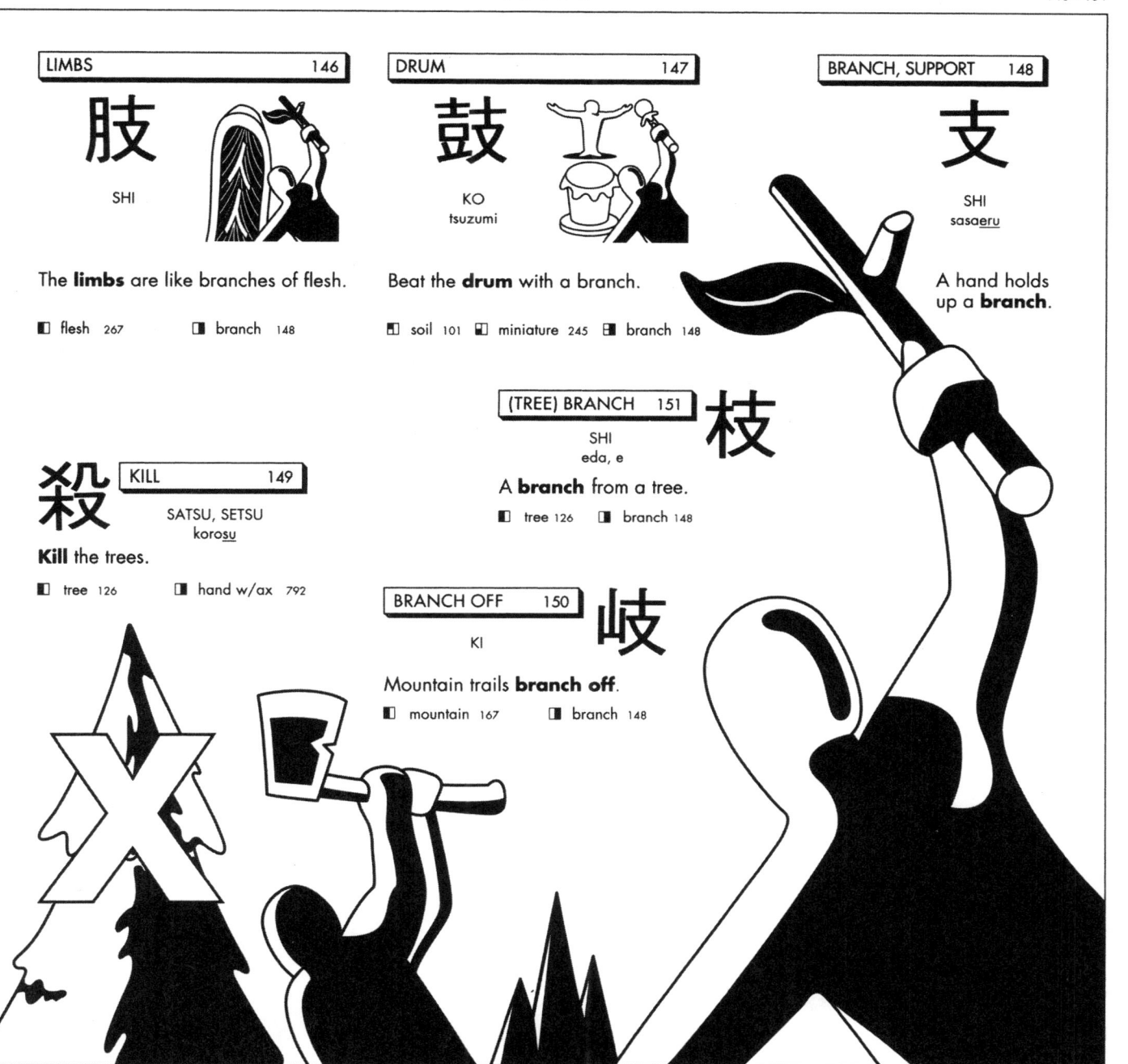

TREES

LIMBS — 146
肢
SHI

The **limbs** are like branches of flesh.

- flesh 267
- branch 148

DRUM — 147
鼓
KO
tsuzumi

Beat the **drum** with a branch.

- soil 101
- miniature 245
- branch 148

BRANCH, SUPPORT — 148
支
SHI
sasaeru

A hand holds up a **branch**.

KILL — 149
殺
SATSU, SETSU
korosu

Kill the trees.

- tree 126
- hand w/ax 792

(TREE) BRANCH — 151
枝
SHI
eda, e

A **branch** from a tree.

- tree 126
- branch 148

BRANCH OFF — 150
岐
KI

Mountain trails **branch off**.

- mountain 167
- branch 148

Timber

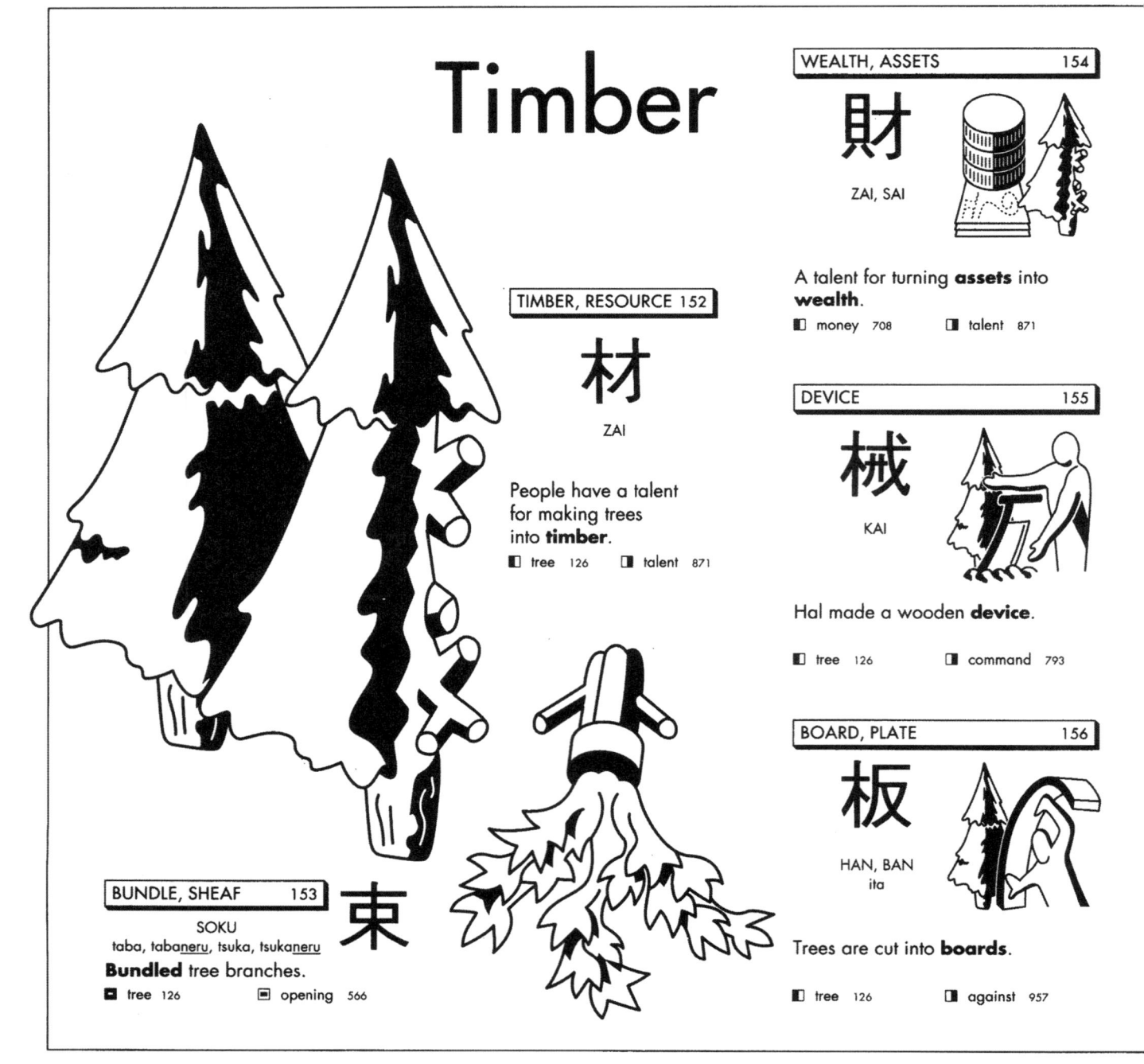

TIMBER, RESOURCE 152
材
ZAI

People have a talent for making trees into **timber**.

- tree 126
- talent 871

BUNDLE, SHEAF 153
束
SOKU
taba, tabaneru, tsuka, tsukaneru

Bundled tree branches.

- tree 126
- opening 566

WEALTH, ASSETS 154
財
ZAI, SAI

A talent for turning **assets** into **wealth**.

- money 708
- talent 871

DEVICE 155
械
KAI

Hal made a wooden **device**.

- tree 126
- command 793

BOARD, PLATE 156
板
HAN, BAN
ita

Trees are cut into **boards**.

- tree 126
- against 957

TIMBER

DESK, TABLE — 157
机 KI / tsukue

A wooden **table**.

- tree 126
- desk n–157

BOOKSHELF, ARCHIVES — 158
档 TŌ

Three books sit atop a wooden **bookshelf**.

- tree 126
- apply 595

SHELF, TRELLIS — 159
棚 tana

It took two months to build these wooden **shelves**.

- tree 126
- month (X2) 14

FENCE — 160
柵 SAKU / shigarami

I read a book on making **fences**.

- tree 126
- book 868

COLUMN, PILLAR — 161
柱 CHŪ / hashira

A tree is cut into a **pillar** for the master's house.

- tree 126
- master 734

POLE, BAR, CLUB — 162
棒 BŌ

A wooden **club**.

- tree 126
- respectful 703

BOX — 163
箱 hako

A **box** made of bamboo and wood.

- bamboo 123
- tree 126
- eye 538

LACQUER, VARNISH — 164
漆 SHITSU / urushi

Varnish resins ooze like water from a tree.

- water 66
- tree 126
- water 57

ARRANGE — 165
整 SEI / totono<u>u</u>/<u>eru</u>

Correctly **arrange** the bundle of sticks.

- bundle 153
- strike 802
- correct 826

CUT BRANCHES — 166
柮 TOTSU

Leave nothing but **cut branches**.

- tree 126
- leave 956

Mountains & Valleys

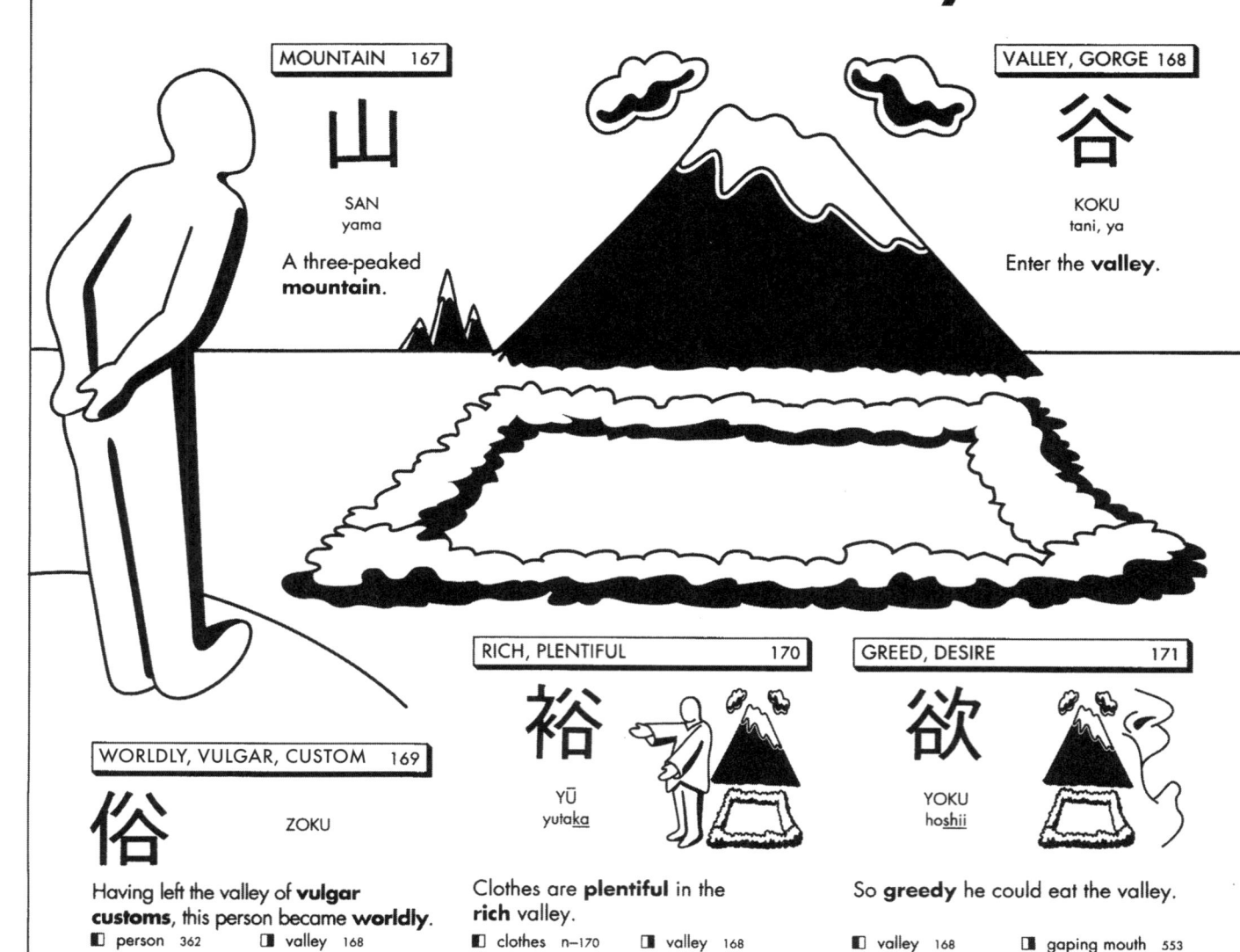

MOUNTAIN 167

山

SAN
yama

A three-peaked **mountain**.

VALLEY, GORGE 168

谷

KOKU
tani, ya

Enter the **valley**.

WORLDLY, VULGAR, CUSTOM 169

俗

ZOKU

Having left the valley of **vulgar customs**, this person became **worldly**.

▫ person 362 ▫ valley 168

RICH, PLENTIFUL 170

裕

YŪ
yuta<u>ka</u>

Clothes are **plentiful** in the **rich** valley.

▫ clothes n–170 ▫ valley 168

GREED, DESIRE 171

欲

YOKU
ho<u>shii</u>

So **greedy** he could eat the valley.

▫ valley 168 ▫ gaping mouth 553

MOUNTAINS & VALLEYS

DARK, OBSCURE, LONELY 172

幽

YŪ
kasu*ka*

Two **dark** and **lonely** paths thread into the mountain.

- mountain 167
- thread (x 2) n–172

PASS, CREST, CRISIS 173

峠

tōge

The **pass** runs above and below the mountain.

- mountain 167
- up 942
- down 943

CRUMBLE, COLLAPSE 174

崩

HŌ
kuzu*reru*/*su*

The mountain will **crumble** in two months.

- mountain 167
- month (x2) 14

PEAK, TOP 175

峰

HŌ
mine

He made slow progress to the **top** of the mountain.

- mountain 167
- slow progress n–175

RAVINE, GORGE 176

峡

KYŌ

A **ravine** between mountain peaks.

- mountain 167
- insert n–176

EXTREMITY, EDGE, UPRIGHT 177

端

TAN
hashi, hata, ha

A person stands **upright** on the **edge** of a cliff.

- stand 627
- mountain 167
- plant n–177

CAPE, STEEP 178

崎

KI
saki

A **steep** mountain.

- mountain 167
- strange 179

STRANGE, ODD 179

奇

KI

How **strange** to step off the cliff.

- big 913
- opening 566

DRAW NEAR, VISIT 180

寄

KI
yo*ru*/*seru*

A **visitor** approaches our house.

- roof 1144
- strange 179

Stones

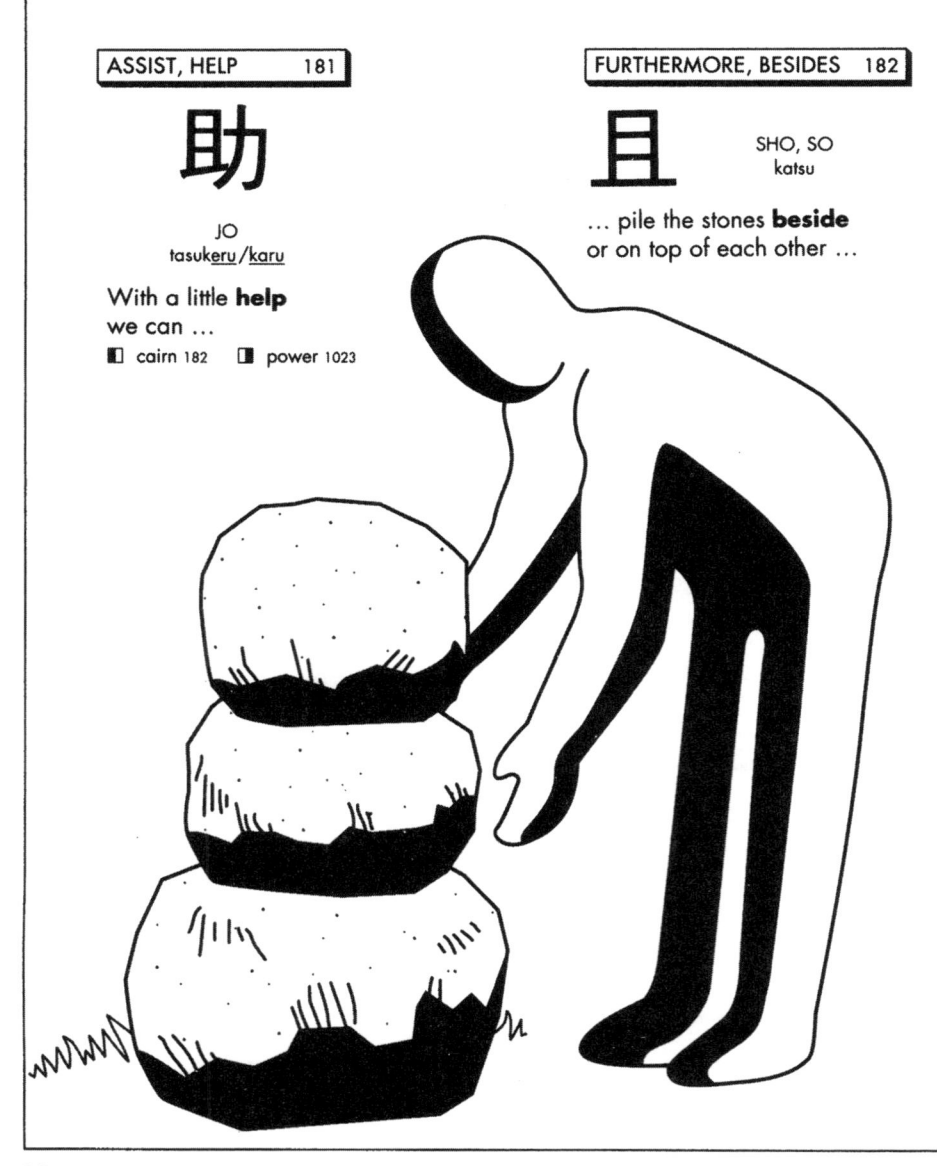

ASSIST, HELP — 181
助
JO
tasuk<u>eru</u>/<u>karu</u>

With a little **help** we can …
- cairn 182
- power 1023

FURTHERMORE, BESIDES — 182
且
SHO, SO
katsu

… pile the stones **beside** or on top of each other …

GROUP, ASSEMBLE — 183
組 
SO
kumi, ku<u>mu</u>

… and **assemble** them with string …
- thread 964
- cairn 182

OBSTRUCT, PREVENT, IMPEDE — 184
阻 
SO
haba<u>mu</u>

… to **obstruct** the hill and **impede** our enemies ….
- hill 1094
- cairn 182

ANCESTOR — 185
祖 
SO

… who took the lives of our **ancestors**.
- religion 696
- cairn 182

STONES

RECLAIM, CLEAR, RUB — 186
拓
TAKU

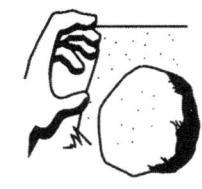

A hand **reclaims** the land by **clearing** it of stones.
- hand 580
- stone 190

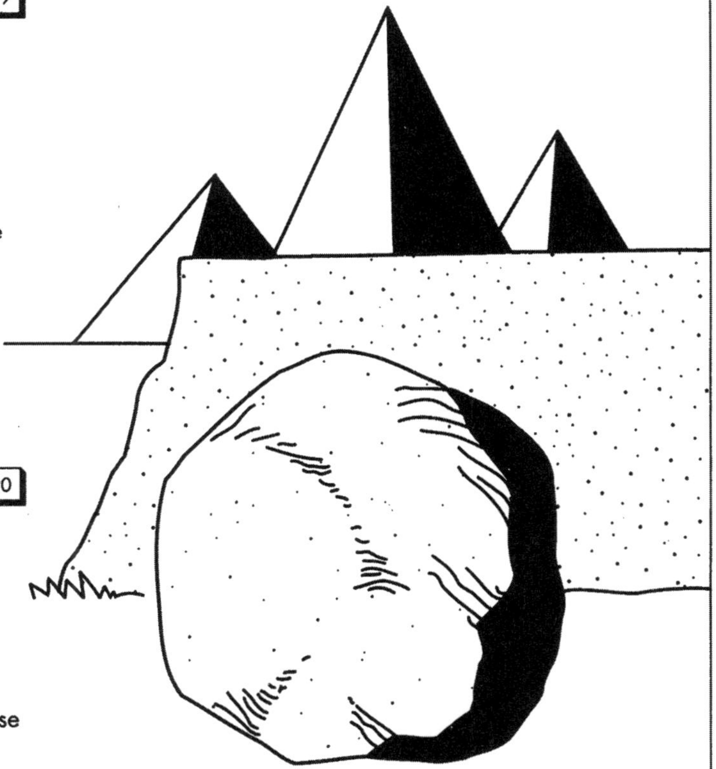

HONE, REFINE — 187
研
KEN
togu

The plow is **honed** on a stone.
- stone 190
- uniformity n–187

MAGNET, PORCELAIN — 188
磁
JI

A **magnet** is a stone with magical threads of force.
- stone 182
- occult (x2) n–172

ROCK, CRAG — 189
岩
GAN
iwa

A **crag** is a stone outcropping on a mountain.
- mountain 167
- stone 190

STONE, ROCK — 190
石
SEKI, SHAKU
ishi

A **rock** at the base of a cliff.

CHARCOAL, COAL — 191
炭
TAN
sumi

Charcoal comes from the mountain.
- mountain 167
- fire 83

ASHES — 192
灰
KAI
hai

Ashes at the foot of the cliff.
- cliff n–81
- fire 83

SAND, GRAVEL — 193
砂
SA, SHA
suna

Sand is small stones.
- stone 190
- little 926

Cave

INVESTIGATE, EXAMINE 194
究 KYŪ

Examine nine caves.

- hole 194
- nine 905

HOLE, CAVE 195
穴 KETSU, ana

The **cave** sheltered eight people.

- roof 1144
- eight 904

SKY, EMPTY 196
空 KŪ, sora, kara, aku

The **empty sky**, seen through a window in a cave.

- hole 194
- construction 1054

KILN, OVEN 197
窯 YŌ, kama

Fire fine pottery in the **kiln**.

- hole 194
- fine 290
- fire 82

SEARCH, PROBE 198
探 TAN, saguru, sagasu

By hand, we **probed** behind a tree to **search** for a cave opening.

- hand 580
- hole 194
- tree 126

THRUST, LUNGE, PROTRUDE 199
突 TOTSU, tsuku

Big John **lunged** from the cave.

- hole 194
- big 913

EXTREME, SUFFER 200
窮 KYŪ, kiwamaru/meru

A body pulled from the cave showed **extreme suffering**.

- hole 194
- body 459
- pull 817

READINGS

A single kanji can have multiple sounds or readings. Kanji were borrowed from China and used both for their phonetic values (the *on-yomi*, shown in capital letters), which shifted over time, and for words of native Japanese origin (the *kun-yomi*, shown in lowercase letters). Which reading to use for a character depends on context and what characters it is grouped with.

FOOD
食物
tabe — eat 232
mono — thing 277

SIGHTSEEING
見物
KEN — see 543
BUTSU — thing 277

DINE
食事
SHOKU — eat 232
JI — act 590

SPLENDID
見事
mi — see 543
goto — thing 590

ONE O'CLOCK
一時
ICHI — one 897
JI — time 691

BRIEF
一時
i(t) — one 897
toki — time 691

2 — FOOD

食物

Field & Plant

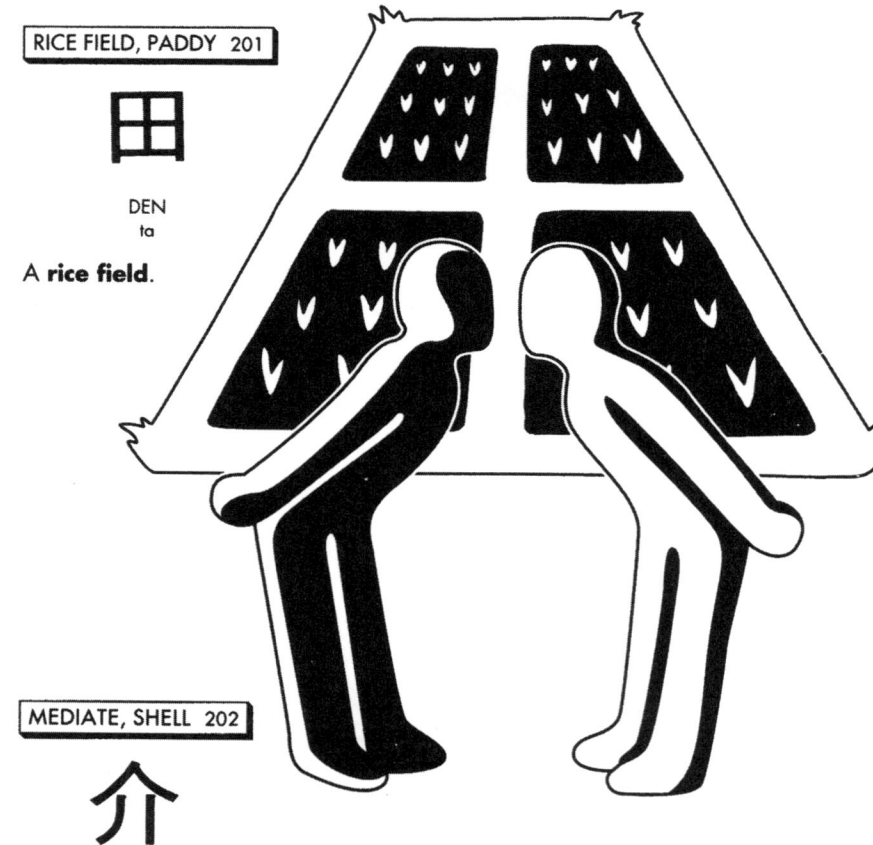

RICE FIELD, PADDY 201

田

DEN
ta

A **rice field**.

MEDIATE, SHELL 202

介

KAI

Two people **mediate** over …

- person n–202
- person n–202

AREA, BOUNDARY 203

界

KAI

… the **boundaries** of the field.

- field 201
- mediate 202

WEALTH, RICHES 204

富

FU, FŪ
tomi, to<u>mu</u>

Under whose roof will go the **riches** of the field?

- roof 1144
- opening 566
- field 201

ABBREVIATE, OUTLINE 205

略

RYAKU

A surveyor walks around the **outline** of each field.

- field 201
- each 1209

FARM, DRY FIELD 206

畑

hata, hatake

The paddy is burned dry and made into a **field**.

- fire 83
- field 201

FIELD & PLANT

RIDGE, EDGE 207
畔
HAN
aze

The **ridges** divide the paddy and hold in water.

- field 201
- half 907

SEEDLING, SAPLING, SHOOT 208
苗
BYŌ, MYŌ
nae, nawa

Seedlings shoot up from the field.

- grass 124
- field 201

TATAMI MAT, SIZE, FOLD, REPEAT 209
畳
JŌ
tatami, tata_mu_

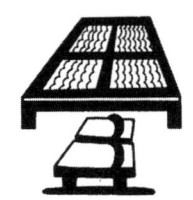

Shoes are for the field, not the **tatami**.

- field 201
- besides 182

POISON 210
毒
DOKU

Mom ate a **poisonous** plant!

- grow 214
- mother 446

BARLEY, WHEAT 211
麦
BAKU
mugi

Check on the growth of the **wheat**.

- grow 214
- slow progress 1218

TILL, PLOW 212
耕
KŌ
tagaya_su_

A **plow tills** the soil well.

- plow n-212
- well n-212

BIRTH, PRODUCE 213
産
SAN
u_mu_

My garden **produces** plants.

- stand 627
- grow 214

LIFE, BIRTH, GROW 214
生
SEI, SHŌ
nama, iki_ru_, u_mu_, u_mareru_, ha_eru_

A **life**-giving plant.

SACRIFICE 215
牲
SEI

A cow's life is **sacrificed**.

- cow 275
- life 214

STAR 216
星
SEI, SHŌ
hoshi

The sun: a life-giving **star**.

- sun 1
- life 214

Rice

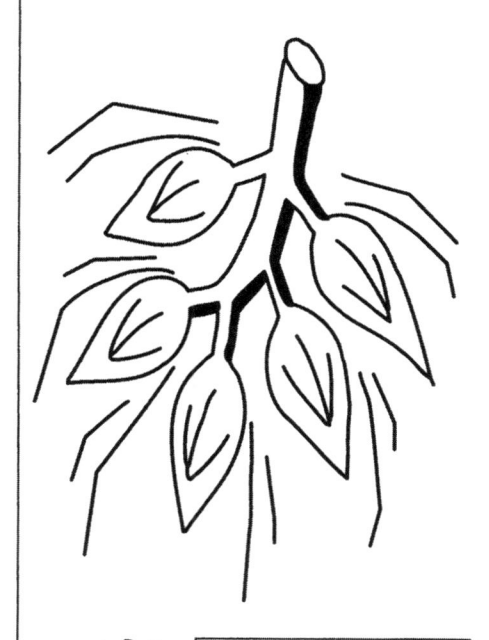

RICE, AMERICA 217
米
SEI, MAI
kome
Japan won't buy **American rice**.

GRAIN, PARTICLE 218
粒
RYŪ
tsubu 
In Japan, rice is bought at **grain** stands.
- rice 217
- stand 627

PROVISIONS, FOOD 219
糧
RYŌ, RŌ
kate 
The town's daily **food** is rice.
- rice 217
- quantity n–219

NEIGHBOR, ADJOIN 220
隣
RIN
tonari 
I'll borrow rice from my **neighbor** on the **adjoining** hill.
- hill 1094
- rice 217
- stop n–220

MATERIALS, MEASURE, CHARGE 221
料
RYŌ 
A ladle is used to **measure** the rice.
- rice 217
- measure 886

POWDER 222
粉
FUN
kona, ko 
Chop the rice into **powder**.
- rice 217
- divide 1025

WORK, EARN MONEY 223
稼
KA
kasegu
Earning money to bring home rice.
- rice plant 231
- home 281

FRAGRANCE, INCENSE 224
香
KŌ, KA
kaoru/ri
The **fragrant** rice dries in the sun.
- rice plant 231
- sun 1

RICE

GRAIN, CEREALS — 225
穀
KOKU

Hands wield axes to harvest the **grains** from the soil.
- soil 101
- rice plant 231
- hand w/ax 792

PROFIT, GAIN, EFFECT — 226
利
RI
ki*ku*

We **profit** by cutting grain …
- rice plant 231
- knife 1037

ORDER, STIPEND — 227
秩
CHITSU

… but lose the grain to workers' **stipends**.
- rice plant 231
- lose 577

PRODUCT, PILE — 228
積
SEKI
tsu*mu* / *moru*

Our rice **products** earn a **pile** of money.
- rice plant 231
- grow 214
- money 708

HARVEST — 230
穫
KAKU

At **harvest** time we feast on fowl.
- rice plant 231
- bird 319
- hand 600

"RICE PLANT" — 231
禾

This **rice plant** radical represents "grain."

COURSE, SECTION — 229
科
KA

Sort the grains of rice in a **sectioned** box.
- rice plant 231
- measure 886

FOOD

Eat

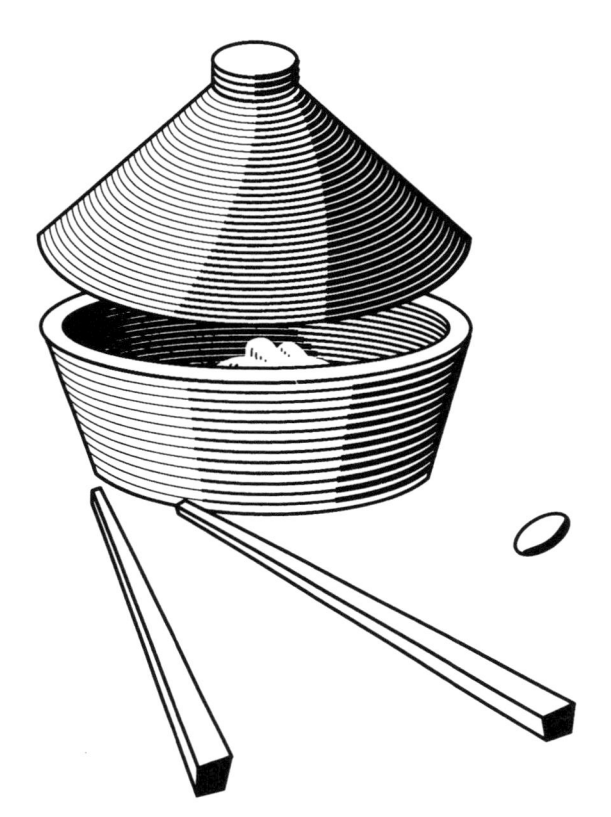

FOOD, EAT 232

食

SHOKU
ta<u>beru</u>, ku<u>u</u>

Eat a bowl of **food**.

LARGE BUILDING, HALL 233

館

KAN

Keep eating and you'll have to keep your butt in a **large building**.

▪ food 323 ▪ roof 1144 ▪ buttocks 466

STARVE 234

餓

GA
u<u>eru</u>

A **starving** body eats itself.

▪ eat 232 ▪ self 450

STARVE, HUNGER 235

飢

KI
u<u>eru</u>

Food on the table makes me **hungry**.

▪ food 232 ▪ table 157

DRINK, SWALLOW 236

飲

IN
no<u>mu</u>

A mouth opens wide to **drink**.

▪ eat 232 ▪ gaping mouth 553

COOKED RICE, FOOD 237

飯

HAN
meshi

Cooked rice eaten in a cupped hand.

▪ eat 232 ▪ turning hand n–237

REAR, SUPPORT 238

養

YŌ
yashina<u>u</u>

I **support** myself by **rearing** sheep.

▪ sheep 290 ▪ eat 232

SECTION, LESSON 239

課

KA

Her speech **lesson** bears fruit.

▪ speak 840 ▪ fruit 240

EAT

FRUIT, RESULT, CARRY OUT — 240
果
KA
ha*te*, hata*su*

Fruit from the trees in the field.

- field 201
- tree 126

JUICE, SOUP, LIQUID — 243
汁
JŪ
shiru

Ten parts water makes a good **soup**.

- water 66
- ten 906

CULTIVATE, GROW — 246
培
BAI
tsuchika*u*

I **grew** a mouth-watering tomato.

- soil 101
- stand 627
- mouth 566

VEGETABLE — 241
菜
SAI
na

Vegetables grow between the grass and the trees.

- grass 124
- hand 609
- tree 126

SALT — 244
塩
EN
shio

I put Earth **salt** on my dish of eggs.

- soil 101
- opening 566
- dish 265

COMPENSATE — 247
賠
BAI

I was **compensated** with money …

- money 708
- stand 627
- mouth 566

EGG, ROE — 242
卵
RAN
tamago

Two **eggs**.

BEANS, MINIATURE — 245
豆
TŌ, ZU
mame

A **tiny** bowl of **beans**.

DIVIDE, CUT UP — 248
剖
BŌ

… when my tomato was **cut up**.

- stand 627
- mouth 566
- knife 1037

Wine

"WINE" 249
酉

A **wine** jar.

ALCOHOL, SAKÉ 250
酒

SHU
sake, saka

Pour out the **saké**.

- water 66
- wine 249

DRUNK, DIZZY 251
酔

SUI
yo<u>u</u>

I get **drunk** after nine or ten bottles.

- wine 249
- nine 903
- ten 906

FERMENT, YEAST 252
酵

KŌ

The young wine needs yeast to **ferment**.

- wine 249
- piety 403

CURD, DAIRY PRODUCE 253
酪

RAKU

Jars of **dairy products** are left on each doorstep.

- wine 249
- each 1209

DISTRIBUTE 254
配

HAI
kuba<u>ru</u>

I'll **distribute** the wine personally.

- wine 249
- me 445

SEVERE, CRUEL, HARSH 255
酷

KOKU

The wine has a **severe, harsh** taste.

- wine 249
- grow 214
- mouth 566

BOTTLE, JUG, JAR 256
瓶

BIN
kame

A **bottle** and a **jug**.

- pair n–256
- vessel n–256

Tray

GAIN, PROFIT, BENEFIT 257
益 
EKI, YAKU
masu

In a **profitable** year my dish overflows.
- water n–257
- dish 261

TRAY, BON FESTIVAL 258
盆
BON

A **tray** is used for cutting.
- divide 1025
- dish 261

REWARD, TOAST 259
酬
SHŪ

Drink a **toast** to the state.
- wine 249
- state 56

TRAY, BOWL, PLATE 260
盤
BAN

Carry the **tray**.
- carry 1182
- dish 261

DISH, BOWL, PLATE, TRAY 261
皿
sara

A **bowl** on a **tray**.

STEAL 262
盗
TŌ 
nusumu

I cry over what'll be **stolen** next—my dish!
- next 553
- dish 261

LIQUID MEASURE 263
升 
SHŌ
masu

Measure ten spoonfuls of **liquid**.
- person 362
- ten 906

SERVE WINE, LADLE, SCOOP 264
酌 
SHAKU
kumu

Serve wine with a **ladle**.
- wine jar 249
- ladle 265

LADLE, MEASURE 265
勺 
SHAKU

Measure liquid with a **ladle**.

Meat

MEAT, FLESH — 266
肉
NIKU

This **meaty** steak serves two people.

"FLESH, MEAT" — 267
月
This radical can mean either **flesh** 266 or **moon** 14 depending on the character it's in.

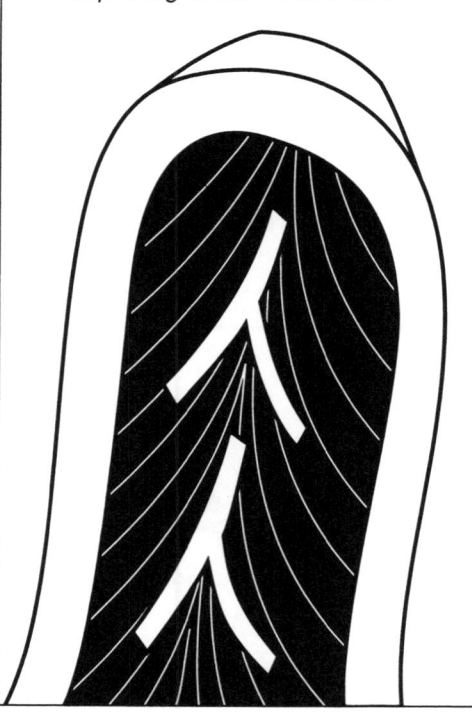

BE LIKE, BE LUCKY — 268
肖
SHŌ
ayaka*ru*

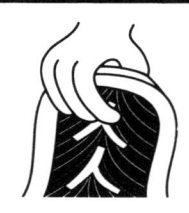

You'll **be lucky** if you get a little meat.
- little 926
- meat 267

PARE, REDUCE — 269
削
SAKU
kezu*ru*

Pare the little piece of meat.
- little 926
- meat 267
- knife 1037

EXTINGUISH, VANISH, CONSUME — 270
消
SHŌ
ke*su*, ki*eru*

A little water **extinguishes** the burning meat.
- water 66
- little 926
- meat 267

FAT, GREASE — 271
脂
SHI
abura, yani

The **fat** of the meat …
- meat 267
- tasty 272

SWEET, PRESUME UPON — 272
甘
KAN
amai/*eru*/*yakasu*

…is **sweet**.

TASTY, GOOD, GIST — 273
旨
SHI
mune, uma*i*

I spoon **tasty** things into my mouth.
- spoon n–273
- mouth n–273

FAT — 274
肪
BŌ

Trim the **fat** off the sides of the meat.
- meat 267
- side 386

3 ANIMALS

INTERESTING WORDS

"Fire-flower" burns a picture in your mind, while "flowering fire" is much more playful than the English "fireworks." Words like "interesting" and "genius" make you wonder how they came to be. Compounds like "adult" and "tomorrow" have assigned readings that can't be guessed at from their kanji. *Dōbutsu*, "animal," at right, literally means "move thing."

動物

FIREWORKS
花火
hana — **bi**
flower 116 — fire 83

SPARK
火花
hi — **bana**
fire 83 — flower 116

INTERESTING
面白
omo — **shiroi**
face 469 — white 936

GENIUS
鬼才
KI — **SAI**
devil 645 — talent 871

ADULT
大人
otona
big 913 — person 363

TOMORROW
明日
asu
bright 8 — sun 1

Cow, Pig, & Sheep

牛 **COW** 275
GYŪ
ushi

This is the **cow** with the crumpled horn.

PASTURE 276

牧 BOKU
maki

Drive the cow to **pasture**.

- cow 275
- strike 802

THING 277

物 BUTSU, MOTSU
mono

To get milk you pull on the cow's **thing**.

- cow 275
- thing n–277

UNRAVEL, EXPLAIN, SOLVE 278

解 KAI, GE
toku

A cow's horn **explains** a lot about its life.

- horn 280
- knife 1023
- cow 275

豕 **"PIG"** 279

This means **pig** when used as an element.

HORN, ANGLE, CORNER 280

角 KAKU
tsuno, kado

A **horn** bends at an **angle**.

COW, PIG, & SHEEP 281–290

HOUSE, SPECIALIST 281
家
KA, KE
ie, ya

A sty is a **house** for pigs.

- roof 1144
- pig 279

GROUP, FLOCK 282
群
GUN
mura, mure/reru

The lord of the sheep attends his **flock**.

- lord 417
- sheep 290

FRESH, VIVID, CLEAR 283
鮮
SEN
azayaka

Fine **fresh** fish.

- fish 354
- sheep 290

DETAILED 284
詳
SHŌ
kuwashii

His was a **detailed** speech on sheep.

- word 840
- sheep 290

PIG, HOG 285
豚
TON
buta

We use a **pig** for its meat.

- meat 267
- pig 279

GOOD FORTUNE, OMEN 286
祥
SHŌ

A sheep is sacrificed on the altar to bring **good fortune**.

- altar 696
- sheep 290

BEAUTIFUL, FINE 287
美
BI
utsukushii

Big **beautiful** sheep.

- sheep 290
- big 913

ARRIVE, WEAR 288
着
CHAKU
tsuku, kiru

I like to **wear** wool myself.

- sheep 290
- self 542

CHASE, PURSUE 289
逐
CHIKU
ou

In **pursuit** of a pig.

- move 1153
- pig 279

SHEEP, FINE, PRAISEWORTHY 290
羊
YŌ
hitsuji

Sheep are **fine** assets.

291 – 294　　　　　　　　　　　　**ANIMALS**

Horse

HORSE	291

馬

BA
uma, ma

A **horse** lies on its side.

This tends to look more like a **horse**, if you picture it on its side.

STOP, STAY	292

駐

CHŪ

A horse **stays** by his master.

- horse 291
- master 734

NOISE, DISTURBANCE	293

騒

SŌ
sawa<u>gu</u>/<u>gashii</u>

The horse is **disturbed** by a snake.

- horse 291
- strike 802
- snake 311

SURPRISE	294

驚

KYŌ
odoro<u>ku</u>/<u>kasu</u>

Surprise a horse with a stick and it will respect you.

- respect 295
- horse 291

60

HORSE

RESPECT 295
敬 
KEI
uya<u>mau</u>

I'll beat some **respect** into you.

- humility n–295
- strike 802

WARN, REPROACH 296
警 
KEI

He **warned** me of the hand with the stick.

- respect 295
- speak 840

EXAMINE 297
験 
KEN

A good scout **examines** his horse …

- horse 291
- all n–297

SWORD, BAYONET 298
剣 
KEN
tsurugi

… checks his **sword** …

- all n–297
- sword 1023

INVESTIGATE 299
検 
KEN

… and **investigates** behind trees …

- tree 126
- all n–297

STEEP, SEVERE, PERILOUS 300
険 
KEN
kewa<u>shii</u>

… before making camp in the **steep** and **perilous** hills.

- hill 1094
- all n–297

STATION 301
駅 
EKI

Load the horse at the **station**.

- horse 291
- measure 884

RIDER 302
騎 
KI

A strange **rider** mounts …

- horse 291
- strange 179

PACK HORSE, POOR QUALITY 303
駄 
DA

… but the **poor pack horse** keels under the weight of the fat man.

- horse 291
- fat 914

Bugs

INSECT, WORM 304

虫

CHŪ
mushi

A **bug**.

FIREFLY 305

蛍

KEI
hotaru

Firefly: a radiant insect.

- fire n–305
- insect 304

MOSQUITO 306

蚊

ka

A textbook case of **mosquito** bites.

- insect 304
- text 834

COCOON 307

繭

KEN
mayu

In the grass, an insect made a **cocoon** of thread.

- grass 124
- thread 964
- insect 304

BARBARIAN 308

蛮

BAN

His **barbaric** smell is attracting bugs.

- red 929
- insect 304

IMPURE, TURBID, VOICED 309

濁

DAKU
nigoru/su

Use a net to rid the **impure** water of insects.

- water 66
- net 987
- insect 304

TOUCH, FEEL, CONTACT 310

触

SHOKU
fureru, sawaru

An insect's hornlike antennae: "**feelers**."

- horn 280
- insect 304

Snakes & Birds

"SNAKE" 311
虫

Insect 304 originally came from a drawing of a snake and in some kanji carries the meaning **snake**.

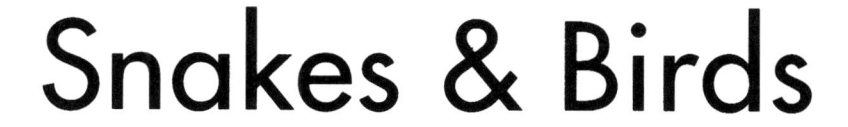

SNAKE, SERPENT 312
蛇
JA, DA
hebi

He fell when bit by a **snake**.

- snake 311
- roof 1144
- person n–312

STRONG 313
強
KYŌ, GŌ
tsuyoi

A **strong** snake can pull with its tail.

- pull 817
- snake 311

BIRD 314
鳥
CHŌ
tori

A **bird** in a nest …

NON-HUMAN CRY 315
鳴
MEI
naku/ru

… **cries** out.

- mouth 566
- bird 314

ISLAND 316
島
TŌ
shima

A bird flies above the **island** mountains.

- mountain 167
- bird 314

CRANE, STORK 317
鶴
KAKU
tsuru

The **crane** is next to another bird.

- heron 331
- bird 314

Plumage

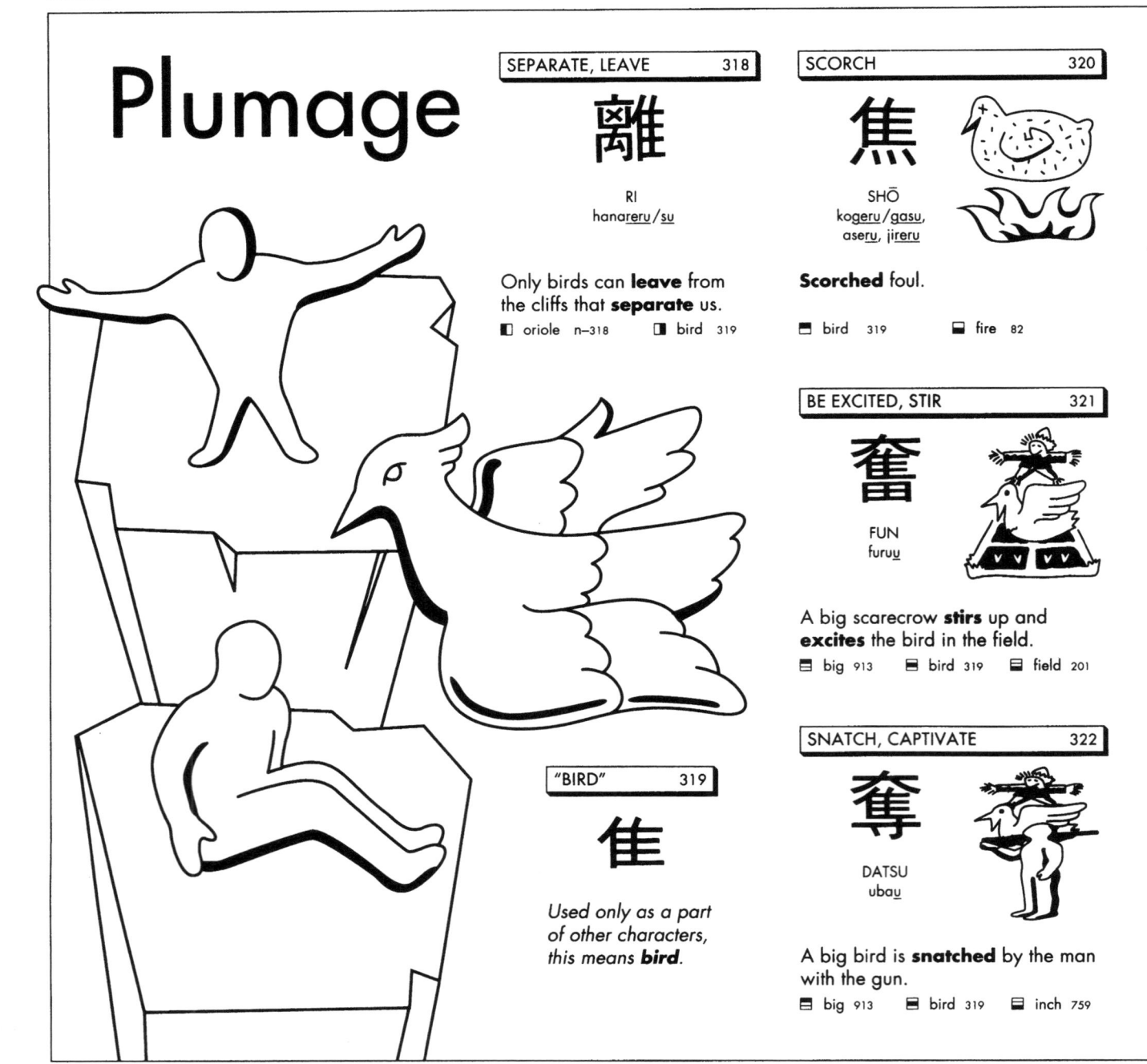

SEPARATE, LEAVE — 318

離

RI
hana<u>reru</u>/<u>su</u>

Only birds can **leave** from the cliffs that **separate** us.

▢ oriole n–318   ▢ bird 319

"BIRD" — 319

隹

Used only as a part of other characters, this means **bird**.

SCORCH — 320

焦

SHŌ
ko<u>geru</u>/<u>gasu</u>,
ase<u>ru</u>, ji<u>reru</u>

Scorched foul.

▢ bird 319   ▢ fire 82

BE EXCITED, STIR — 321

奮

FUN
furu<u>u</u>

A big scarecrow **stirs** up and **excites** the bird in the field.

▢ big 913   ▢ bird 319   ▢ field 201

SNATCH, CAPTIVATE — 322

奪

DATSU
uba<u>u</u>

A big bird is **snatched** by the man with the gun.

▢ big 913   ▢ bird 319   ▢ inch 759

PLUMAGE

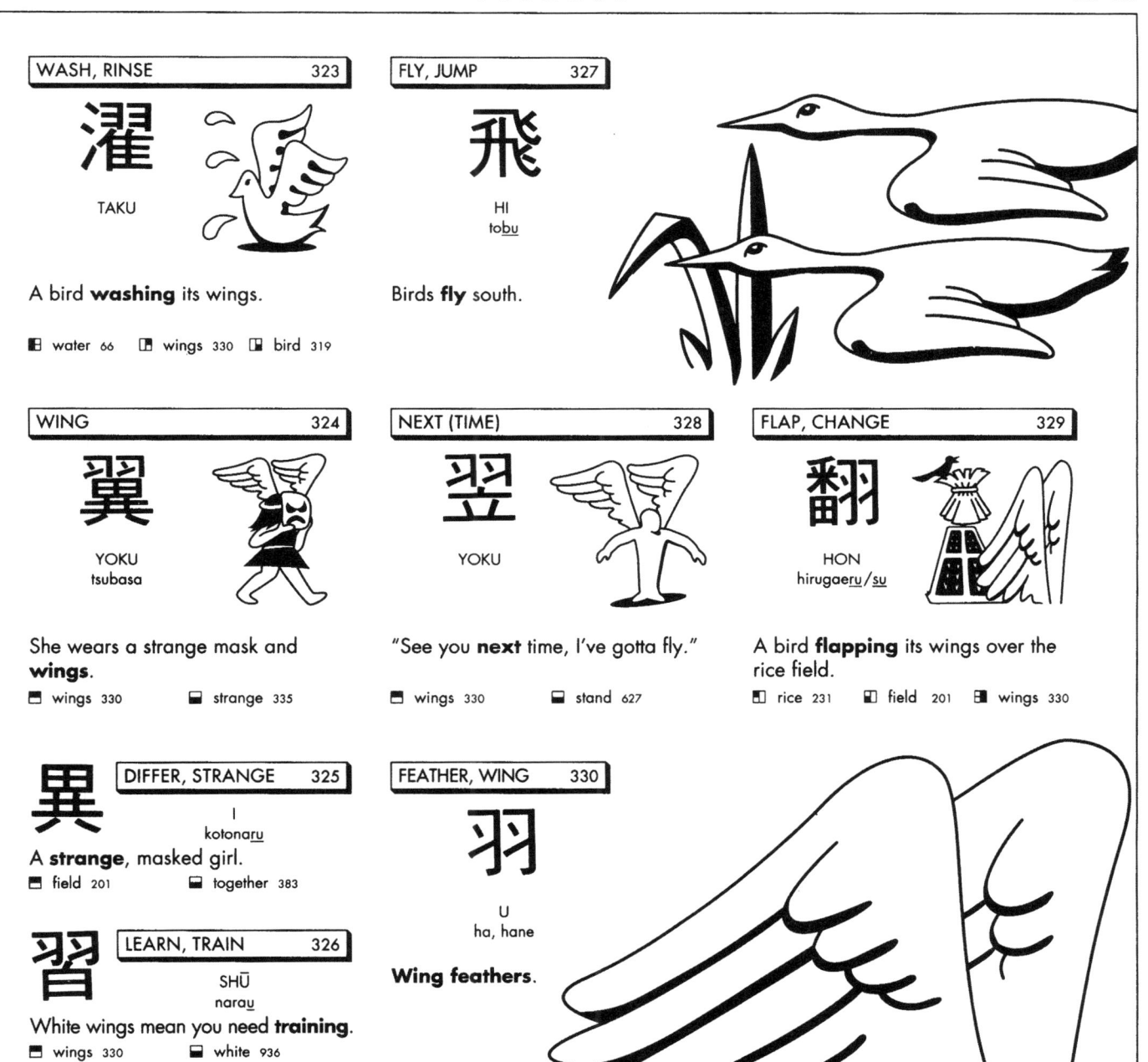

WASH, RINSE — 323
濯
TAKU

A bird **washing** its wings.

- water 66
- wings 330
- bird 319

FLY, JUMP — 327
飛
HI
to<u>bu</u>

Birds **fly** south.

WING — 324
翼
YOKU
tsubasa

She wears a strange mask and **wings**.

- wings 330
- strange 335

NEXT (TIME) — 328
翌
YOKU

"See you **next** time, I've gotta fly."

- wings 330
- stand 627

FLAP, CHANGE — 329
翻
HON
hirugae<u>ru</u>/<u>su</u>

A bird **flapping** its wings over the rice field.

- rice 231
- field 201
- wings 330

DIFFER, STRANGE — 325
異
I
kotona<u>ru</u>

A **strange**, masked girl.

- field 201
- together 383

LEARN, TRAIN — 326
習
SHŪ
nara<u>u</u>

White wings mean you need **training**.

- wings 330
- white 936

FEATHER, WING — 330
羽
U
ha, hane

Wing feathers.

ANIMALS

Heron

"HERON" 331
隹

This element means **heron**.

WATCH, OBSERVE 332
観

KAN

Bird **watching**.

- heron 331
- watch 543

ENCOURAGE, ADVISE 333
勧

KAN
susu<u>meru</u>

Encourage heron preservation.

- heron 331
- power 745

REJOICE, MERRY 334
歓

KAN
yoroko<u>bu</u>

Rejoice and sing like a bird.

- heron 331
- gaping mouth 553

HERON / DOG

Dog

DOG 335
犬
KEN
inu

A big, spotted **dog**.

- spot n-335
- big 913

BEAST, ANIMAL 336
獣
JŪ
ke(du)mono

The mask of a **beast**.

- protect n-336
- dog 338

FIERCE, RAGING, BRAVE 337
猛
MŌ

The child **bravely** touches the **fierce** dog's dish.

- dog 338
- child 447
- dish 261

"DOG" 338
犭

This element means **dog**.

PROTECT 339
守
SHU, SU
mamoru

A man **protects** the house ...

- roof 1144
- inch 759

HUNT 340
狩
SHU
kari/ru

... and **hunts** with his dog.

- dog 338
- protect 335

HUNTING 341
猟
RYŌ

They go **hunting** for birds ...

- dog 45
- leap n-341

CATCH, SEIZE, GET 342
獲
KAKU
eru, toru

... usually **catching** one in the grass.

- dog 338
- grass 124 + bird 319
- hand 580

Forest Animals

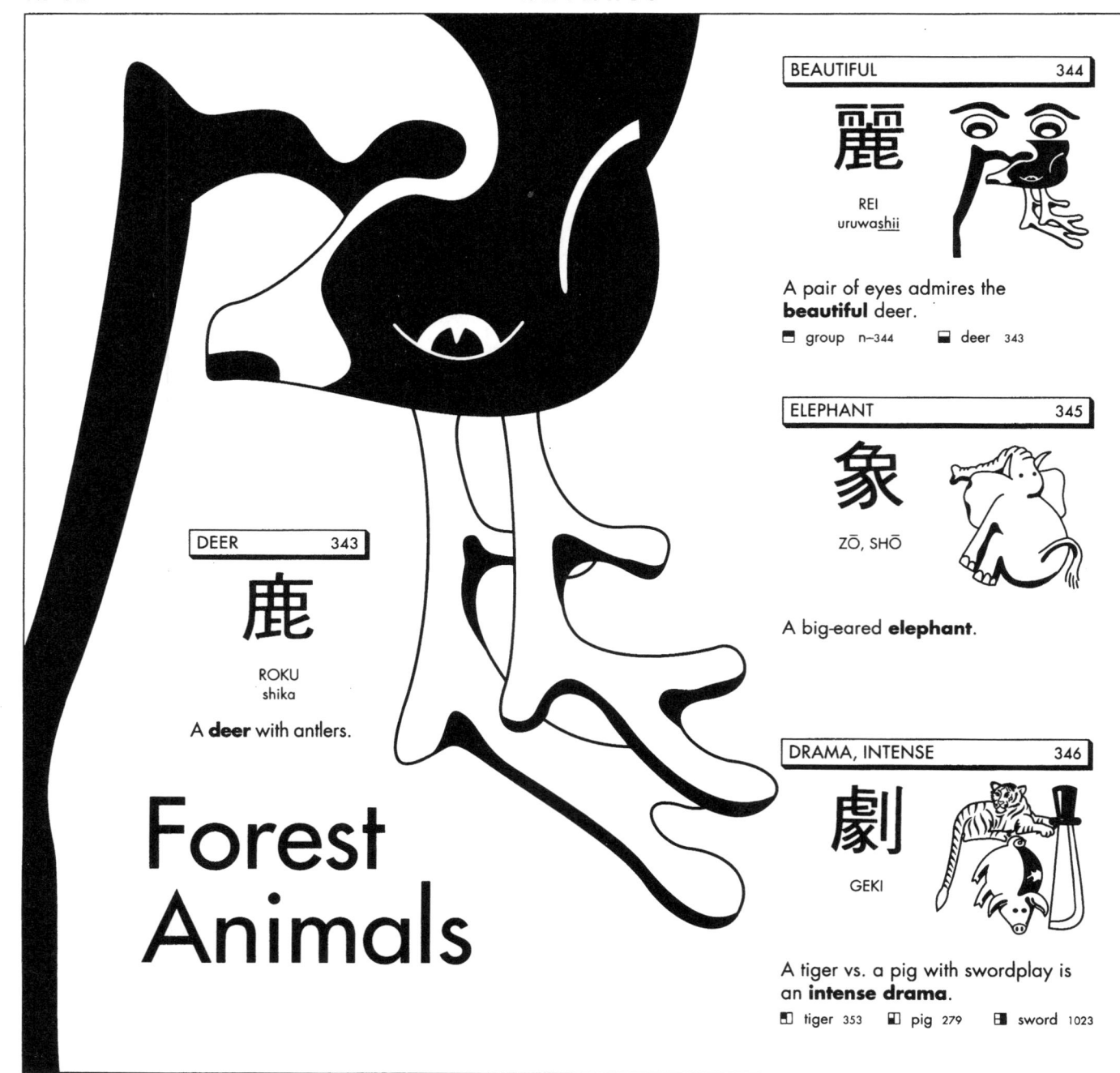

DEER 343
鹿
ROKU
shika

A **deer** with antlers.

BEAUTIFUL 344
麗
REI
uruwa<u>shii</u>

A pair of eyes admires the **beautiful** deer.
- group n–344
- deer 343

ELEPHANT 345
象
ZŌ, SHŌ

A big-eared **elephant**.

DRAMA, INTENSE 346
劇
GEKI

A tiger vs. a pig with swordplay is an **intense drama**.
- tiger 353
- pig 279
- sword 1023

FOREST ANIMALS

CRUELTY, OPPRESS — 347
虐 
GYAKU
shiita*geru*

The tiger's **cruel**, **oppressive** paw …

- tiger 353
- hand n–347

CAPTIVE, PRISONER OF WAR — 348
虜 
RYO
toriko

… guards the **prisoner of war** …

- tiger 353
- man 419

FEAR, ANXIETY — 349
虞 
GU
osore

… and this gives the prisoner's wife **anxiety**.

- tiger 353
- give 834

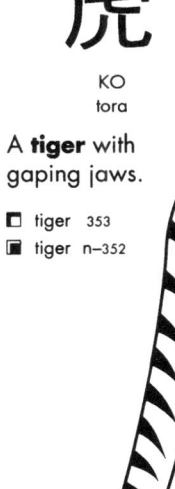

PLAY, FROLIC, JOKE — 350
戯
GI
tawamu*reru*

The circus tiger **plays** around the fire.

- tiger 353
- play n–350
- halberd 801

TIGER — 352
虎
KO
tora

A **tiger** with gaping jaws.

- tiger 353
- tiger n–352

SKIN — 351
膚
FU
hada

A tiger rips open a man's **skin** and eats his guts.

- tiger 353
- stomach n–351

"TIGER" — 353
虍

*This element means **tiger**.*

Sea Creatures

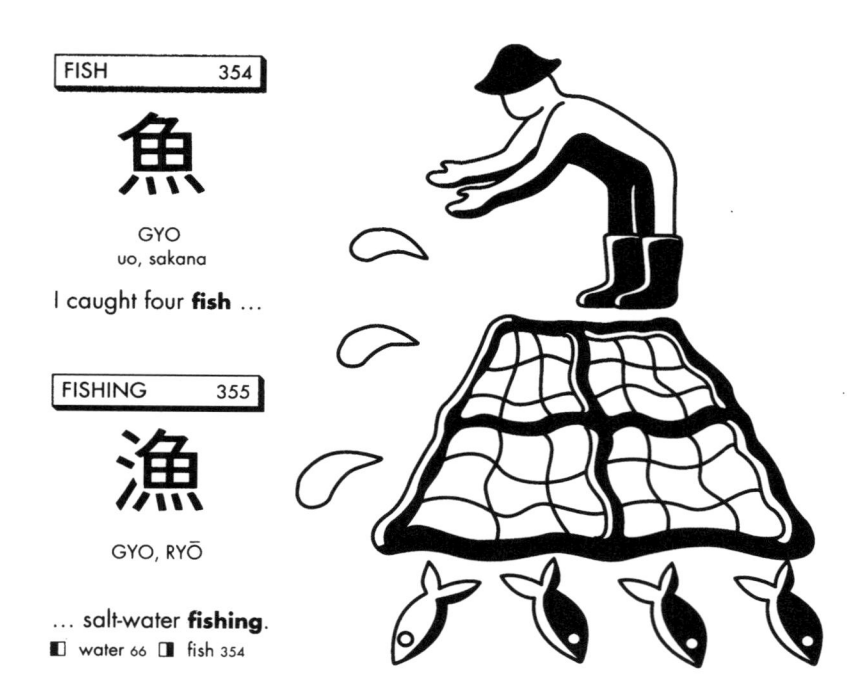

FISH 354
魚
GYO
uo, sakana

I caught four **fish** ...

FISHING 355
漁
GYO, RYŌ

... salt-water **fishing**.
◼ water 66 ◼ fish 354

TORTOISE, TURTLE 356
亀
KI
kame

The **turtle** wears a shell.

SHELL, ARMOR, HIGH, 1ST 357
甲
KŌ, KAN
kōra

A turtle's **shell** is its **armor**.

DRAGON 358
竜
RYŪ, RYŌ
tatsu

A roaring **dragon**.

ATTACK 359
襲
SHŪ
osou

The dragon **attacks** by burning clothing.
◼ dragon n–359 ◼ clothing 1021

WATERFALL 360
滝
taki

The **waterfall** roars like a dragon.
◼ water 66 ◼ dragon 358

WHALE 361
鯨
GEI
kujira

The **whale** is a capital fish!
◼ fish 354 ◼ capital 1077

REPEATING KANJI

A word for "people" in Japanese is *hitobito*, shown at right. The upper kanji is **hito** 363, PERSON. The lower character is a graphic device similar to ditto marks (") in English, indicating that the previous character is repeated. Sometimes, the pronunciation of the second character is changed slightly to make it easier to say.

SOMETIMES	GRAND
時々	堂々
toki doki	DŌ DŌ
time 691 (X2)	hall 1130 (X2)

VARIOUS	WE
色々	我々
iro iro	ware ware
colors 927 (X2)	self 794 (X2)

INCREASINGLY	A LITTLE BIT
益々	少々
masu masu	SHŌ SHŌ
gain 257 (X2)	few 925 (X2)

人
々

4 PEOPLE

People

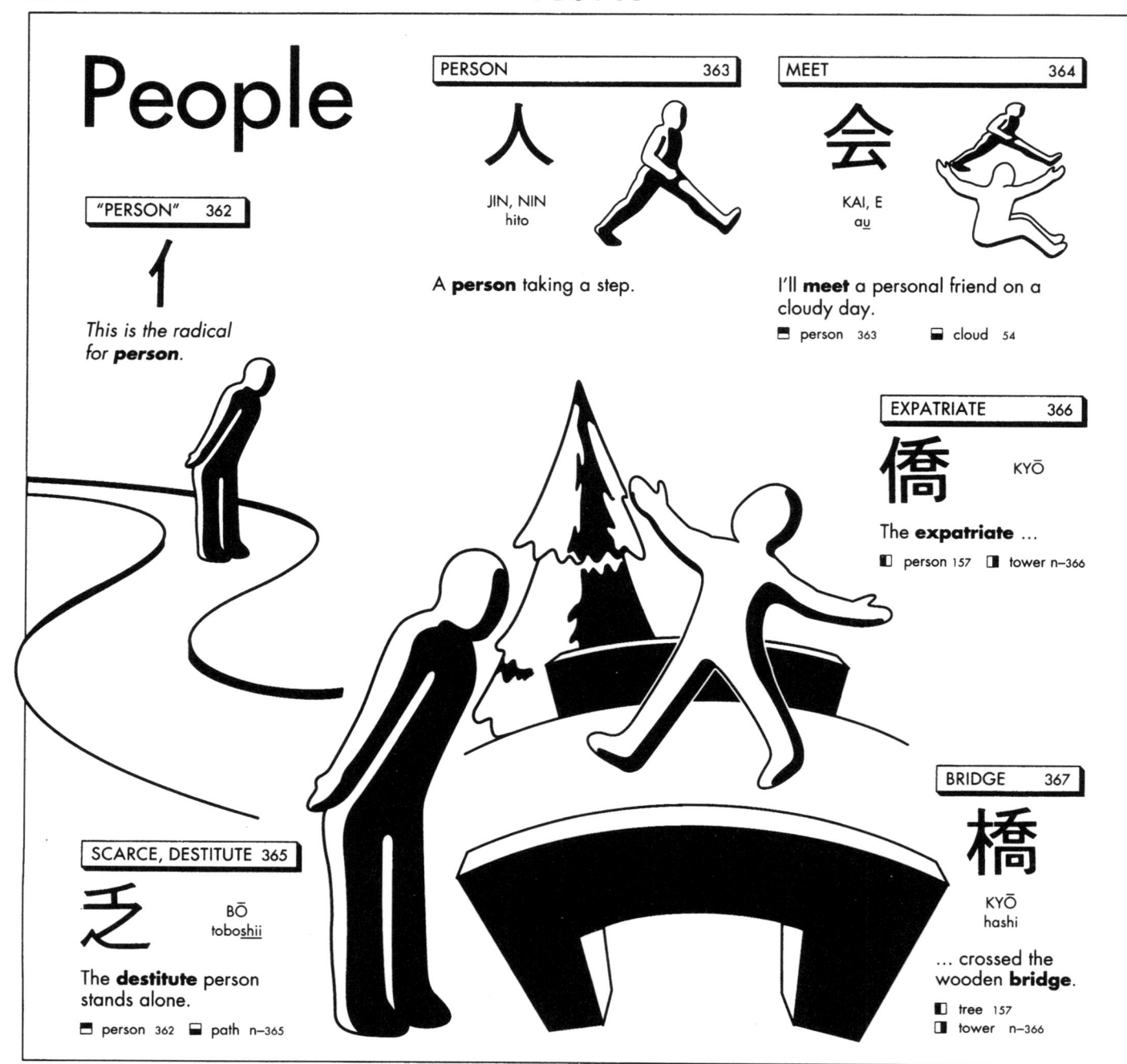

"PERSON" 362

亻

This is the radical for **person**.

PERSON 363

人

JIN, NIN
hito

A **person** taking a step.

MEET 364

会

KAI, E
a<u>u</u>

I'll **meet** a personal friend on a cloudy day.

- person 363
- cloud 54

EXPATRIATE 366

僑

KYŌ

The **expatriate** ...

- person 157
- tower n–366

SCARCE, DESTITUTE 365

乏

BŌ
tobo<u>shii</u>

The **destitute** person stands alone.

- person 362
- path n–365

BRIDGE 367

橋

KYŌ
hashi

... crossed the wooden **bridge**.

- tree 157
- tower n–366

PEOPLE

BENEVOLENT, HUMANITY — 368
仁
JIN, NI

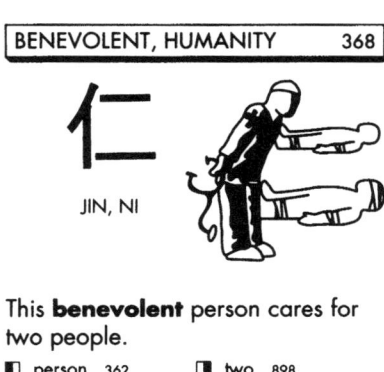

This **benevolent** person cares for two people.

- person 362
- two 898

SUBMIT, FOLLOW, LIE DOWN — 369
伏
FUKU
fu<u>su</u>/<u>seru</u>

The dog **lies** down before its master.

- person 362
- dog 335

RANK, EXTENT — 370
位
I
kurai

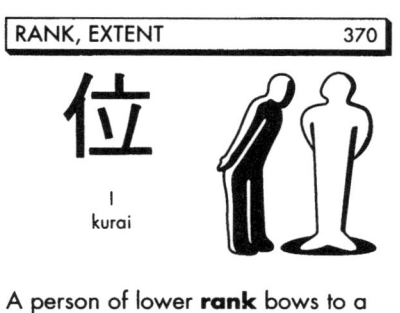

A person of lower **rank** bows to a person of higher standing.

- person 362
- stand 627

LOAD, BURDEN — 371
荷
KA
ni

What is that person's **load**? Grass?

- tree 157
- what? n–371

SERVE, WORK, DO — 372
仕
SHI, JI
tsuka<u>eru</u>

This person **serves** the samurai.

- person 362
- samurai 753

REACH, EXTEND — 373
及
KYŪ
oyo<u>bi</u>/<u>bu</u>/<u>bosu</u>

Reach out and **extend** an open hand.

- person 362
- hand n–373

PEOPLE

CHANGE 374
化
KA, KE
ba<u>keru</u>

A young person **changes** into a seated old man.

- person 362
- fallen person n–374

PRINCIPLES, ETHICS 375
倫
RIN

People in Washington have big **principles** and few **ethics**.

- person 362
- order n–375

REPLACE, GENERATION, FEE 376
代
DAI, TAI
ka<u>waru</u>/<u>eru</u>, yo

Every **generation** must pay its dues.

- person 362
- halberd 801

HERMIT, WIZARD 377
仙
SEN

A **hermit** lives in the mountains.

- person 362
- mountain 167

SEAT, SIT, GATHER 378
座
ZA
suwa<u>ru</u>

Two people **sit** on the ground floor.

- building 1143
- soil + person (x2) 101

PEOPLE

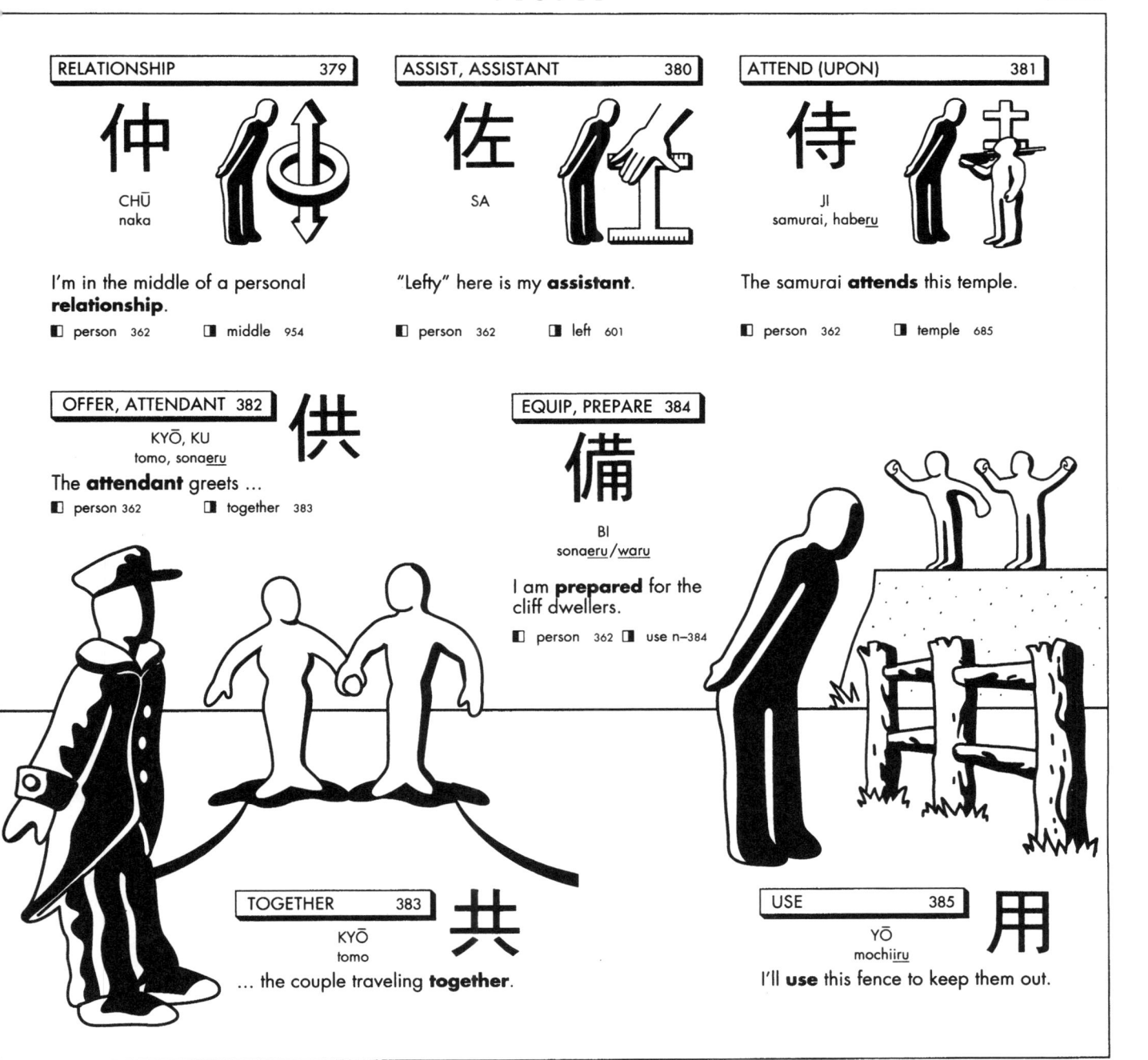

RELATIONSHIP 379
仲
CHŪ
naka

I'm in the middle of a personal **relationship**.

- person 362
- middle 954

ASSIST, ASSISTANT 380
佐
SA

"Lefty" here is my **assistant**.

- person 362
- left 601

ATTEND (UPON) 381
侍
JI
samurai, habe*ru*

The samurai **attends** this temple.

- person 362
- temple 685

OFFER, ATTENDANT 382
供
KYŌ, KU
tomo, sona*eru*

The **attendant** greets …

- person 362
- together 383

EQUIP, PREPARE 384
備
BI
sona*eru*/*waru*

I am **prepared** for the cliff dwellers.

- person 362
- use n–384

TOGETHER 383
共
KYŌ
tomo

… the couple traveling **together**.

USE 385
用
YŌ
mochi*iru*

I'll **use** this fence to keep them out.

Person

PERSON, SIDE, WAY, DIRECTION, SQUARE 386
方
HŌ
kata

The **person** points in that **direction**.

FLAG 387
旗
KI
hata

A person waves a **flag**.

- flag n-387
- device n-387

PERFORM, CHARITY 388
施
SHI, SE
hodoko_su_

A drama is **performed** for charity.

- flag n-387
- creature n-102

RELEASE, EMIT 389
放
HŌ
hana_su_/_tsu_

This person was **released** after being beaten.

- person 386
- strike 802

SIDE, BESIDES 390
傍
BŌ
katawara

Put it **beside** that standing person.

- person 362
- stand 627
- person 386

VISIT, INQUIRE 391
訪
HŌ
otozu_reru_, tazu_neru_

I asked him directions during my **visit**.

- speak 840
- person 386

PERSON / POPULACE

Populace

LOW — 392
低
TEI
hiku*i*

A person comforts a family member who is **low**.

- person 362
- family 396
- one 897

TO REACH, RESIST, OPPOSE — 393
抵
TEI

A hand reaches out for a **resistant** family member.

- hand 580
- family 396
- one 897

COMPARE, RATIO — 394
比
HI
kura*beru*

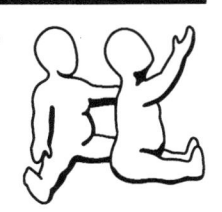

Twins are always **compared**.

- sitting person n–374
- sitting person n–374

MULTITUDE, BUG, DESCENDANTS — 397
昆
KON

A **multitude** of **descendants** sit under the sun.

- sun 394
- compare 394

PEOPLE, POPULACE — 395
民
MIN
tami

There are no **people** with big heads …

CLAN, FAMILY, MR — 396
氏
SHI
uji

… in my **family**.

RESIDENCE, MANSION — 398
邸
TEI

My family **resides** in a **mansion**.

- family 396
- one 897
- hill 1094

CRITICIZE, STRIKE, PASS — 399
批
HI

A hand **strikes** out at the sit-in.

- hand 580
- compare 394

People's Burdens

INDUSTRIOUS 400
孜
SHI

If you're not **industrious**, I'll beat you with a stick.
- child 447
- strike 802

GOVERNMENT OFFICE, SIGN 401
署
SHO

The big eye of **government** watches the ever-burdened people.
- net 987
- person 408

"BURDENS" 402
歩

This element means **burdens**.

TEACH 404
教
KYŌ
oshi<u>eru</u>

I'll **teach** piety to you with this stick.
- piety 403
- strike 802

FILIAL PIETY 403
孝
KŌ

The burden a child bears: **filial piety**.
- burden 402
- child 447

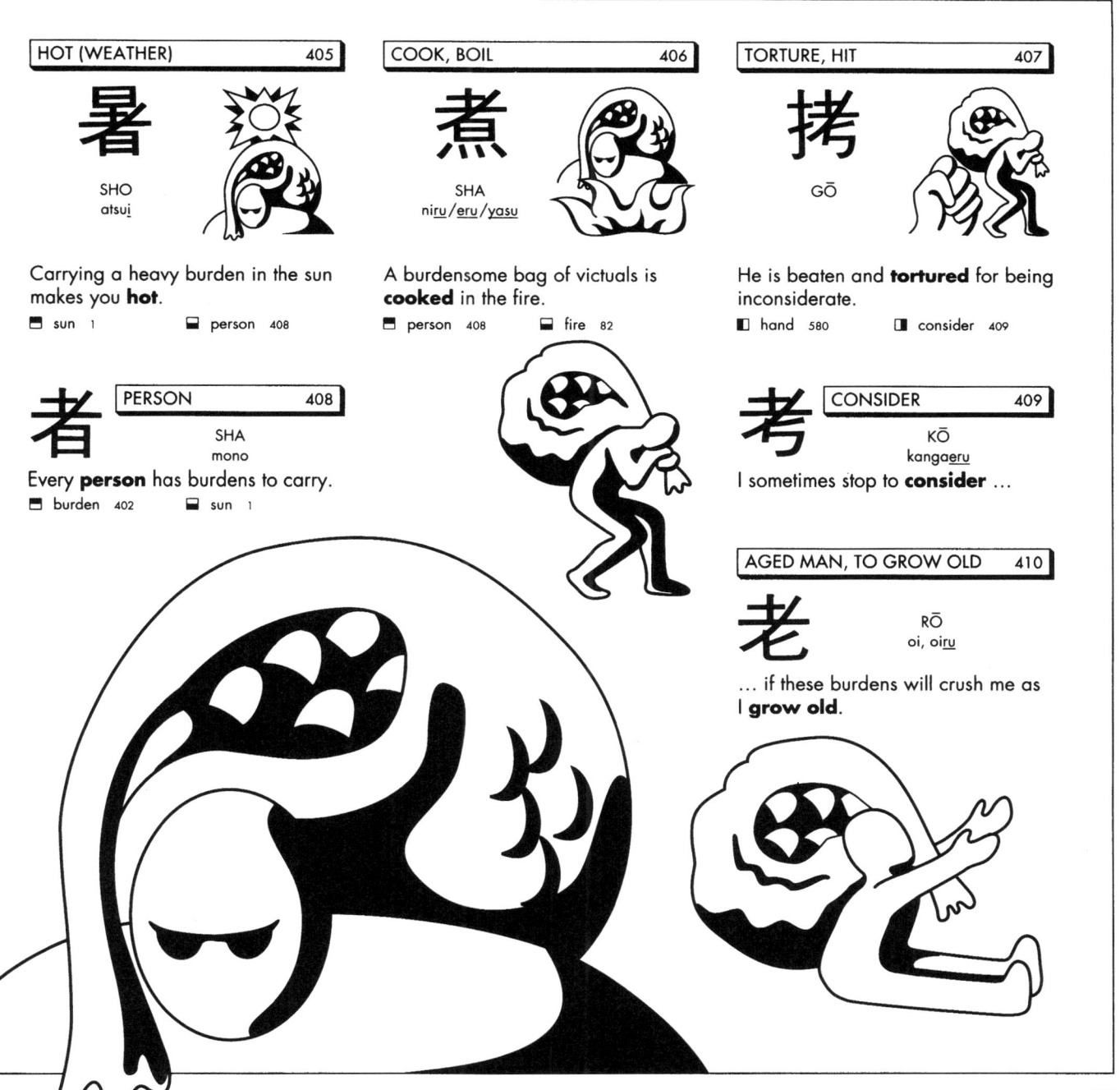

PEOPLE'S BURDENS

HOT (WEATHER) 405
暑
SHO
atsu*i*

Carrying a heavy burden in the sun makes you **hot**.
- sun 1
- person 408

COOK, BOIL 406
煮
SHA
ni*ru*/*eru*/*yasu*

A burdensome bag of victuals is **cooked** in the fire.
- person 408
- fire 82

TORTURE, HIT 407
拷
GŌ

He is beaten and **tortured** for being inconsiderate.
- hand 580
- consider 409

PERSON 408
者
SHA
mono

Every **person** has burdens to carry.
- burden 402
- sun 1

CONSIDER 409
考
KŌ
kanga*eru*

I sometimes stop to **consider** …

AGED MAN, TO GROW OLD 410
老
RŌ
oi, oi*ru*

… if these burdens will crush me as I **grow old**.

Woman & Man

女 | WOMAN 411
JO, NYŌ, NYO
onna, me

This **woman** ...

姦 | NOISY, IMMORAL 412
KAN
kashima<u>shii</u>

... tends to be **noisy** in groups.
◻ woman 411 ◻ woman 411 ◻ woman 411

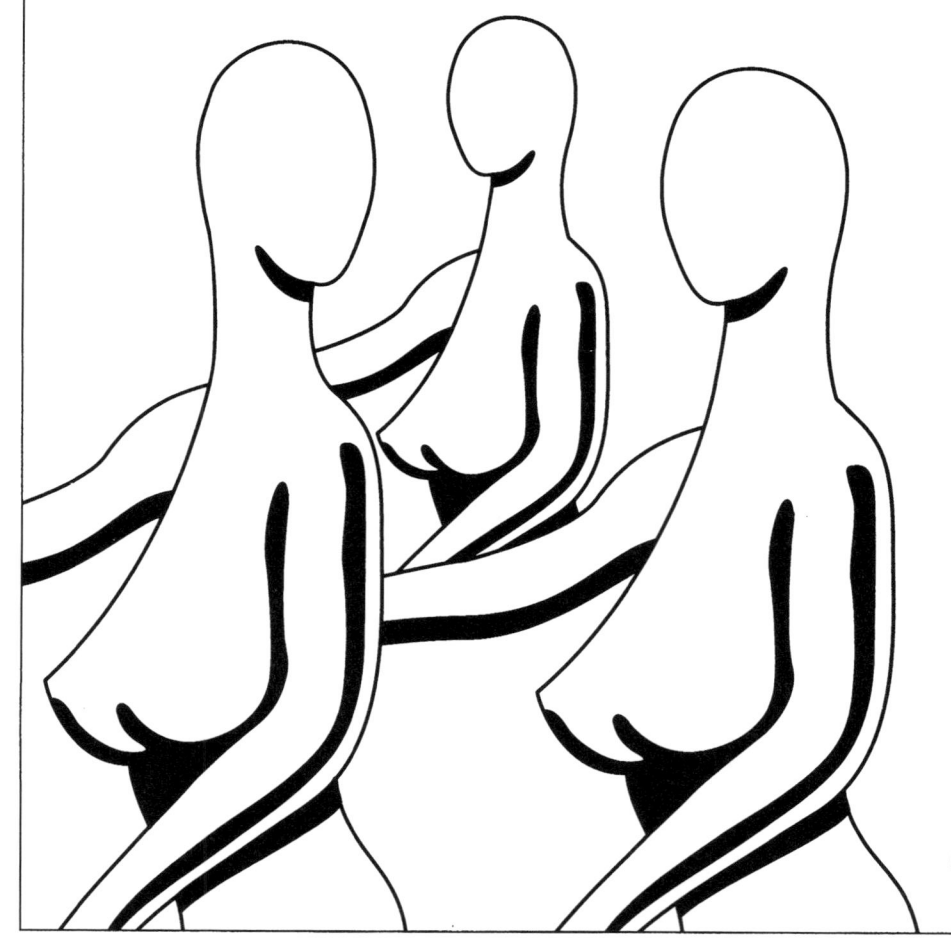

娯 | PLEASURE, AMUSEMENT 413
GO

She takes **pleasure** in giving advice ...
◻ woman 411   ◻ give 835

始 | BEGIN, FIRST 414
SHI
ha<u>ji</u>meru/<u>maru</u>

... but is the **first** to open her mouth ...
◻ woman 411   ◻ self 411   ◻ mouth 566

姿 | FIGURE, SHAPE 415
SHI
sugata

... and cry over her **figure**.
◻ next 555   ◻ woman 411

WOMAN & MAN 416–421

MAKE FUN OF, TEASE, RIDICULE 416

嬲

JŌ
nabu**ru**

Two women **tease** a man from both sides.

- woman (x2) 411
- man 419

Many characters containing the elements for "woman" and "man" reflect the times in which they were created.

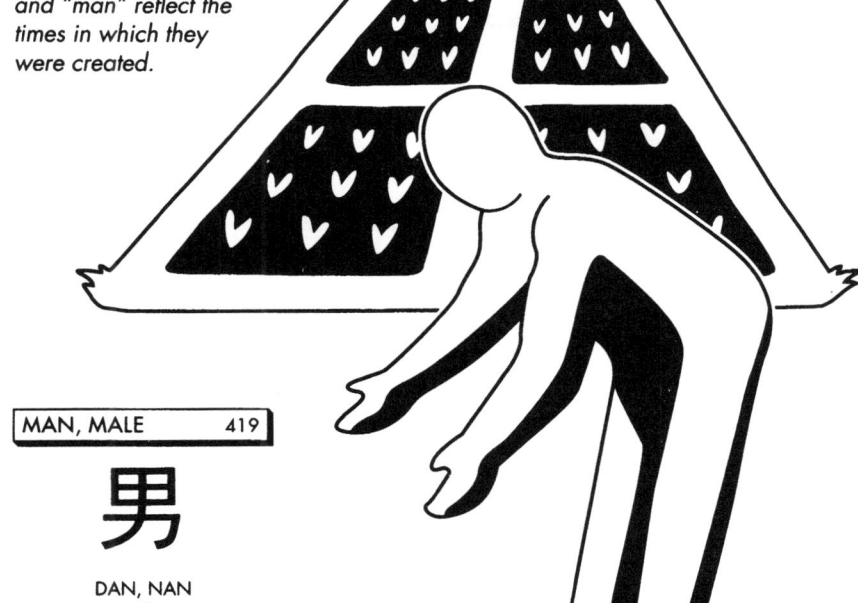

LORD, YOU, MR. 417

君

KUN
kimi

A **tycoon** with a cigar.

- hand w/stick n–417
- mouth 566

MAN, MALE 419

男

DAN, NAN
otoko

A **man** works in the field.

- field 201
- power 745

MALE, POWERFUL 418

雄

YŪ
osu, o-

Falconry is a sport for **powerful males**.

- elbow n–418
- bird 319

MANLY, STRONG 420

壮

SŌ

The samurai shows his **strength**.

- big n– 420
- samurai 753

VILLA, MANOR, MAJESTIC 421

荘

SŌ, SHŌ

The samurai strikes a **majestic** pose on the lawn of his **villa**.

- grass 124
- manly 420

81

Marriage

MARRIAGE 422
姻
IN

If you're too dependent, **marriage** will box you in.

- woman 66
- depend n–422

WOMAN, WIFE 423
婦
FU

A **wife** is a **woman** holding a broom.

- woman 411
- hand w/broom 1052

WIFE 424
妻
SAI
tsuma

The **wife** is handed a broom.

- woman 411
- hand w/broom 1052

CONTACT, JOIN 425
接
SETSU
tsugu

His hand reaches out to **join** hers.

- hand 1052
- stand 627
- woman 411

MISTRESS 426
妾
SHŌ
mekake

A man stands by his **mistress**.

- stand 627
- woman 411

EXQUISITE, ODD 427
妙
MYŌ

This woman is a little **odd**.

- woman 411
- little 924

MARRIAGE

MARRY, BRIDE — 428
嫁 
KA
yome, totsugu

The house of the **bride** looks like a pigsty.

- woman 411
- house 281

RESTFUL, EASE, CHEAP — 429
安 
AN
yasui/maru

A woman under the roof makes for **cheap** labor.

- roof 1144
- woman 411

BANQUET — 430
宴 
EN
utage

The woman gave us everything under the sun at the **banquet**.

- roof 1144
- sun 1
- woman 411

PEACE, SETTLED — 431
妥
DA

A woman's hand brings **peace**.

- hand 580
- woman 411

AUTHORITY, THREATEN — 432
威
I
odosu

The woman **threatens** Hal's **authority**.

- halberd 801
- woman 411

MARRIAGE — 433
婚 
KON

A person sits on a hopechest next to a woman, waiting for **marriage**.

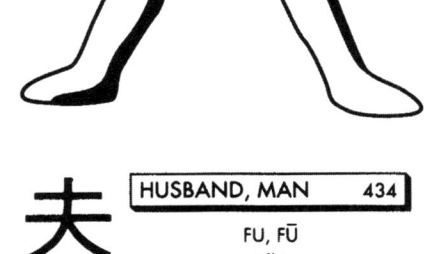

- woman 411
- family 396
- sun 1

HUSBAND, MAN — 434
夫
FU, FŪ
otto

Her **husband** wears a hairpin.

HELP, SUPPORT — 435
扶
FU

A husband lends a **helping** hand.

- hand 580
- husband 434

STANDARD, MEASURE — 436
規
KI

Look to the husband as the **standard**.

- husband 434
- watch 543

Family

FATHER 437
父
FU
chichi

A **father** picks up his child.

ELDER BROTHER 438
兄
KEI, KYŌ
ani

An **elder brother** is a mouth on two legs.

- mouth 566
- legs n–438

YOUNGER BROTHER 439
弟
TEI, DAI, DE
otōto

My snot-nosed **younger brother**.

ELDER SISTER 440
姉
SHI
ane

My **older sister** lives in the city.

- woman 411
- city 1084

YOUNGER SISTER 441
妹
MAI
imōto

My immature **younger sister** lives in the country.

- woman 411
- immature 144

CLAN, FAMILY 442
族
ZOKU

A **family's** coat of arms is displayed on a flag.

- flag n–387
- arrow 818

FAMILY

EACH, EVERY 443
毎
MAI
-goto

Every person has a mother.

■ person 363   ■ mother 446

DESCENDANTS, GRANDCHILDREN 444
孫
SON
mago

The **grandchild** is my **descendant**.

■ child 363   ■ lineage 977

I, ME, SELF, YOU 445
己
KO, KI
onore

I, **myself**, kneel before **you**.

MOTHER 446
母
BO
haha

A woman's nipples become dark during **motherhood**.

CHILD 447
子
SHI, SU 
ko

A **child** ...

LIKE, GOOD, FINE 448
好
KŌ
su<u>ku</u>, kono<u>mu</u>/<u>mashii</u>

... **likes** to be held by a woman.

■ woman 411   ■ child 447

BREASTS, MILK 449
乳
NYŪ
chichi, chi

A woman holds a child to her **breast**.

■ hand 609   ■ child 447   ■ breast n–449

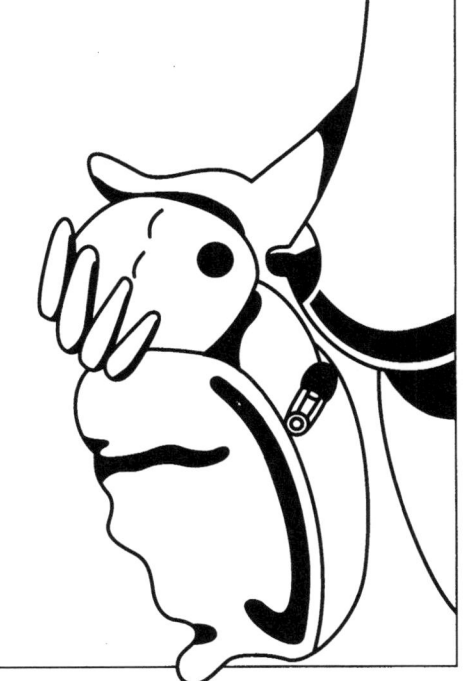

Self

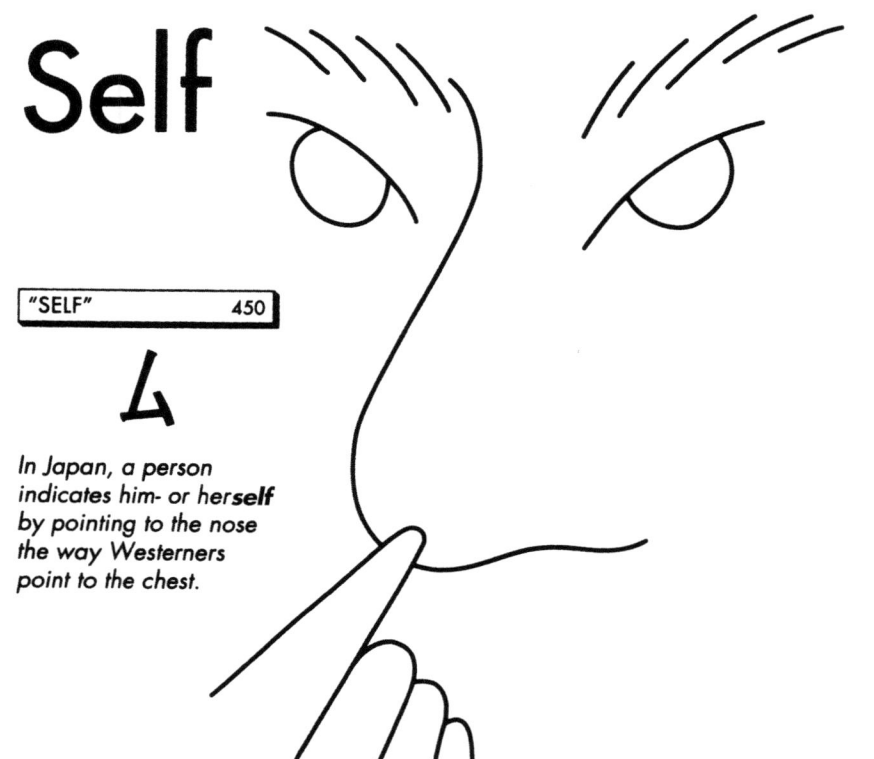

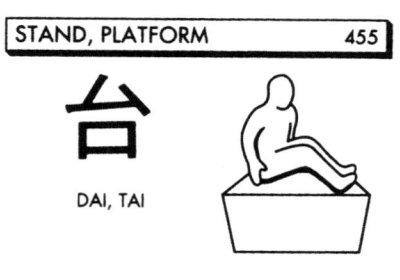

In Japan, a person indicates him- or her**self** by pointing to the nose the way Westerners point to the chest.

"SELF" 450
ム

STAND, PLATFORM 455
台 — DAI, TAI

He's sitting on the **platform** by himself.
- self 450
- mouth 566

SPLIT 456
八

This element means **splitting** or **dividing**.

WOMB 451
胎 — TAI

Wombs are flesh-launching platforms.
- flesh 267
- platform 455

ACCUSE, SUE 453
訟 — SHŌ

I **sued** him for his public **accusation**.
- speak 840
- public 457

PUBLIC, FAIR, LORD 457
公 — KŌ, ōyake

Split open the self and make it **public**.
- split 456
- self 450

DISCUSSION 452
議 — GI

We had a righteous **discussion**.
- speak 849
- righteousness 794

I, PRIVATE, PERSONAL 454
私 — SHI, wata(ku)shi

I keep a **personal** supply of rice.
- rice plant 231
- self 450

PINE 458
松 — SHŌ, matsu

The **pine** tree is in public parks.
- tree 126
- public 457

LOOK-ALIKE KANJI

In a writing system that uses more than 2,000 characters it is not surprising that some characters look very similar. (Imagine the difficulty of Chinese: one dictionary lists more than 48,000 characters.) The kanji **karada** 134, BODY, at right can easily be mistaken for **yasumi** 138, REST. Note the horizontal line within the right-hand element of BODY.

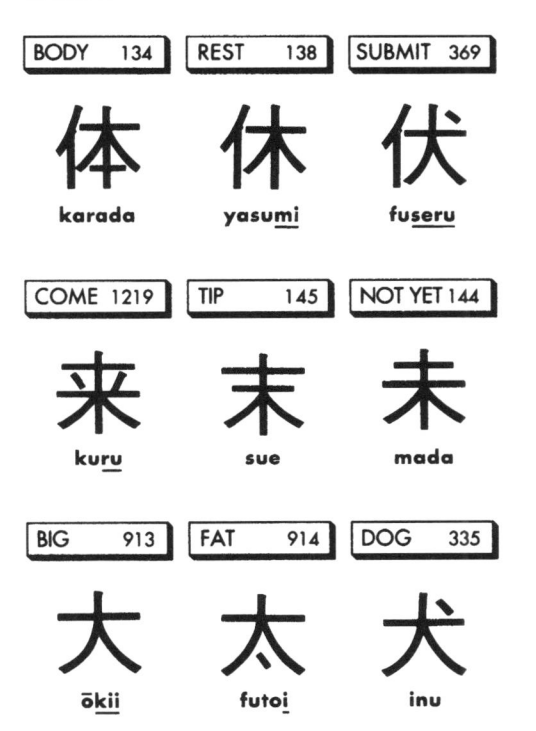

BODY 134	REST 138	SUBMIT 369
体	休	伏
karada	yasumi	fuseru

COME 1219	TIP 145	NOT YET 144
来	末	未
kuru	sue	mada

BIG 913	FAT 914	DOG 335
大	太	犬
ōkii	futoi	inu

体

5
BODY

Body

BODY 459
身
SHIN
mi

A corpulent **body**.

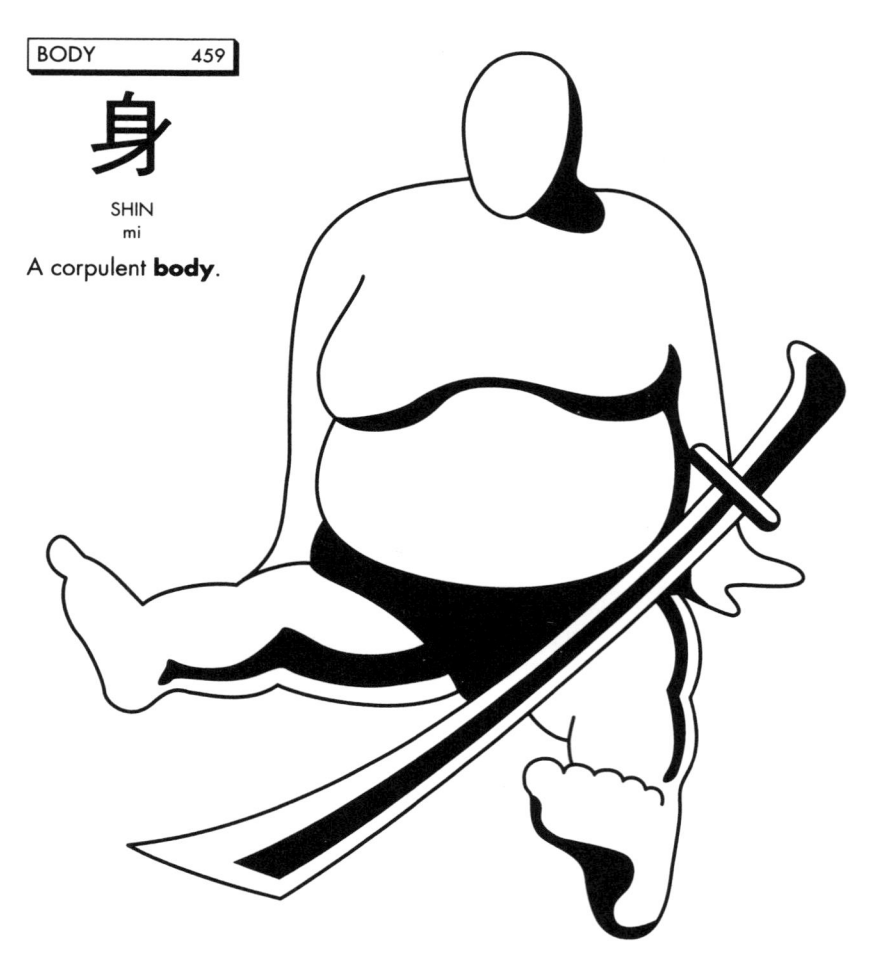

"BODY" 460
尸

This element can mean **body**, and sometimes appears as a miscopying of DOOR 1113.

URINE 461
尿
NYŌ

Urine drops from a bent-over body.

▫ body 460   ▪ water 57

BRAIN 462
脳
NŌ

An evil **brain** thinks only of the flesh.

▪ flesh 267   ▫ hand 611   ▫ evil 647

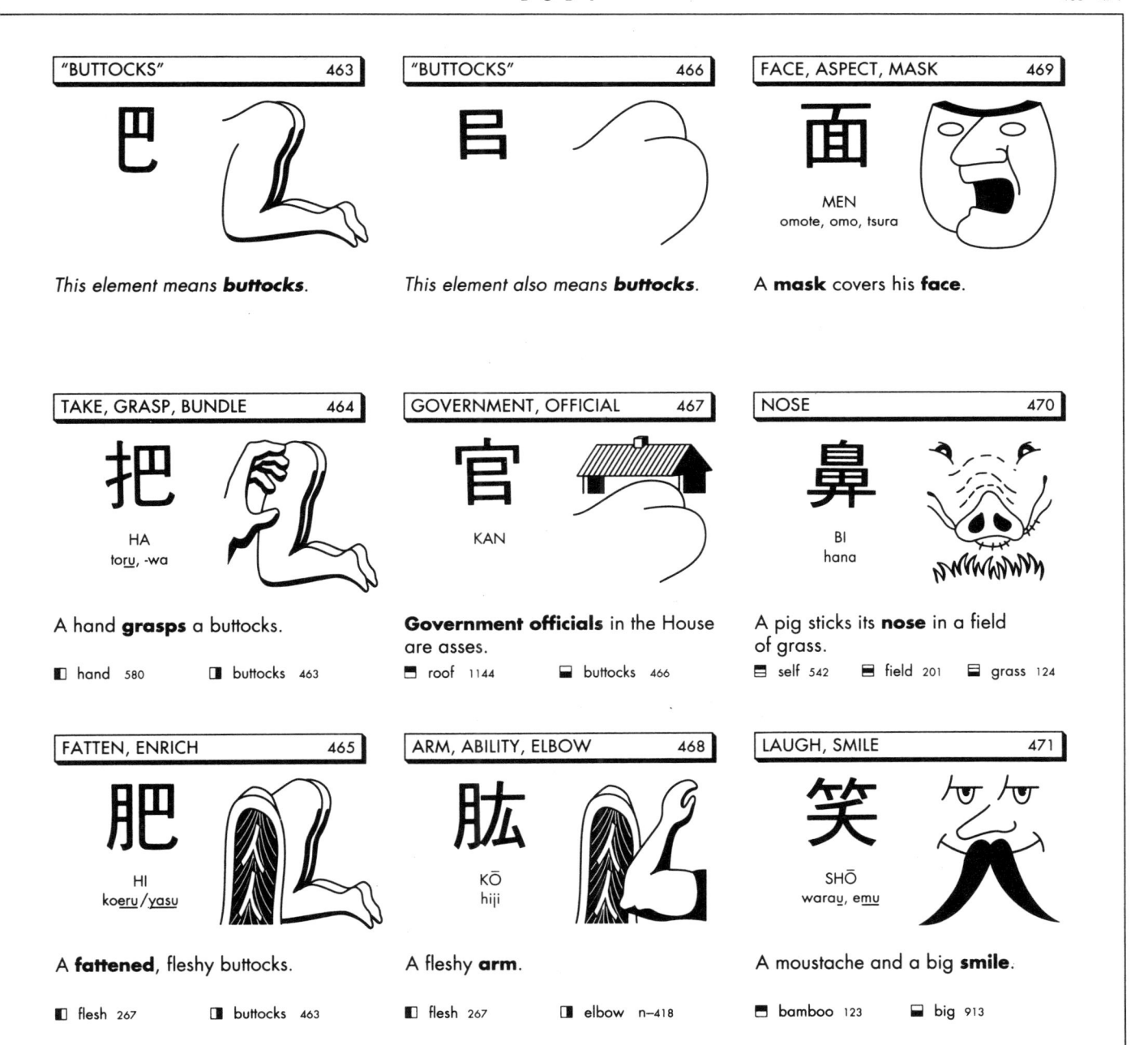

BODY

"BUTTOCKS" 463
巴

This element means **buttocks**.

"BUTTOCKS" 466
呂

This element also means **buttocks**.

FACE, ASPECT, MASK 469
面
MEN
omote, omo, tsura

A **mask** covers his **face**.

TAKE, GRASP, BUNDLE 464
把
HA
to<u>ru</u>, -wa

A hand **grasps** a buttocks.

- hand 580
- buttocks 463

GOVERNMENT, OFFICIAL 467
官
KAN

Government officials in the House are asses.

- roof 1144
- buttocks 466

NOSE 470
鼻
BI
hana

A pig sticks its **nose** in a field of grass.

- self 542
- field 201
- grass 124

FATTEN, ENRICH 465
肥
HI
ko<u>eru</u>/<u>yasu</u>

A **fattened**, fleshy buttocks.

- flesh 267
- buttocks 463

ARM, ABILITY, ELBOW 468
肱
KŌ
hiji

A fleshy **arm**.

- flesh 267
- elbow n–418

LAUGH, SMILE 471
笑
SHŌ
wara<u>u</u>, e<u>mu</u>

A moustache and a big **smile**.

- bamboo 123
- big 913

Flesh & Bone

BONE — 472
骨
KOTSU
hone

A **bone** protrudes from the flesh.

- vertebrae 474
- flesh 267

SKIN, TEXTURE, GRAIN — 473
肌
KI
hada

The **skin** covers the flesh.

- flesh 267
- desk n-157

"VERTEBRA" — 474
This element means **vertebra**.

TORSO, TRUNK, BODY — 475
胴
DŌ

He has the same fleshy **torso** as always.

- flesh 267
- same 889

INTESTINE — 476
腸
CHŌ
harawata

The meat I ate wasn't easy on my **intestines**.

- flesh 267
- sun 1
- rays n-26

SLIP, SLIDE, SMOOTH — 477
滑
KATSU
suberu, nameraka

A wet, **slippery** bone.

- water 66
- bone 472

FLESH & BONE

CHEST, BREAST, HEART — 478

胸

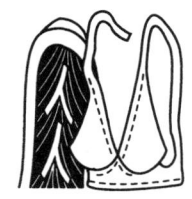

KYŌ
mune, muna

A cross-your-**heart** bra supports fleshy **breasts**.

- flesh 267
- lungs n–478

PLACENTA, WOMB — 479

胞

HŌ

The flesh of the **womb** protects the child.

- flesh 267
- protect 944

MUSCLE, SINEW — 480

筋

KIN
suji

Muscles as **sinewy** as bamboo.

- bamboo 123
- flesh 267
- power 745

SWELL, BULGE — 481

脹

CHŌ
fuku<u>ramu</u>/<u>reru</u>

Long, **bulging** muscles.

- flesh 267
- long 915

VEIN, PULSE — 482

脈

MYAKU

Veins are little streams in the flesh.

- flesh 267
- river 55

SHOULDER — 484

肩

KEN
kata

Like a door on a hinge, the arm swings from the **shoulder**.

- door 1113
- flesh 267

BACK, STATURE, DEFY — 483

背

HAI
se, sei, somu<u>ku</u>/<u>keru</u>

Two professors sit **back** to back and **defy** each other.

- north n–483
- flesh 267

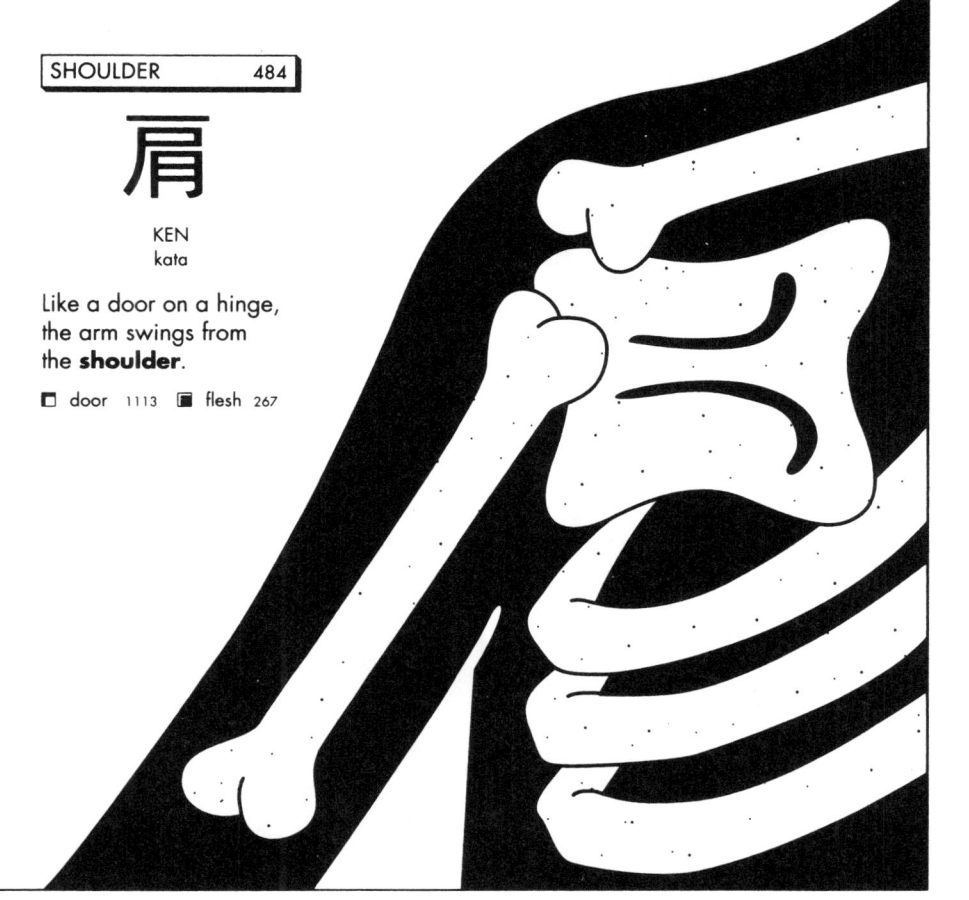

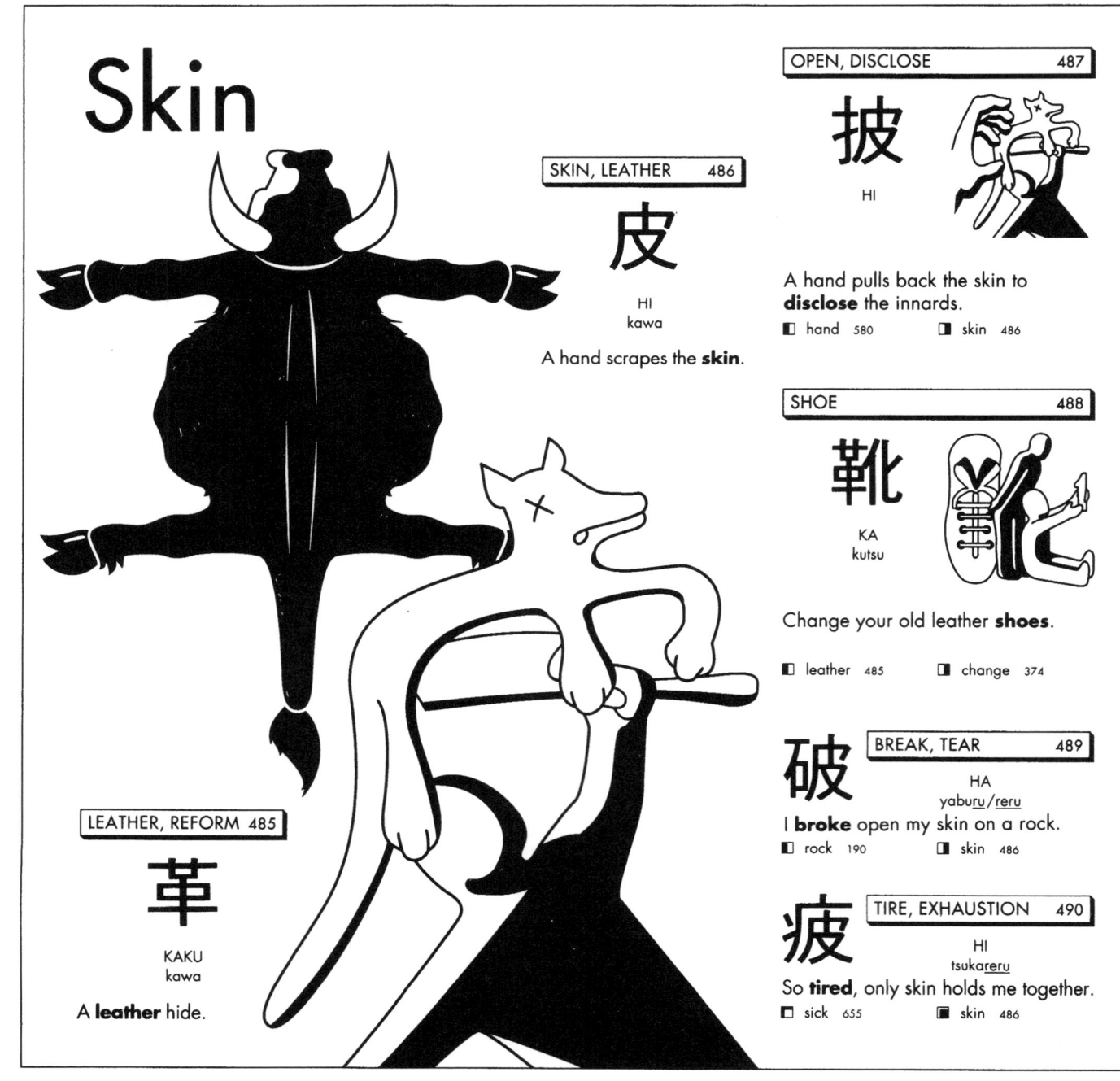

Skin

SKIN, LEATHER 486
皮
HI
kawa

A hand scrapes the **skin**.

LEATHER, REFORM 485
革
KAKU
kawa

A **leather** hide.

OPEN, DISCLOSE 487
披
HI

A hand pulls back the skin to **disclose** the innards.

- hand 580
- skin 486

SHOE 488
靴
KA
kutsu

Change your old leather **shoes**.

- leather 485
- change 374

BREAK, TEAR 489
破
HA
yaburu/reru

I **broke** open my skin on a rock.

- rock 190
- skin 486

TIRE, EXHAUSTION 490
疲
HI
tsukareru

So **tired**, only skin holds me together.

- sick 655
- skin 486

Tooth, Fang, & Claw

SKIN / TOOTH, FANG, & CLAW

TOOTH 491
歯
SHI
ha

Bits of rice get stuck in your **teeth**.
- stop 1205
- rice 217

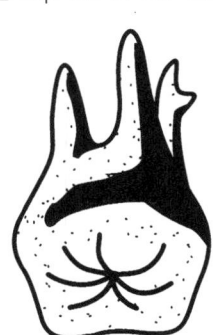

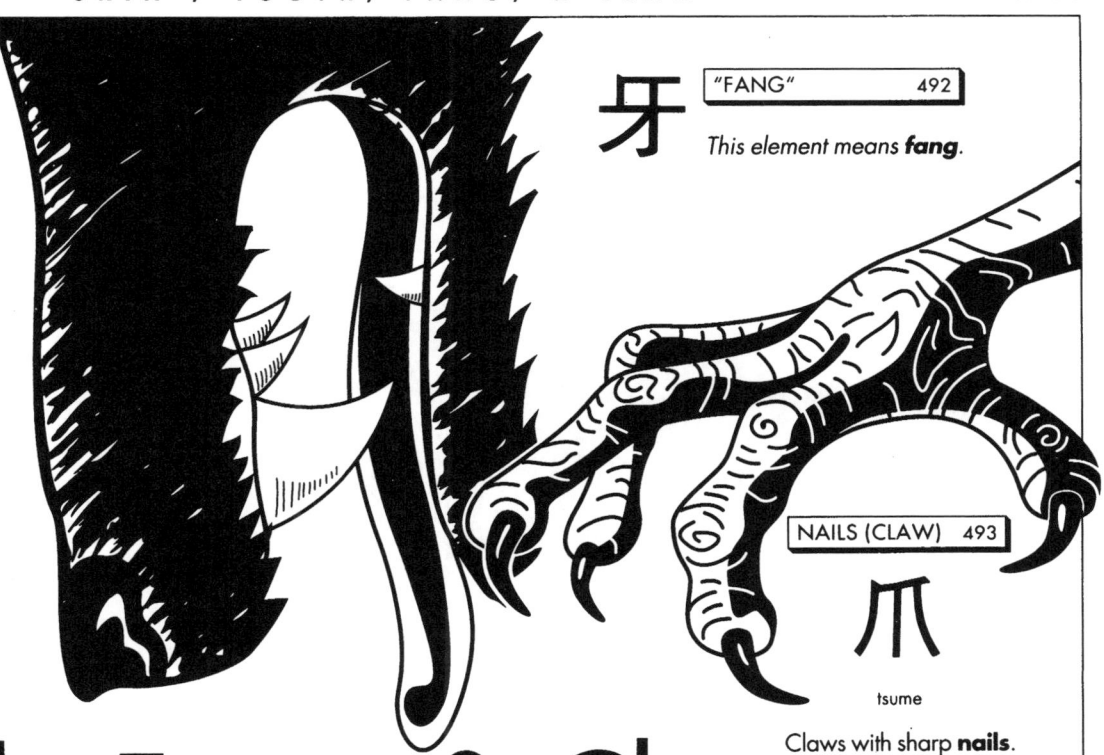

"FANG" 492
牙
This element means **fang**.

NAILS (CLAW) 493
爪
tsume

Claws with sharp **nails**.

AGE 494
齢
REI

The **aged** man ordered some new teeth.
- tooth 491
- order n–494

ELEGANCE, TASTE 495
雅
GA

Sink your fangs into a **tasty** bird.
- fang 492
- bird 319

PINCH, GRASP 496
抓
SŌ
tsumamu, tsuneru

Hands that **pinch**, claws that **grasp**.
- hand 580
- claw 493

93

Heart

FLOW, SECRETE — 497
泌
HITSU, HI

Blood **flows** from a stabbed heart.
- water 66
- necessarily n-497

"HEART" — 498
忄

This form of the **heart** radical looks like bood rushing through one's veins. It often suggests feelings.

HEART, MIND, CORE, FEELINGS — 499
心
SHIN
kokoro

My **feelings** come from the **core** of my **heart**.

PLEASANT, CHEERFUL — 500
快
KAI
kokoroyo<u>i</u>

I started out on a **pleasant** hike.
- heart 498
- pull apart n-500

DECIDE, SETTLE, COLLAPSE — 501
決
KETSU
ki<u>maru</u>/<u>meru</u>

After a while I **decided** to **settle** down before I **collapsed**.
- water 66
- pull apart n-500

SUDDEN, EMERGENCY, HURRY — 502
急
KYŪ
iso<u>gu</u>, se<u>ku</u>

Suddenly, I grasped my heart. It was an **emergency**.
- crouch n-502
- hand 597
- heart 499

HEART

SUSPICIOUS, WEIRD, MYSTERY 503

怪

KAI, KE
aya<u>shii</u>/<u>shimu</u>

It's a **mystery** who stabbed the samurai.

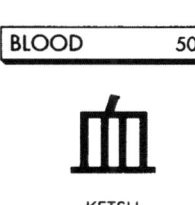

- heart 499
- hand 600
- soil 101

SAD 504

悲

HI
kana<u>shii</u>/<u>shimu</u>

My heart is not happy, but **sad**.

- opposite 960
- heart 498

FEAR, AFRAID 505

怖

FU
kowa<u>i</u>

Fear spread through our hearts.

- heart 499
- spread 1008

BLOOD 506

血

KETSU
chi

He's **bloody**.

GRIEVE, MOURN 507

悼

TŌ
ita<u>mu</u>

Our hearts will **grieve** and **mourn** the deceased.

- heart 498
- table 508

TABLE, EXCEL, HIGH 508

卓

TAKU

Set the **table** for the wake.

- up 942
- sun 1
- ten 906

SEX, NATURE 509

性

SEI, SHŌ
saga

It's his **nature** to express his feelings.

- heart 499
- life 214

ENDURE, STEALTH 510

忍

NIN
shino<u>bu</u>

Can you **endure** a blade in your heart?

- blade 1024
- heart 499

WILL, INTENT 511

志

SHI
kokorozashi, kokoroza<u>su</u>

His heart has the **will** of a samurai.

- samurai 753
- heart 499

RECORD, JOURNAL 512

誌

SHI

The samurai **recorded** his speech.

- speak 840
- samurai 753
- heart 499

Love

LOVE, BELOVED 513

恋

REN
koi, koi*shii*

His heart's filled with **love**.

- red 65
- heart 498

LOVE 516

愛

AI

Unless you uncover your heart, **love's** progress is slow.

- hand 609
- heart 499
- progress n–516

THINK 517

思

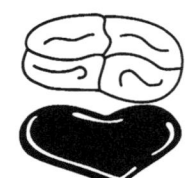

SHI
omo*u*

Thinking involves both the heart and brain.

- field 201
- heart 499

ANXIOUS, DISEASE, BE ILL 514

患

KAN
wazura*u*

He is so **anxious** his heart is tied in knots.

- pierce n–514
- heart 499

LOYALTY, DEVOTION 515

忠

CHŪ

My **loyalty** comes straight from the middle of my heart.

- middle 954
- heart 499

JOY 518

悦

ETSU

Shout for **joy**.

- heart 498
- brother 438

LOVE / HATE

Hate

ANGER, RAGE — 519
怒
DO
ika*ru*, oko*ru*

His heart filled with **rage** ...

- slave 520
- heart 499

SLAVE, SERVANT, GUY — 520
奴
DO
yatsu, yakko

... he beats the **slave** woman.

- woman 520
- hand 600

BAD, HATE — 522
悪
AKU, O
waru*i*

A **bad** heart, full of hatred.

- Asia 1082
- heart 499

COMPOSED, DISTANT — 521
悠
YŪ

Composed, a person behind a wall watches the beating from a **distance**.

- person 362
- strike 802
- heart 499

INDIGNANT, ANGRY — 523
憤
FUN
ikidō*ru*

The crowd becomes **angry** about money.

- heart 498
- ten (x3) 906
- money 708

ANGRY, IN ILL HUMOR — 524
怫
FUTSU

The blood of his heart boils and gushes with **anger**.

- heart 498
- boil n–78

Head, Neck, & Hair

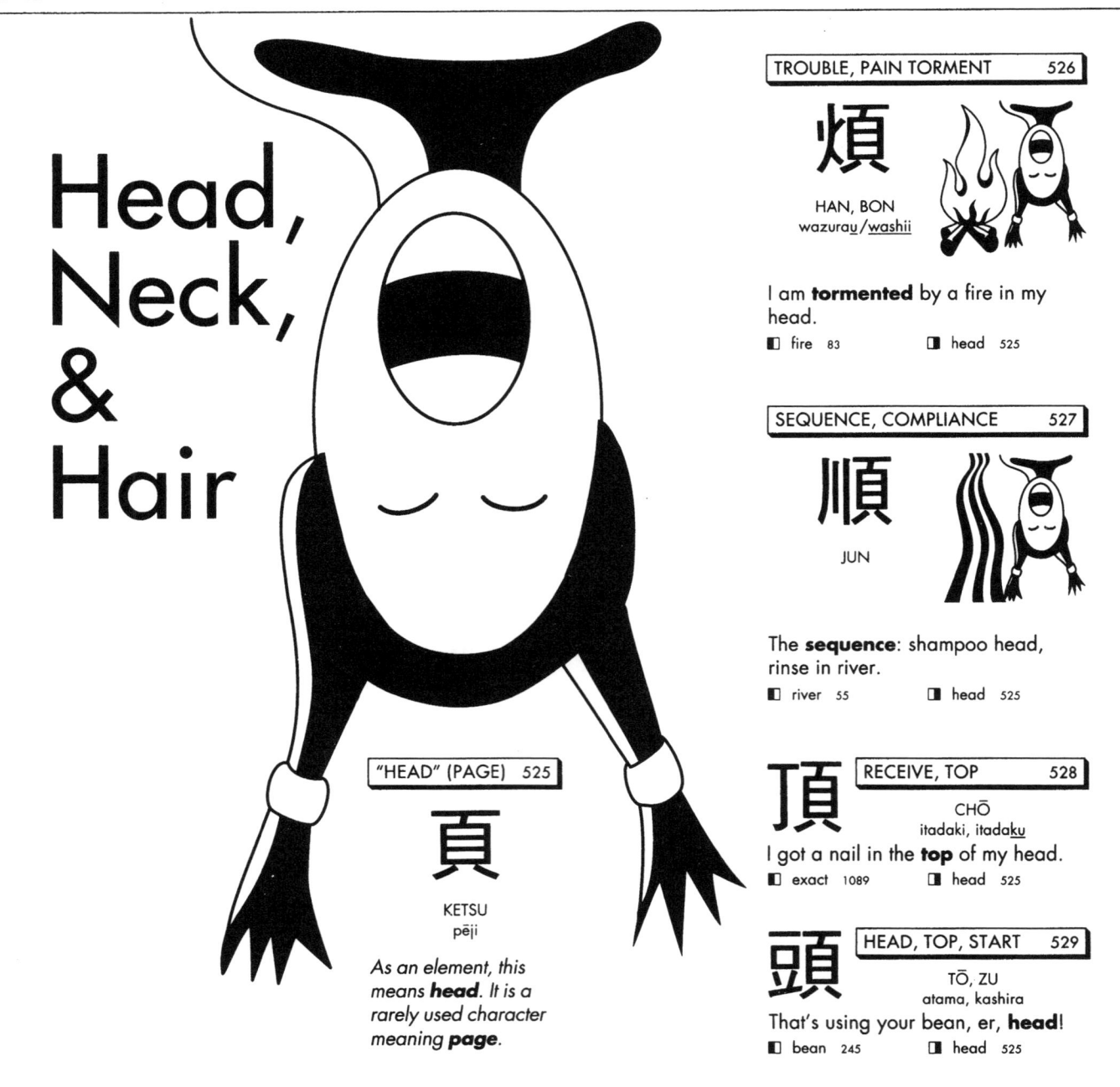

"HEAD" (PAGE) 525

頁

KETSU
pēji

*As an element, this means **head**. It is a rarely used character meaning **page**.*

TROUBLE, PAIN TORMENT 526

煩

HAN, BON
wazura<u>u</u>/<u>washii</u>

I am **tormented** by a fire in my head.

- fire 83
- head 525

SEQUENCE, COMPLIANCE 527

順

JUN

The **sequence**: shampoo head, rinse in river.

- river 55
- head 525

RECEIVE, TOP 528

頂

CHŌ
itadaki, itada<u>ku</u>

I got a nail in the **top** of my head.

- exact 1089
- head 525

HEAD, TOP, START 529

頭

TŌ, ZU
atama, kashira

That's using your bean, er, **head**!

- bean 245
- head 525

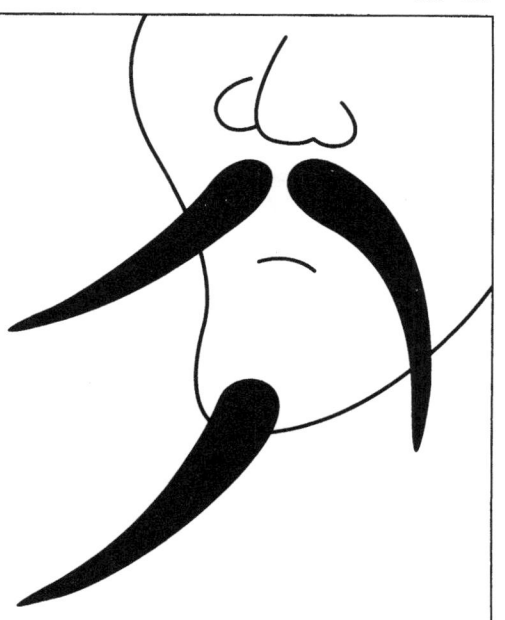

HEAD, NECK, & HAIR

JAW, CHIN 530
顎
GAKU
ago

His **jaw** hangs from his head.

- jaw n–530
- head 530

NECK 531
首
SHU
kubi

A **neck** X-ray.

HAIR 532
毛
MŌ
ke

Hair in a comb.

TAIL 533
尾
BI
o

A **tail** is often a tuft of hair.

- body 460
- hair 532

WAY, ROAD 534
道
DŌ, TŌ
michi

Which **way** in this neck of the woods?

- move 1153
- neck 525

GUIDE, LEAD 535
導
DŌ
michibiku

Lead the way, inch by inch.

- way 534
- inch 534

"HAIR" (DELICATE) 536
彡

This element means **hair**, delicate, or attractive.

HAIR (OF THE HEAD) 537
髪
HATSU
kami

Long **hair** is a girl's best friend.

- long 915
- hair 536
- friend 599

BODY

Eye

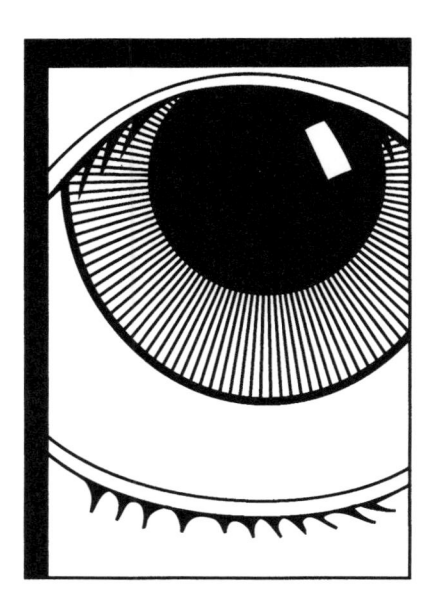

EYE — 538
目
MOKU, BOKU
me, ma-

An **eye** looks through a keyhole.

WATCH, TO LOOK AT — 539
看 
KAN
mi<u>ru</u>

I shade my eye to **look**.

- hand 579
- eye 538

SLEEP, FALL ASLEEP, SLEEPY — 540
眠 
MIN
nemu<u>i</u>/<u>ri</u>/<u>ru</u>

The eyes of the people are **sleepy**.

- eye 538
- people 395

MINISTRY, OMIT, EXAMINE — 541
省 
SEI, SHŌ
habu<u>ku</u>, kaeri<u>miru</u>

The **ministry's examination** will **omit** a few things.

- few 924
- eye 538

SELF — 542
自 
JI, SHI
mizuka<u>ra</u>

The eye is the window to your **self**.

- nose n–542
- eye 538

LOOK, SEE, SHOW — 543
見 
KEN
mi<u>ru</u>/<u>seru</u>/<u>eru</u>

Looking on your hands and knees.

- eye 538
- bent legs n–543

SEE, LOOK, REGARD — 544
視 
SHI
mi<u>ru</u>

Get on your hands and knees when **looking** upon the altar.

- altar 696
- look 543

EYE / EAR

REMEMBER, WAKE — 545

覚

KAKU
obo<u>eru</u>, sam<u>eru</u>/<u>masu</u>

I **remember waking** to see the sun shine over the roof.

- learn n–543
- look 543

SEE, LOOK — 546

覧

RAN

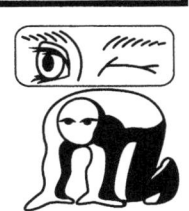

A watchful eye **looks** over the subjects.

- subject n–546
- person n–546
- look 543

INTIMATE, PARENT — 547

親

SHIN
shita<u>shii</u>/<u>shimu</u>
oya

Your **parents** keep a sharp eye on you.

- needle 1006
- look 543

SHAME, ASHAMED — 548

恥

CHI
haji, ha<u>jiru</u>/<u>zukashii</u>

My heart pumps blood to my ears when I'm **ashamed**.

- ear 551
- heart 499

LISTEN (CAREFULLY) — 549

聴

CHŌ
ki<u>ku</u>

Use your ears, eyes, and heart to **listen carefully**.

- ear 551
- net 987
- heart 499

SAINT, SAGE, SACRED — 550

聖

SEI
hijiri

A **sage** is a leader who listens to what his people have to say.

- ear 551
- mouth 566
- king 743

Ear

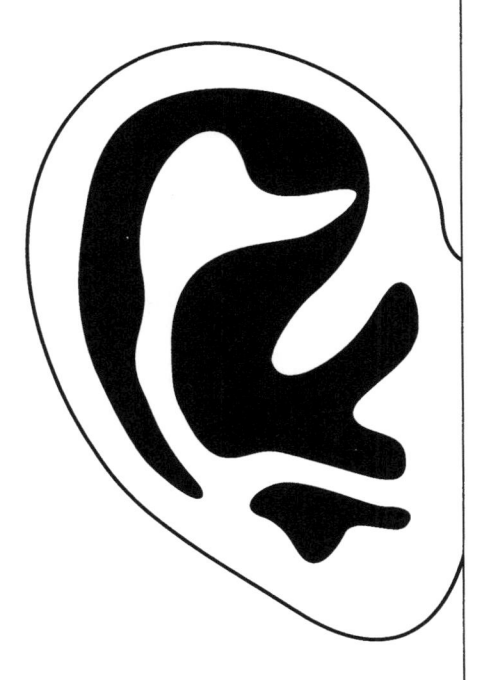

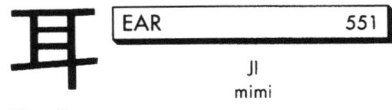

EAR — 551

耳

JI
mimi

Here's an **ear**.

Mouth

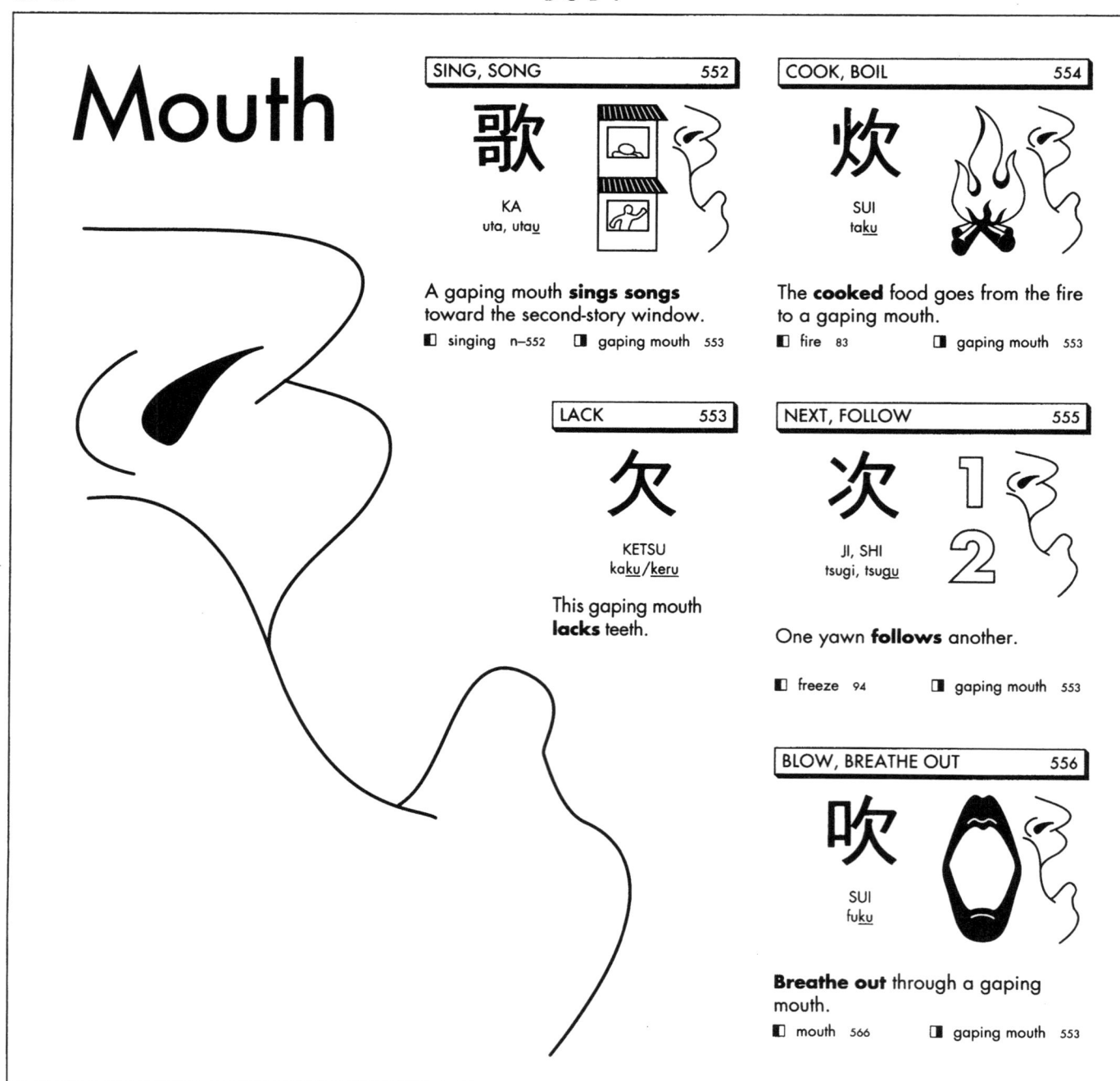

SING, SONG — 552
歌
KA
uta, uta<u>u</u>

A gaping mouth **sings songs** toward the second-story window.

- singing n–552
- gaping mouth 553

LACK — 553
欠
KETSU
ka<u>ku</u>/<u>keru</u>

This gaping mouth **lacks** teeth.

COOK, BOIL — 554
炊
SUI
ta<u>ku</u>

The **cooked** food goes from the fire to a gaping mouth.

- fire 83
- gaping mouth 553

NEXT, FOLLOW — 555
次
JI, SHI
tsugi, tsu<u>gu</u>

One yawn **follows** another.

- freeze 94
- gaping mouth 553

BLOW, BREATHE OUT — 556
吹
SUI
fu<u>ku</u>

Breathe out through a gaping mouth.

- mouth 566
- gaping mouth 553

MOUTH

GOOD LUCK, JOY — 557
吉
KICHI, KITSU

A samurai shouts for **joy**.
- samurai 753
- mouth 566

SHOUT, YELL — 558
叫
KYŌ
sake**bu**

A golfer **shouts** "FORE!"
- mouth 566
- sudden n–558

DISGORGE, VOMIT — 559
吐
TO
ha**ku**

A mouth **vomits** dirt.
- mouth 566
- soil 101

KNOW — 560
知
CHI
shi**ru**

If you **know**, words fly like arrows.
- arrow 818
- mouth 566

TO SUCK, INHALE — 561
吸
KYŪ
su**u**

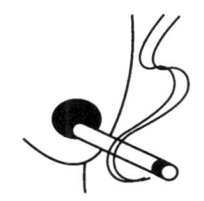

Inhale carbon monoxide, **suck** on a cigarette.
- mouth 566
- reach 373

CALL, BREATHE — 562
呼
KO
yo**bu**

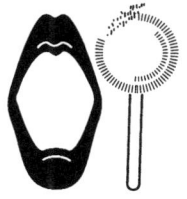

In one **breath**, I blew away the milkweed flower.
- mouth 566
- exhale n–562

INSCRIBE, SIGN — 563
銘
MEI

Inscribe your name in metal.
- metal 105
- name 565

PEACE, SOFT, JAPAN — 564
和
WA, O
yawa**ragu**, nago**yaka**

Peace is a mouth full of **soft** rice.
- rice plant 231
- mouth 566

NAME, FAME — 565
名
MEI, MYŌ
na

His **name** is on everyone's lips.
- moon 14
- mouth 566

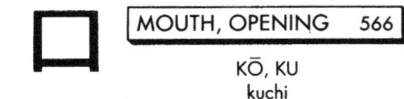

MOUTH, OPENING — 566
口
KŌ, KU
kuchi

The **mouth** is an **opening** in the face.

BODY

CARRY IN ONE'S HAND, BRING 567
携
KEI
tazusa<u>waru</u>/<u>eru</u>

To carry a bird in one's hand.

- hand 580
- bird 319
- hand n–567

MANAGE, MANIPULATE 570
操
SŌ
misao, ayatsu<u>ru</u>

He **manages** to **manipulate** the packages by the Christmas tree.

- hand 580
- goods 1038
- tree 126

CHALLENGE, DEFY 573
挑
CHŌ
ido<u>mu</u>

Others flee, but I **defy** the omen.

- hand 580
- omen 1170

CHOOSE, SELECT 568
択
TAKU
era<u>bu</u>, yo<u>ru</u>

I'll hand pick my **selection** after studying all the measurements.

- hand 580
- measure 884

CLUMSY, POOR 571
拙
SETSU
tsutana<u>i</u>, mazu<u>i</u>

My hands are as **clumsy** as two left feet.

- hand 580
- leave 956

PAY, SWEEP AWAY, RID 574
払
FUTSU
hara<u>u</u>

Rid yourself of people who don't **pay**.

- hand 580
- nose 450

SEARCH 569
捜
SŌ
saga<u>su</u>

To **search** with a lantern in one's hand.

- hand 580
- expound 698
- hand 600

THROW, CAST 572
投
TŌ
na<u>geru</u>

I will **throw** this ax.

- hand 580
- hand w/ax 792

INSERT, PINCH, SQUEEZE 575
挟
KYŌ
hasa<u>maru</u>/<u>mu</u>

I need a hand—they put the big **squeeze** on me.

- hand 580
- squeeze n–575

Hand

BEAT, TAP, CLAP — 576
拍
HAKU, HYŌ

A hand **taps** a white drum.

- hand 580
- white 936

LOSE — 577
失
SHITSU
ushina*u*

It slipped out of my hand and was **lost**.

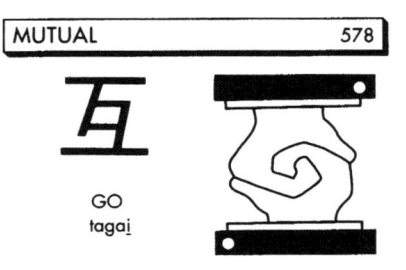

MUTUAL — 578
互
GO
taga*i*

Mutual dependency.

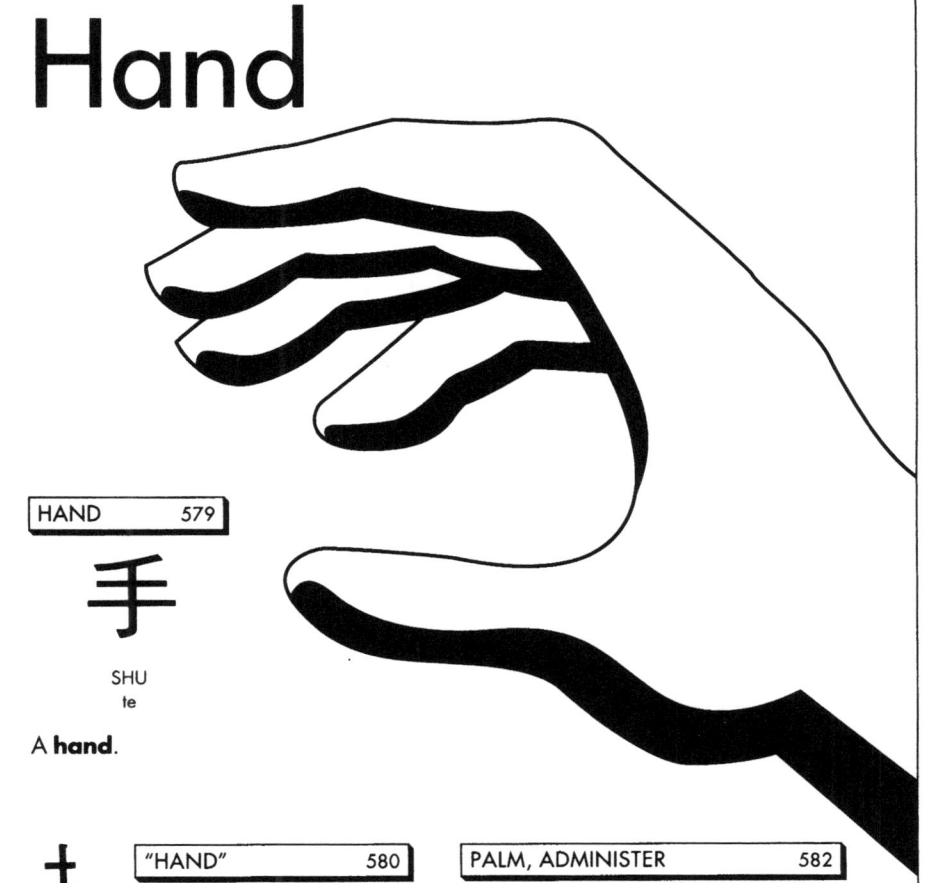

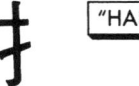

HAND — 579
手
SHU
te

A **hand**.

"HAND" — 580
扌

A common **hand** radical looks like this.

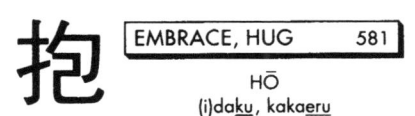

EMBRACE, HUG — 581
抱
HŌ
(i)da*ku*, kaka*eru*

I was wrapped in an **embrace**.

- hand 580
- wrap 944

PALM, ADMINISTER — 582
掌
SHŌ,
tsukasado*ru*,
tanagokoro

I have a shiny coin in the **palm** of my hand.

- shine n–582
- mouth 566
- hand 579

MEET, JOIN, FIT — 583

合

GŌ
a<u>u</u>/<u>waseru</u>

The lid **fits** the mouth of the jar.

- person 363
- one 897
- mouth 566

PICK UP, GATHER, TEN — 584

拾

SHŪ, JŪ
hiro<u>u</u>

A hand **picks up** the lid.

- hand 580
- fit 583

LOAD, BOARD — 585

搭

TŌ

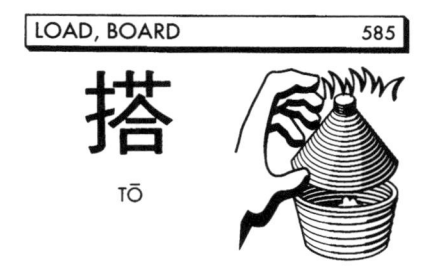

Load grass into the container.

- hand 580
- grass 124
- fit 583

ERASE, RUB, PAINT — 586

抹

MATSU

Erase the **paint** with the end of my brush.

- hand 580
- end 145

PULL OUT, PLUCK — 587

抽

CHŪ
nu<u>ku</u>

Pull out in this direction.

- hand 580
- cause 76

PUSH — 588

押

Ō
o<u>su</u>, os<u>aeru</u>

Push in this direction.

- hand 580
- shell 357

CHASE, SEIZE — 589

逮

TAI

Chase the animal and **seize** it by the tail.

- move 1153
- hand grasping n–589

THING, MATTER, ACT — 590

事

JI, ZU
koto

What is that **thing** in your hand?

- signboard n–1153
- hand 597

LAW, CONTROL — 591

律

RITSU, RICHI

The written **law** of the road.

- road 1192
- writing n–591

WRITING BRUSH — 592

筆

HITSU
fude

A bamboo **brush**.

- bamboo 123
- writing n–592

Hold

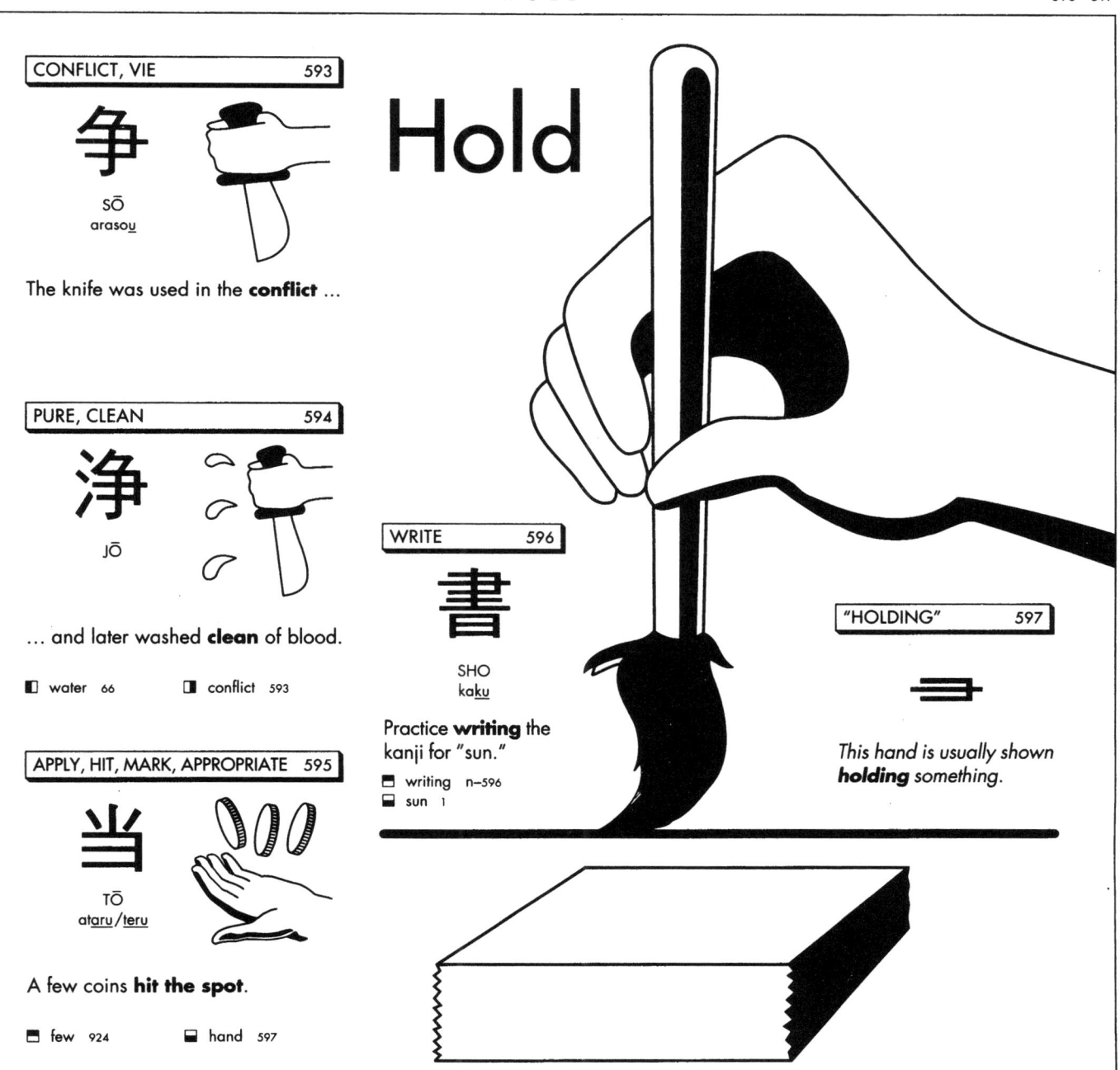

CONFLICT, VIE — 593
争
SŌ
arasou

The knife was used in the **conflict** ...

PURE, CLEAN — 594
浄
JŌ

... and later washed **clean** of blood.

- water 66
- conflict 593

APPLY, HIT, MARK, APPROPRIATE — 595
当
TŌ
ataru/teru

A few coins **hit the spot**.

- few 924
- hand 597

WRITE — 596
書
SHO
kaku

Practice **writing** the kanji for "sun."

- writing n–596
- sun 1

"HOLDING" — 597
ヨ

This hand is usually shown **holding** something.

Reach

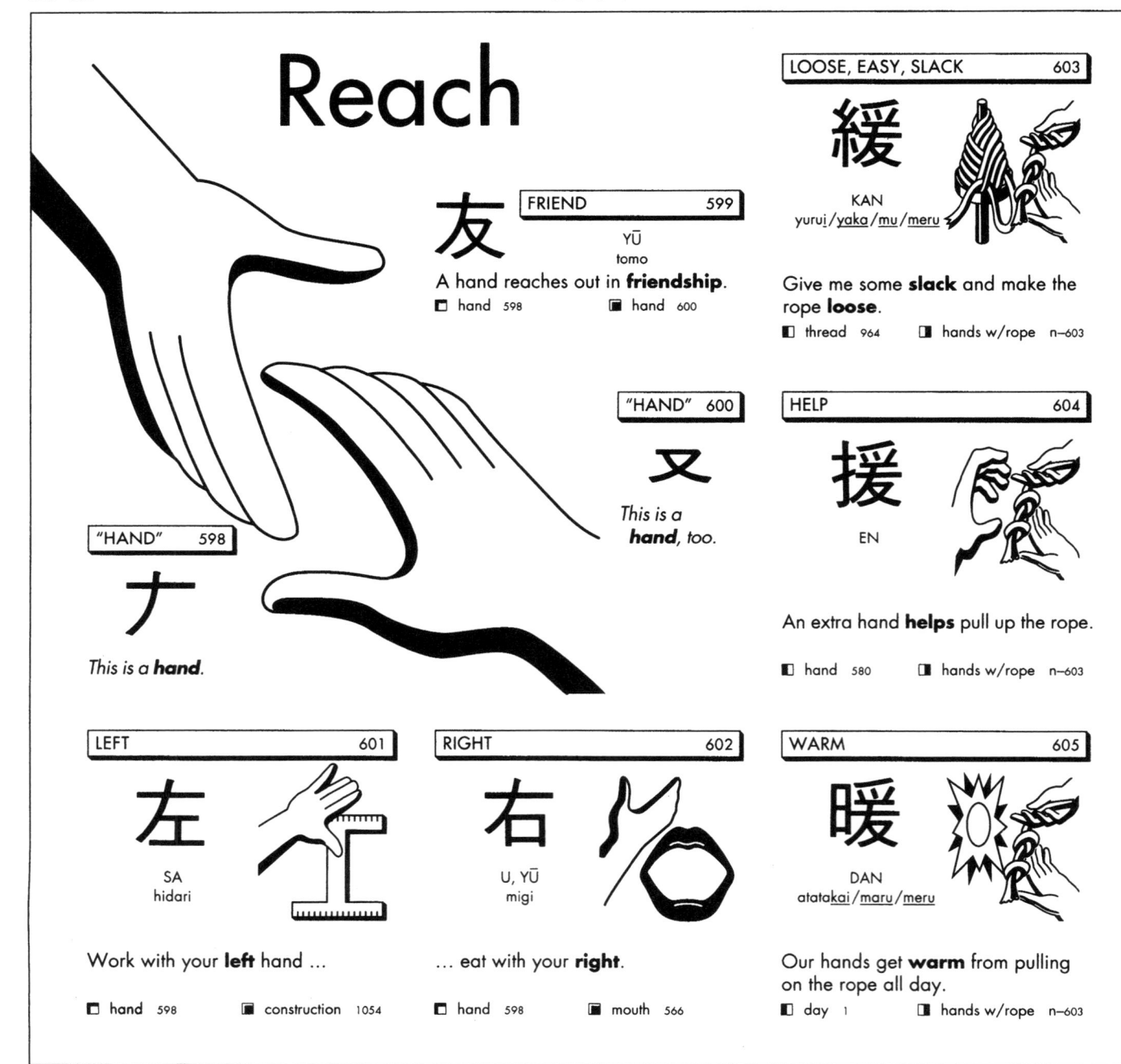

"HAND" 598
ナ

*This is a **hand**.*

FRIEND 599
友

YŪ
tomo

A hand reaches out in **friendship**.

□ hand 598   ■ hand 600

"HAND" 600
又

*This is a **hand**, too.*

LEFT 601
左

SA
hidari

Work with your **left** hand ...

□ hand 598   ■ construction 1054

RIGHT 602
右

U, YŪ
migi

... eat with your **right**.

□ hand 598   ■ mouth 566

LOOSE, EASY, SLACK 603
緩

KAN
yurui / yaka / mu / meru

Give me some **slack** and make the rope **loose**.

□ thread 964   ■ hands w/rope n–603

HELP 604
援

EN

An extra hand **helps** pull up the rope.

□ hand 580   ■ hands w/rope n–603

WARM 605
暖

DAN
atatakai / maru / meru

Our hands get **warm** from pulling on the rope all day.

□ day 1   ■ hands w/rope n–603

REACH / GIVE

Give

PLUCK, EXTRACT, MISS 606
抜
BATSU
nu*ku*/*karu*/*keru*/*kasu*

A hand **plucks** a friend from danger.

- hand 580
- friend 599

"HAND" 609

This is a **hand**.

"HAND" 611

This is a **hand**, *too*.

SHAKE, SWING, ROCK 607
揺
YŌ
yu*ru*/*reru*/*ragu*/*suru*,
yu*suburu*

A basket **swings** from one hand to the other.

- hand 580
- hand 609
- basket n–607

RECEIVE 610
受
JU
u*keru*

A hand **receives** the diploma.

- hand 609
- hand 600

GIVE, GRANT, BESTOW 608
授
JU
sazu*keru*

A **grant** is **given**.

- hand 580
- receive 610

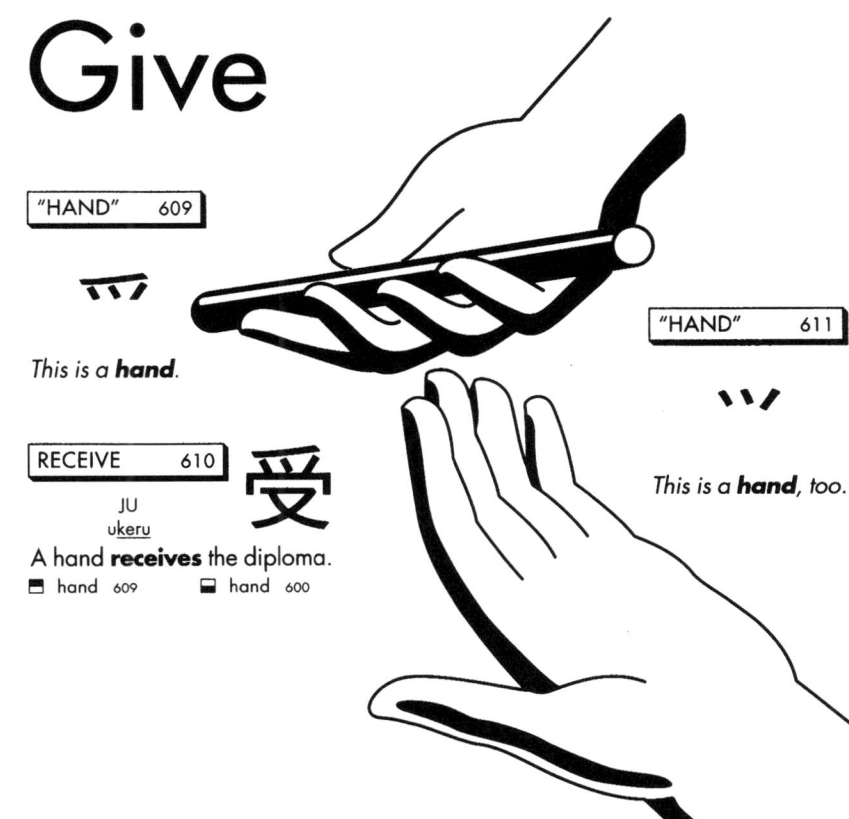

OFFER, RAISE, ACT, PERFORM 612
挙
KYO
a*geru*, kozo*tte*

A **raised** hand is **offered** a diploma in the **performing** arts.

- hand 611
- hand 579

HONOR, FAME, PRAISE 613
誉
YO
homa*re*

A baccalaureate address filled with **praise** and **honor**.

- hand 611
- speak 840

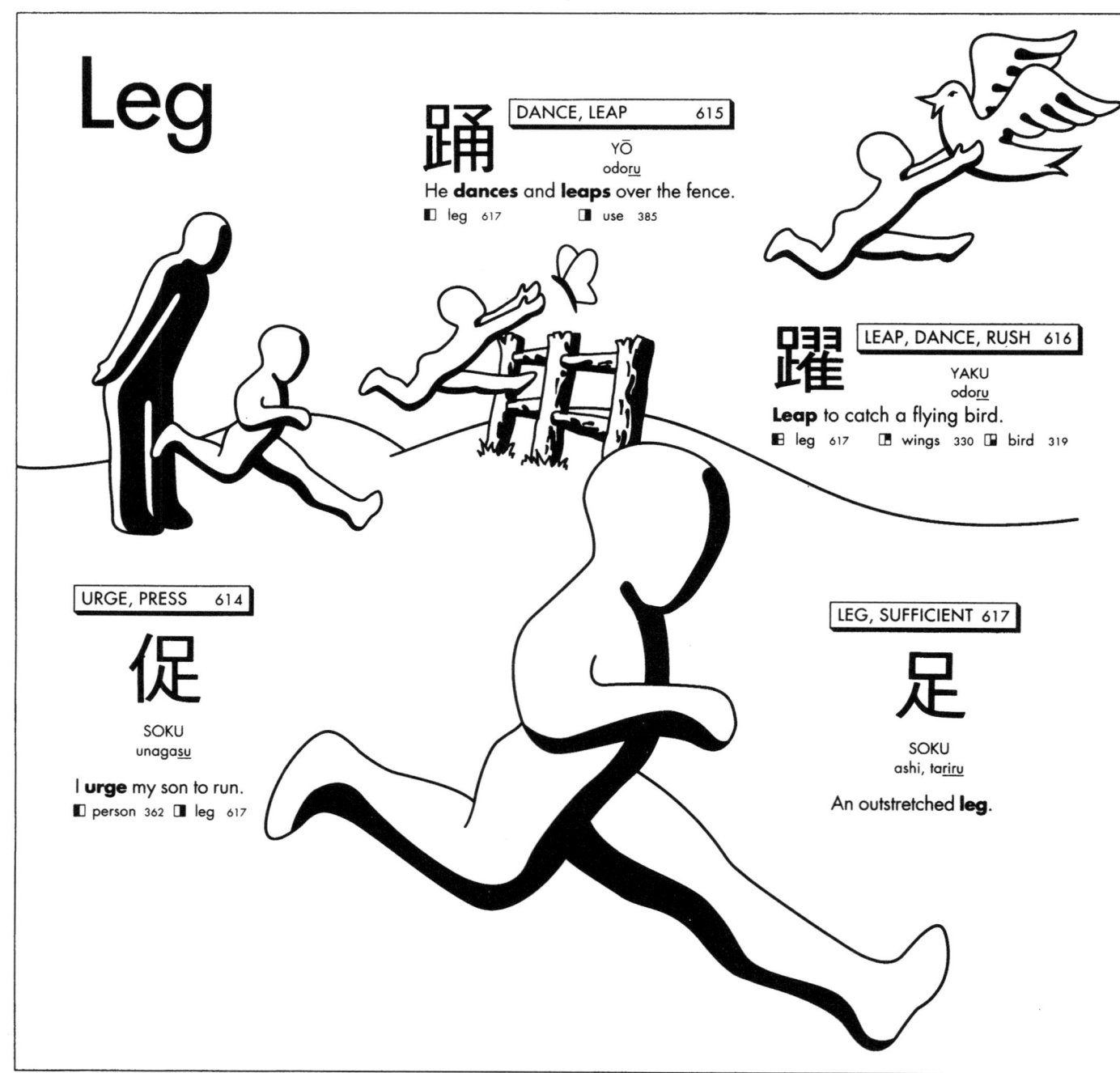

Leg

踊 DANCE, LEAP 615
YŌ
odo*ru*

He **dances** and **leaps** over the fence.
- leg 617
- use 385

躍 LEAP, DANCE, RUSH 616
YAKU
odo*ru*

Leap to catch a flying bird.
- leg 617
- wings 330
- bird 319

促 URGE, PRESS 614
SOKU
unaga*su*

I **urge** my son to run.
- person 362
- leg 617

足 LEG, SUFFICIENT 617
SOKU
ashi, ta*riru*

An outstretched **leg**.

TRACE, REMAINS — 618

跡 SEKI / ato

A bird left **traces** of **footprints** in the sand.

- leg 617
- red n-65

SPRING, JUMP, LEAP — 619

跳 CHŌ / haneru, tobu

Leap a trillion feet

- leg 617
- trillion 1170

ARISE, WAKE, CAUSE — 620

起 KI / okiru / koru / kosu

I **arise**, stretch, and run out of the house in the morning.

- run 625
- self 445

FOLLOW, COMPLY — 621

従 JŪ / shitagau

I run from the path of the **complacent followers** …

- path 1192
- follow n-621
- leg 617

CROSS, EXCEED, EXCEL — 622

越 ETSU / koeru/su

… and run to **cross** beyond the lance-wielding sentry.

- run 625
- halberd 801

HOLD, CARRY, OFFER — 623

提 TEI, CHŌ / sageru

My legs and hands **carry** the day.

- hand 580
- sun 1
- leg 617

FOLLOWER, FUTILITY — 624

徒 TO / ada, itazura

It's **futile** to **follow** such a fast runner.

- path 1192
- run 625

RUN — 625

走 SŌ / hashiru

Run on the ground.

- ground 101
- leg 617

PROCEED, GO — 626

赴 FU / omomuku

Proceed when the signal permits.

- run 625
- announce n-626

Stand

立 STAND, RISE, LEAVE 627
RITSU, RYŪ
ta*tsu* / *teru*

A **standing** person.

競 COMPETE, BID 628
KYŌ, KEI
ki*sou*

A standing-room-only crowd watches two brothers **compete**.
- stand (x2) 627
- brother (x2) 438

泣 WEEP, CRY 629
KYŪ
na*ku*

Stand **weeping** in a puddle of tears.
- water 66
- stand 627

商 TRADE, DEAL, SELL 630
SHŌ
aki*nau*

Stand at a booth and make a **deal**.
- stand 627
- prostitution n–630

倍 DOUBLE, FOLD 631
BAI

The person's height is **double** that of the standing man.
- person 362
- stand 627
- mouth 566

陪 ATTEND, ACCOMPANY 632
BAI

The **attendant** stood on a box on a hill.
- hill 1094
- stand 627
- mouth 566

並 ROW, LINE, RANK, ORDINARY 633
HEI
nami, nara*bi* / *bu*

Stand in **line**.

FURIGANA

Small hiragana (and sometimes katakana) symbols can be placed above or to the side of a kanji character to indicate its correct pronunciation. These small kana, called *furigana*, are commonly given for younger readers and whenever there is some question as to how a kanji is read. Kanji used in personal names, for example, often have nonstandard readings, while some kanji are only used in particular contexts and may not be familiar even to educated adult readers. The word "spirit" at right, is read *bōrei*.

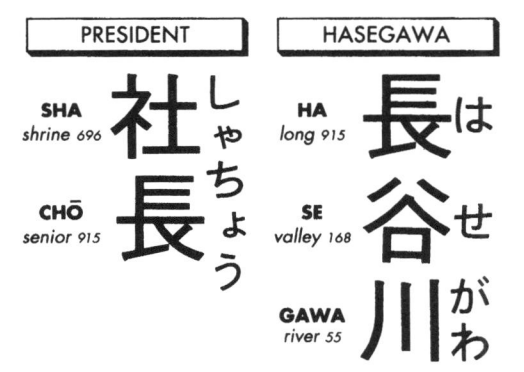

PRESIDENT	HASEGAWA
SHA shrine 696 **CHŌ** senior 915	**HA** long 915 **SE** valley 168 **GAWA** river 55

社長 しゃちょう

長谷川 はせがわ

The same kanji, **nagai** 915, is used in Mr. Hasegawa's title, **shachō**, and in his family name. The different readings of the kanji are indicated by *furigana*.

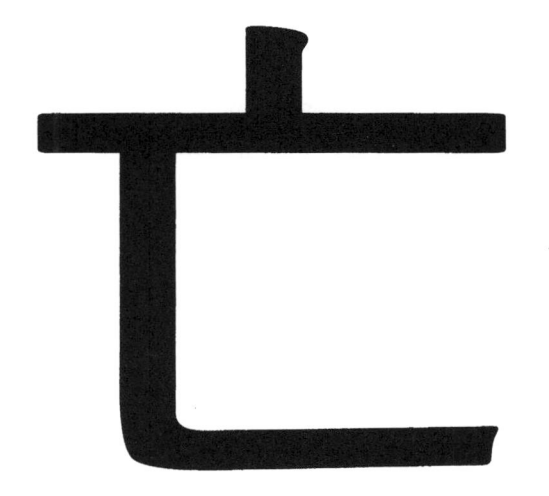

亡霊

6 SPIRIT

Spirit

A SOUL, SPIRIT — 634
REI, RYŌ
tama

A **spirit** stands in the falling rain.

- rain 45
- stand 627

DEATH — 635
SHI
shinu

One fallen **dead** in the moonlight …

- one 897
- bones 637
- fallen person n–374

BURY — 636
SŌ
hōmuru

… and buried in the grass

- grass (x2) 124
- death 635

LEAVE, CRUEL, HARM — 637
ZAN
nokoru/su

To stab them to the bones is **cruel**.

- bones n–637
- halberd 801

SPLIT, RIP, REND — 638
RETSU
saku/keru

Rip the clothes to shreds.

- bones n–637
- knife 1037
- clothes 1021

FIERCE, INTENSE — 639
RETSU

A **fierce** line of fire.

- bones n–637
- knife 1037
- fire 82

SPIRIT

UGLY, INDECENT — 640
醜 SHŪ / minikui

Alcohol is an **ugly** devil in a bottle.

- alcohol 251
- devil 645

DEMON, WITCH, EVIL SPIRIT — 641
魔 MA

A **demon** lives in a building in the forest.

- building 1143
- forest 142
- devil 645

BEWITCH, CHARM — 642
魅 MI

The devil easily **charms** the immature.

- devil 645
- immature 145

SOUL, SPIRIT — 643
魂 KON / tama, tamashii

A **spirit** in a cloud.

- cloud 54
- devil 645

LOWLY, MEAN, DESPISE — 644
卑 HI / iyashii / shimu

The devil is **lowly** and **mean**.

DEVIL, DEMON — 645
鬼 KI / oni

A horned **devil** roams the fields.

TOMBSTONE, MONUMENT — 646
碑 HI

The devil hides near the **tombstone**.

- stone 190
- mean 644

Pain

BAD LUCK, EVIL, DISASTER 647
凶 KYŌ

Bad luck . . .

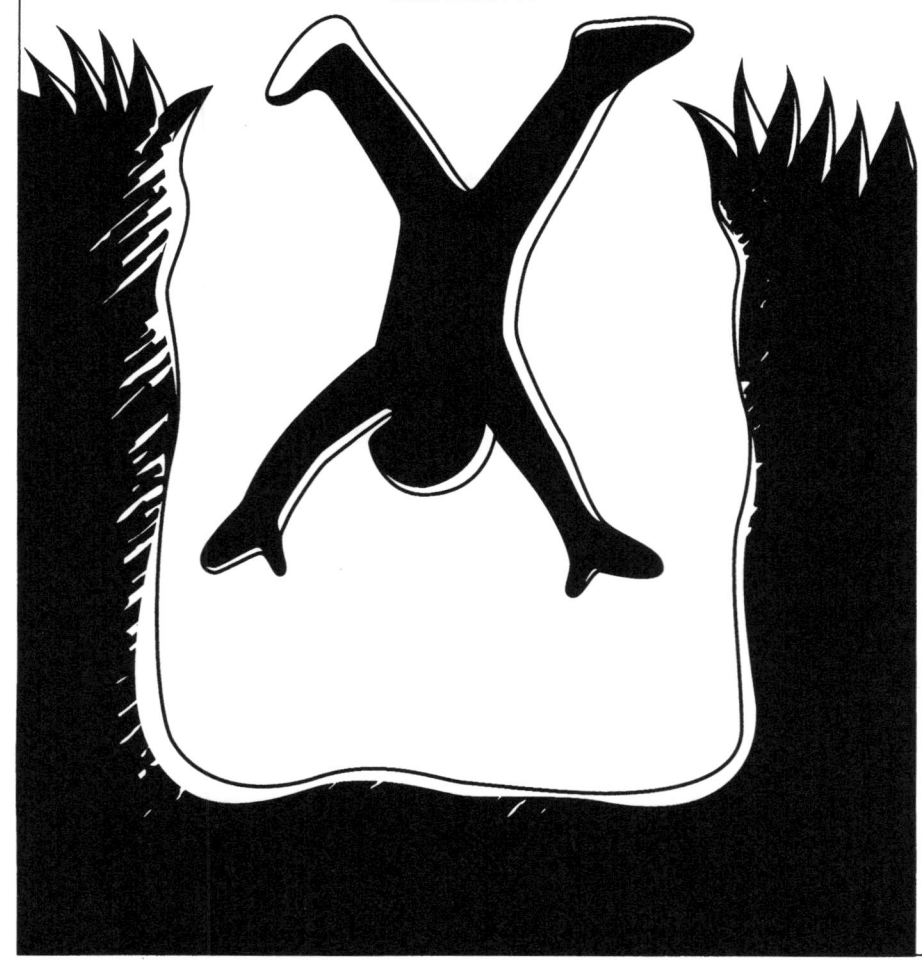

EVIL 648
兇 KYŌ

. . . to be eaten by an **evil** monster.

- bad luck 647
- legs 647

WORRY, DISTRESS, ANNOY 649
悩 NŌ
nayamashii/mu/masu

My heart and brain are **worried**.

- heart 498
- brain n–649

SPIRIT 650
気 KI, KE

My **spirit** rises like steam.

- vapors n–650
- rice n–650

PAIN 651–659

ILLNESS, SWIFTLY 651

疾

SHITSU

The arrow causing the **illness** is removed **swiftly** …
- illness 655
- arrow 818

HEAL, MEDICAL 652

医

I
iya*su*

… and is put in the **medic**'s box when a patient **heals**.
- enclosed n–652
- arrow 818

CAUSE, BASED ON, DEPEND ON 653

因

IN
yo*ru*

A big illness **caused** me to stay in bed.
- enclosed 778
- big 913

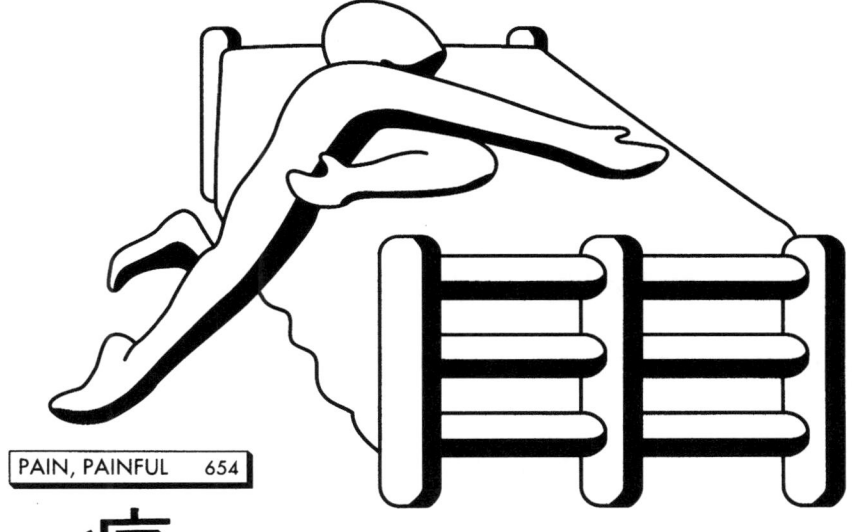

PAIN, PAINFUL 654

痛

TSŪ
ita*i* / *mu* / *meru*

He has a **painful** illness.
- illness 655
- use 385

FOOLISH 656

痴

CHI

To **fools**, knowledge is a sickness.
- illness 655
- know 560

FAVOR, KINDNESS 657

恩

ON

He did a **kind**-hearted **favor**.
- cause 653
- heart 499

"ILLNESS" 655

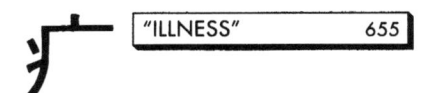

疒

As an element this means **illness**.

EPIDEMIC 658

疫

EKI, YAKU

An **epidemic** strikes.
- illness 655
- hand w/ax 792

SYMPTOM, ILLNESS 659

症

SHŌ

Symptoms correctly identify **illness**.
- illness 655
- correct 826

Dead Bodies

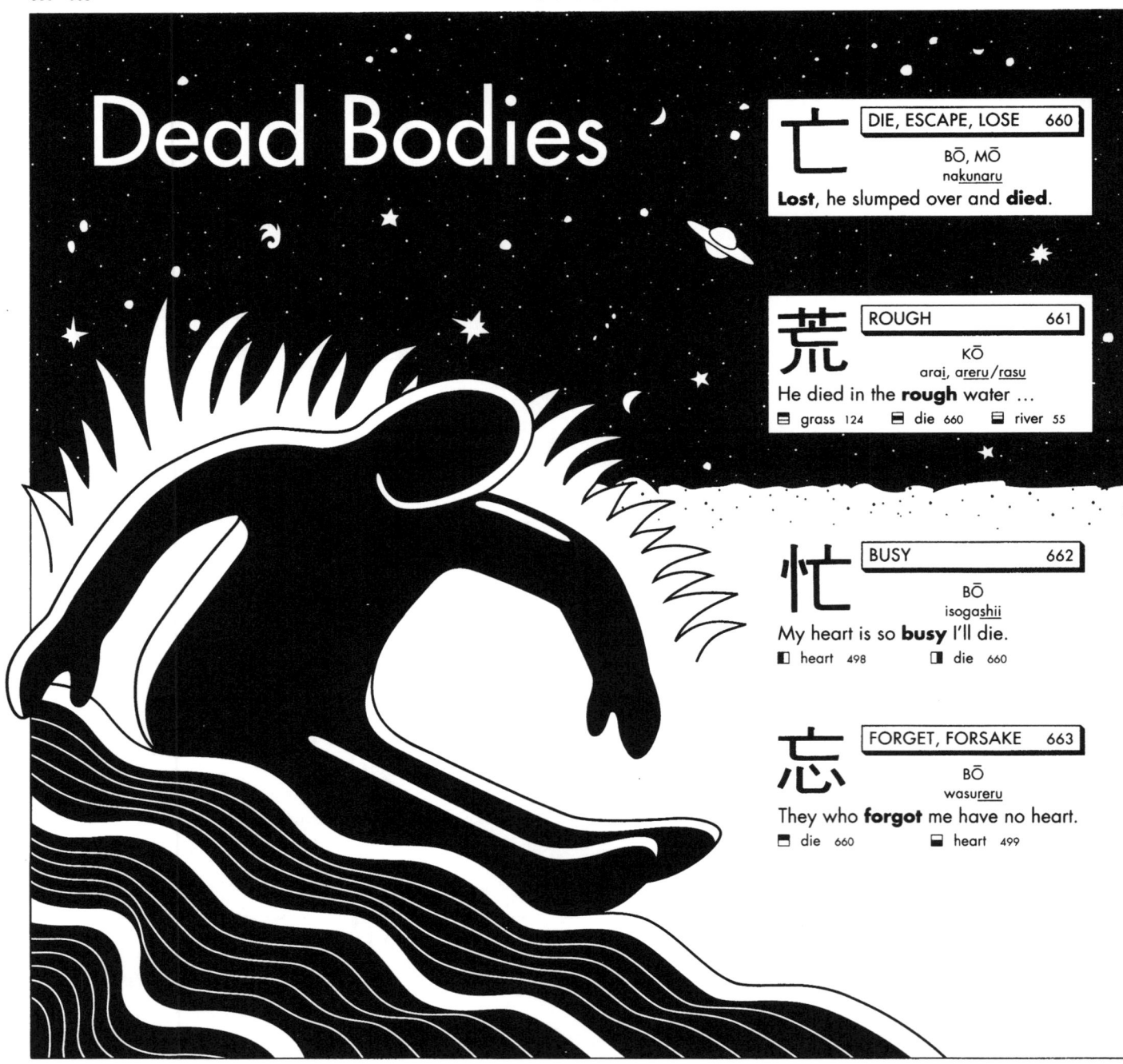

SPIRIT

| 亡 | **DIE, ESCAPE, LOSE** 660 |
BŌ, MŌ
na<u>kunaru</u>
Lost, he slumped over and **died**.

| 荒 | **ROUGH** 661 |
KŌ
ara<u>i</u>, a<u>reru</u>/<u>rasu</u>
He died in the **rough** water …
▢ grass 124 ▢ die 660 ▢ river 55

| 忙 | **BUSY** 662 |
BŌ
iso<u>gashii</u>
My heart is so **busy** I'll die.
▢ heart 498 ▢ die 660

| 忘 | **FORGET, FORSAKE** 663 |
BŌ
wasu<u>reru</u>
They who **forgot** me have no heart.
▢ die 660 ▢ heart 499

DEAD BODIES 664–670

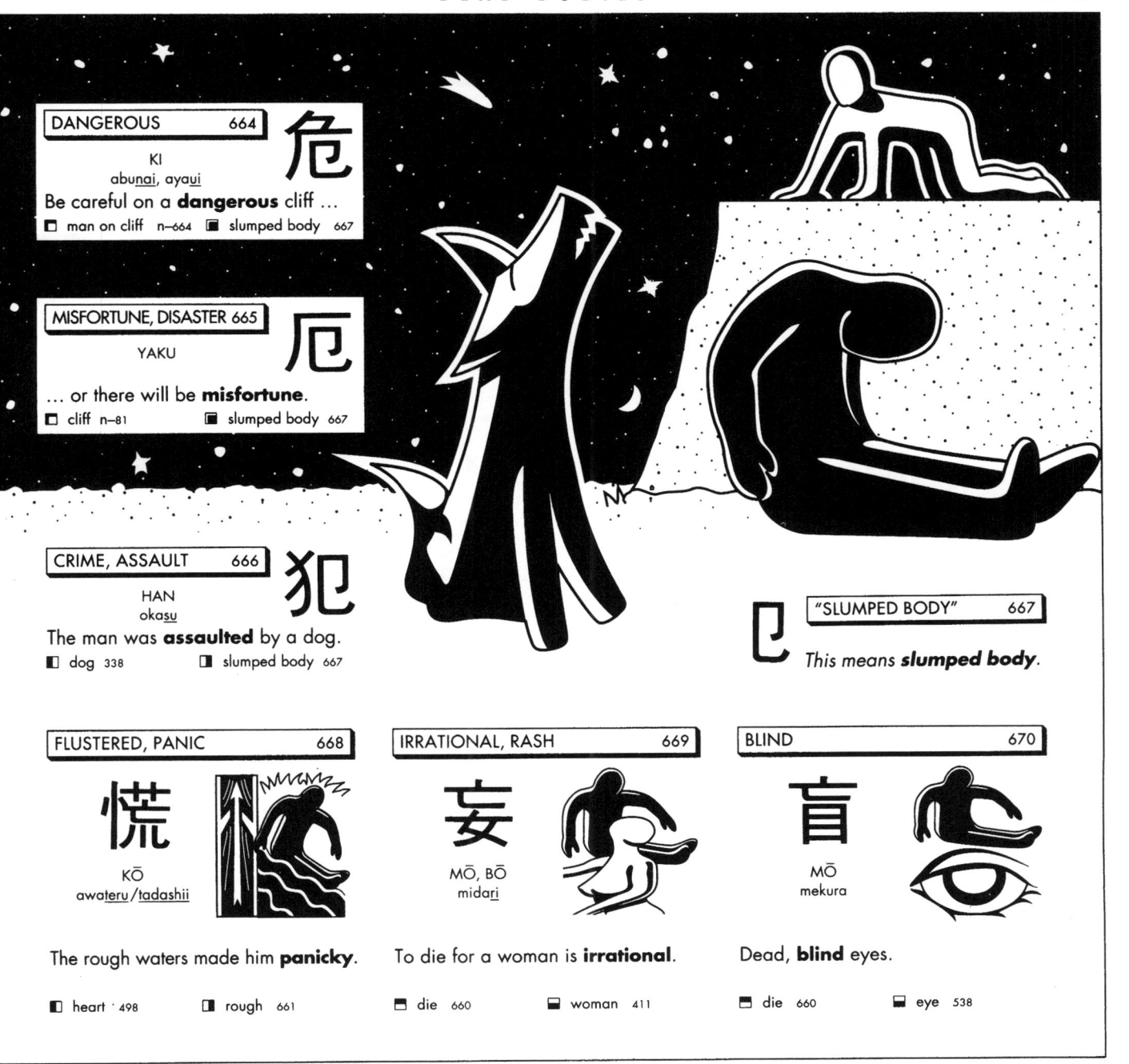

DANGEROUS 664
危
KI
abunai, ayaui
Be careful on a **dangerous** cliff ...
- man on cliff n–664
- slumped body 667

MISFORTUNE, DISASTER 665
厄
YAKU
... or there will be **misfortune**.
- cliff n–81
- slumped body 667

CRIME, ASSAULT 666
犯
HAN
okasu
The man was **assaulted** by a dog.
- dog 338
- slumped body 667

"SLUMPED BODY" 667
巳
This means **slumped body**.

FLUSTERED, PANIC 668
慌
KŌ
awateru / tadashii
The rough waters made him **panicky**.
- heart 498
- rough 661

IRRATIONAL, RASH 669
妄
MŌ, BŌ
midari
To die for a woman is **irrational**.
- die 660
- woman 411

BLIND 670
盲
MŌ
mekura
Dead, **blind** eyes.
- die 660
- eye 538

119

Past

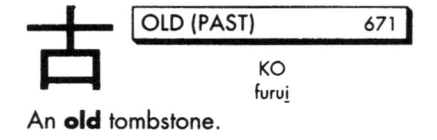

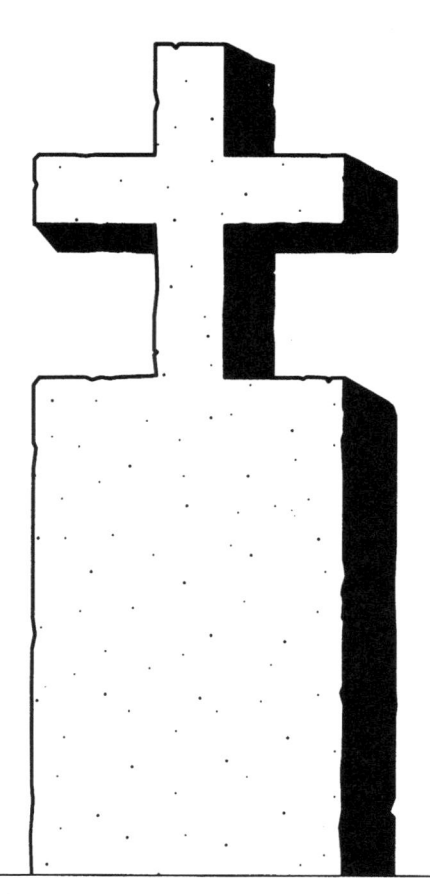

OLD (PAST) 671
古
KO
furu*i*

An **old** tombstone.

WITHER, DECAY 672
枯
KO
ka*reru*/*rasu*

An old tree **withers**.

▪ tree 126   ▪ old 671

PAST, REASON 673
故
KO
yue

A violent **past** gives way to reason.

▪ old 671   ▪ strike 802

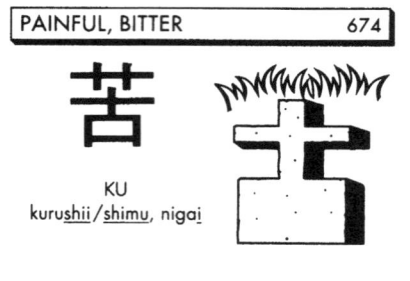

PAINFUL, BITTER 674
苦
KU
kuru*shii*/*shimu*, niga*i*

The old grass tastes **bitter**.

▪ grass 124   ▪ old 671

CONQUER, OVERCOME 675
克
KOKU

Brothers, we shall **overcome**.

▪ old 671   ▪ legs n–675

BURY 676
埋
MAI
u*maru*/*meru*, uzu*moreru*

He is **buried** outside the village.

▪ soil 101   ▪ village 1088

SUITABLE, FIT, GO 677
適
TEKI

It's **suitable** to visit the grave.

▪ move 1153   ▪ appropriate n–677

MATCH, ENEMY 678

敵

TEKI
kataki

He struck his **enemy** and killed him.

- appropriate n–678
- strike 802

DROP, DRIP 679

滴

TEKI
shizuku, shitata*ru*

His tear**drops drip** …

- water 66
- appropriate n–679

LEGITIMATE HEIR 680

嫡

CHAKU

… because she, not he, is the **legitimate heir**.

- woman 411
- appropriate n–680

GRAVE 681

墓

BO
haka

A sunny **grave**, dug in the grassy soil.

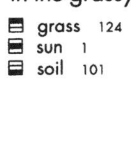

- grass 124
- sun 1
- soil 101

MOURN 682

弔

CHŌ
tomura*u*

A look of **mourning**.

MOURN, ABHOR, ODIOUS 683

忌

KI
imu/*mawashii*

I **hate** how my heart still **mourns**.

- self 445
- heart 499

Temple

BUDDHA, FRANCE 684
仏

BUTSU, FUTSU
hotoke

Buddhist meditation is popular in **France**.

- person 362
- self 450

HEAVEN 688
天

TEN
ama

Heaven is one big place.

- one 897
- big 913

GREEDY 689
罪

ZAI
tsumi

The **greedy** miser revels in his net worth.

- net 987
- oppose 957

TEMPLE 685
寺

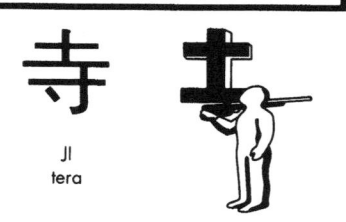

JI
tera

He guards every inch of the **temple**.

- soil 101
- inch 759

WAIT 686
待

TAI
matsu

Wait in the road by the temple.

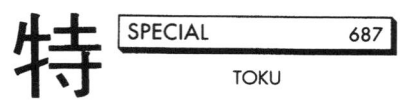

- road 1192
- temple 685

SPECIAL 687
特

TOKU

Cows were **special** and worshiped.

- cow 276
- temple 685

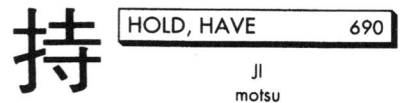

HOLD, HAVE 690
持

JI
motsu

Holding hands in the temple.

- hand 580
- temple 685

TIME, HOUR 691
時

JI
toki

The temple sun dial tells the **time**.

- sun 1
- temple 685

TEMPLE / SHRINE

PROPRIETY, BOW — 692
礼
REI

Bow at the altar.

- altar 696
- kneeling figure n–692

CALAMITY — 693
禍
KA
wazawai

The **calamity** was remembered at the altar.

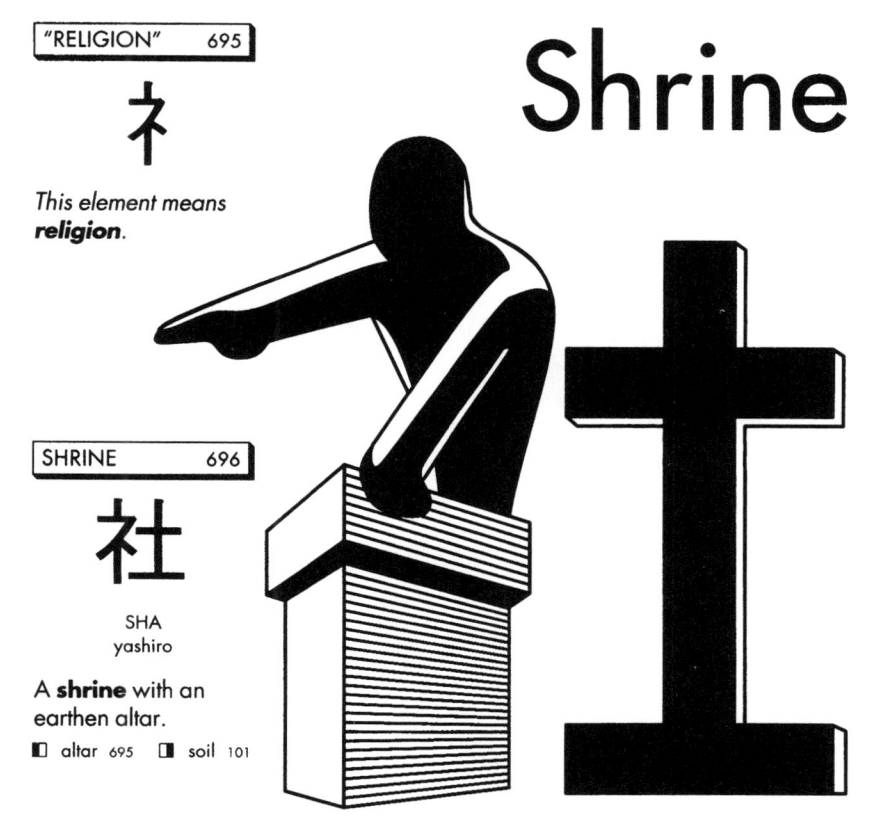

- altar 696
- bones 474

PASS, EXCEED, ERROR — 694
過
KA
sugiru / gosu, ayamachi

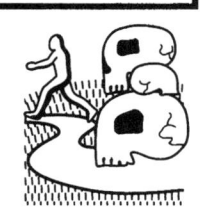

Quickly **pass** the pile of bones.

- move 1153
- bones 474

"RELIGION" — 695
礻

This element means religion.

SHRINE — 696
社
SHA
yashiro

A **shrine** with an earthen altar.

- altar 695
- soil 101

GOD, SPIRIT — 697
神
SHIN, JIN
kami

The preacher expounds the word of **God**.

- altar 696
- expound 698

SAY, EXPOUND — 698
申
SHIN
mōsu

Ten words he **spoke** out of his mouth.

- mouth 566
- ten 906

HAPPINESS — 699
祉
SHI

Stop at the altar for **happiness**.

- altar 696
- stop 1205

Shrine

Religion

FESTIVAL, WORSHIP 700
祭
SAI
matsu*ru*, matsuri

Offering meat at the **festival**.

- meat 267
- hand 600
- show 701

SHOW 701
示
JI, SHI
shime*su*

Show devotion at the altar.

PRIEST, BOY, TOWN 702
坊
BŌ

The **boy** becomes the **town priest**.

- soil 101
- person 362

OFFER, RESPECTFUL 703
奉
HŌ, BU
tatematsu*ru*

I **respectfully offer** my prayer.

RELIGION, MAIN 704
宗
SHŪ, SŌ

Practice religion at the main **altar**.

- roof 1144
- show 701

LOFTY, NOBLE, REVERE 705
崇
SŪ
aga*meru*

In the **lofty** mountains is a **noble** religion.

- mountain 167
- religion 704

OCCASION, EDGE, CONTACT 706
際
SAI
kiwa

On this **occasion** we worship on the **edge** of the hill.

- hill 1094
- festival 700

ORIGINAL FORMS

The development of kanji characters began in China in about 2,000 B.C. when people scratched designs into clay pots and tortoise shells to represent the world around them. Lacking a written language, the Japanese borrowed the writing system (and many pronunciations) of Chinese and Korean migrants in the 3rd or 4th century A.D. Simplified, stylized, and miscopied over the centuries by both the Chinese and the Japanese, many kanji today look very different from their pictographic ancestors.

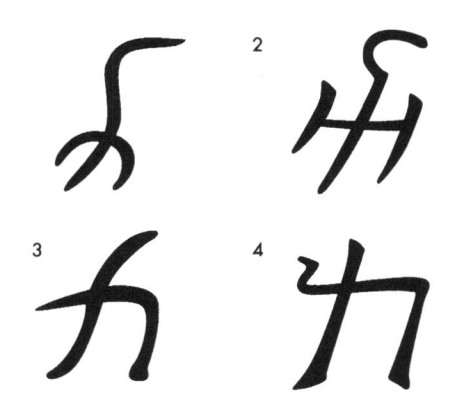

Chikara *745, POWER, shown at right, may come from a drawing of an arm with bulging biceps. Others see it as a stooping man working with a spade or pitchfork or as a hand forcefully pressing down.*

7 POWER

Money

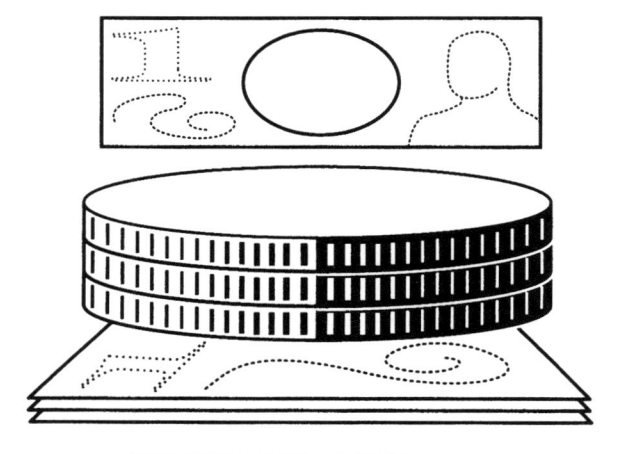

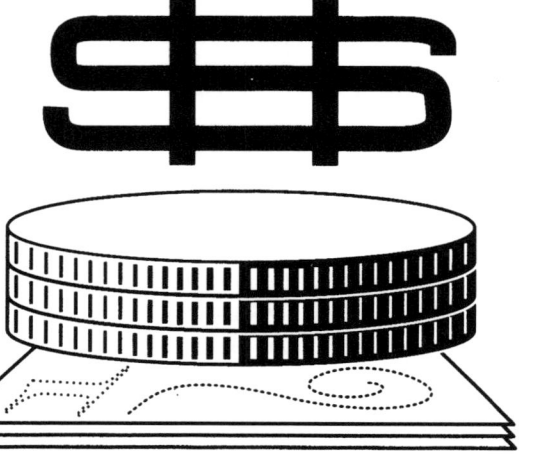

BUY 707
買
BAI
ka<u>u</u>

I **buy** a lot with my net income.
- net 987
- money 708

SHELL 708
貝
KAI

Shells were once used as money.

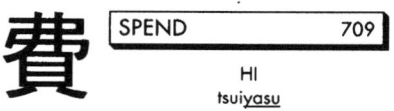

SPEND 709
費
HI
tsui<u>yasu</u>

Spend money.
- gush 78
- money 708

POOR, MEAGER 710
貧
HIN, BIN,
mazu<u>shii</u>

Cutting my **meager** income made me **poor**.
- divide 1025
- money 708

RULE, MODEL, STANDARD 711
則
SOKU
nori, notto<u>ru</u>

Money and weapons are **standard** measures.
- money 708
- knife 1037

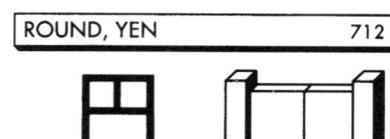

ROUND, YEN 712
円
EN
maru<u>i</u>

Yen from a banker's window.

MONEY

RECOMPENSE, REDEEM 713

償

SHŌ
tsugunau

A person **redeems** ...

- person 362
- prize 714

PRIZE, PRAISE 714

賞

SHŌ

... a monetary **prize**.

- shine n-714
- mouth 566
- money 708

BESTOW 715

賜

SHI
tamawaru

Money was **bestowed** on the field hand.

- money 708
- easy 23

DEFEAT, BEAR, LOSE 716

負

FU
makeru/kasu, ou

The one **defeated bears** the financial burden.

- bent figure n-716
- money 708

LOSS, SPOIL, MISS 717

損

SON
sokonau

The official's money is **lost**. There's zero left!

- hand 580
- official n-717

PIERCE 718

貫

KAN
tsuranuku

Old coins were **pierced** for threading.

- pierce n-708
- money 708

DEBT, LOAN 719

債

SAI

A farmer goes into **debt**.

- person 362
- grow 214
- money 708

DUTY, ENTRUST 720

任

NIN
makaseru

My master **entrusts** me with my **duties**.

- person 362
- burden n-720

WAGES, FEE 721

賃

CHIN

My duties are high, my **wages** are low.

- duty 720
- money 720

CHASTITY, VIRTUE 722

貞

TEI

Virtue is being above taking money.

- above 942
- money 720

Wealth

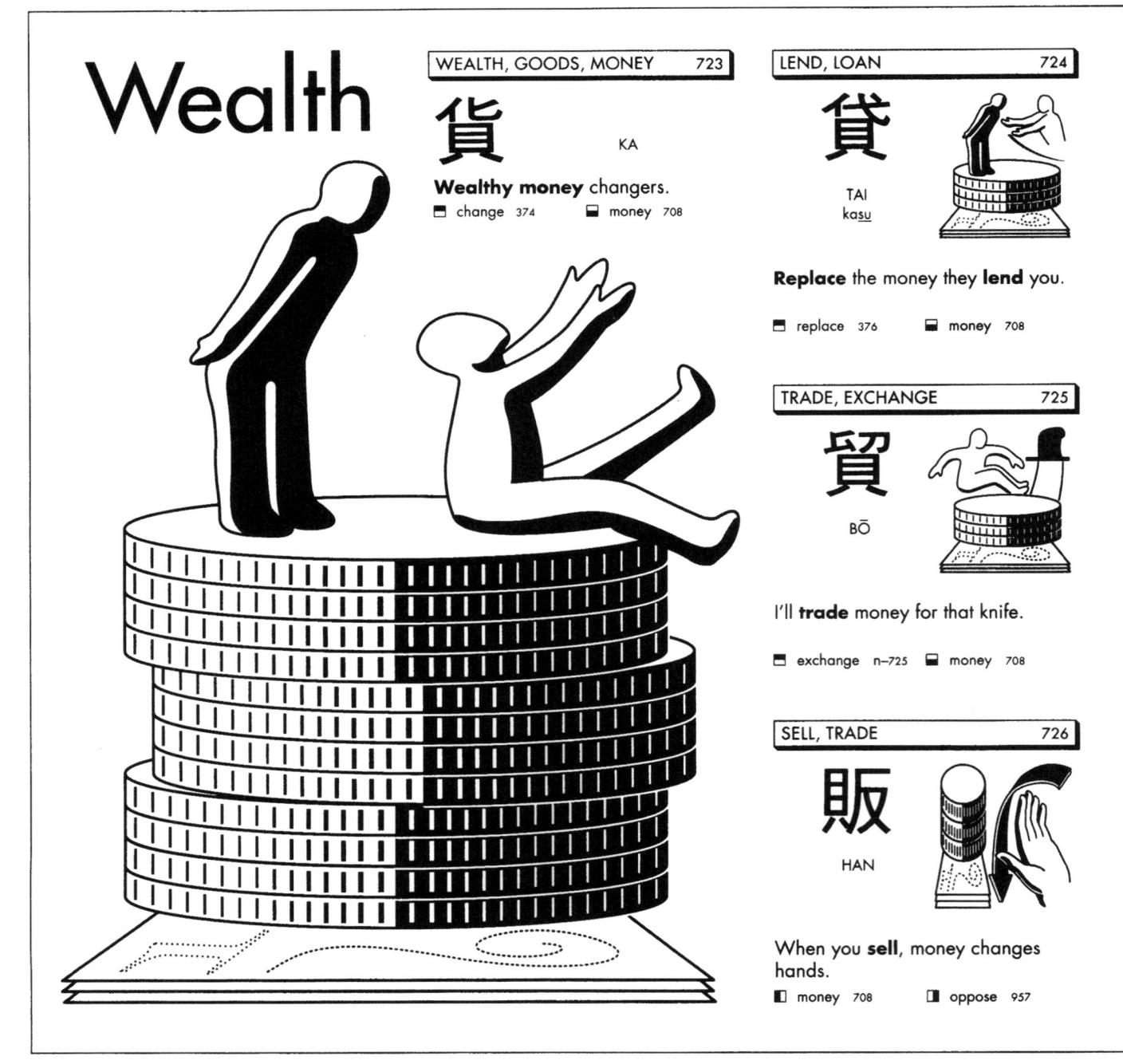

WEALTH, GOODS, MONEY — 723

貨 KA

Wealthy money changers.
- change 374
- money 708

LEND, LOAN — 724

貸 TAI / ka<u>su</u>

Replace the money they **lend** you.
- replace 376
- money 708

TRADE, EXCHANGE — 725

貿 BŌ

I'll **trade** money for that knife.
- exchange n–725
- money 708

SELL, TRADE — 726

販 HAN

When you **sell**, money changes hands.
- money 708
- oppose 957

WEALTH

STORE, SAVE 727
貯
CHO
takuwa<u>eru</u>

Store your **savings** under our roof.

- money 708
- roof 1144
- exact 1089

HAPPINESS, LUCK 731
幸
KŌ
saiwa<u>i</u>, shiawa<u>se</u>, sachi

What **luck** to find yen on the ground.

- soil 101
- person n–731

BRIBE, PROVIDE, BOARD 732
賄
WAI
makana<u>u</u>

Bribed with money and steaks.

- money 708
- hand 100
- meat 267

PRECIOUS, REVERED 728
貴
KI
tatto<u>i</u>/<u>bu</u>, tōto<u>i</u>

My **precious** things ...

- basket 990
- person 100

LEAVE, BEQUEATH 729
遺
I, YUI

... I **leave** behind.

- move 1153
- precious 728

MEMBER, OFFICIAL 730
員
IN

An **official** makes money with his mouth.

- mouth 566
- money 708

PRESENT, GIVE 733
贈
ZŌ, SŌ
oku<u>ru</u>

These **presents** cost a pile of money.

- money 708
- give n–733

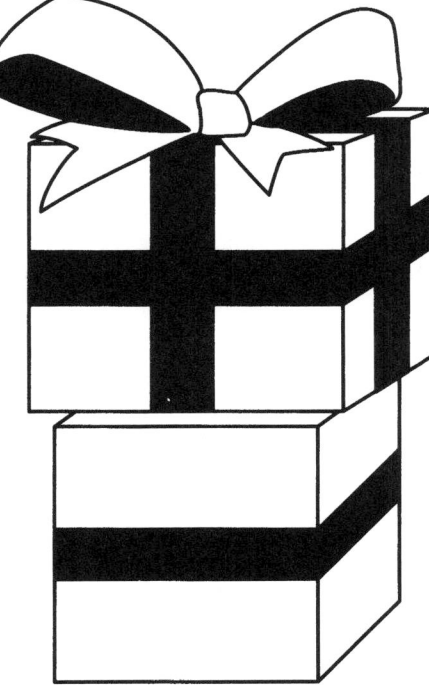

Master

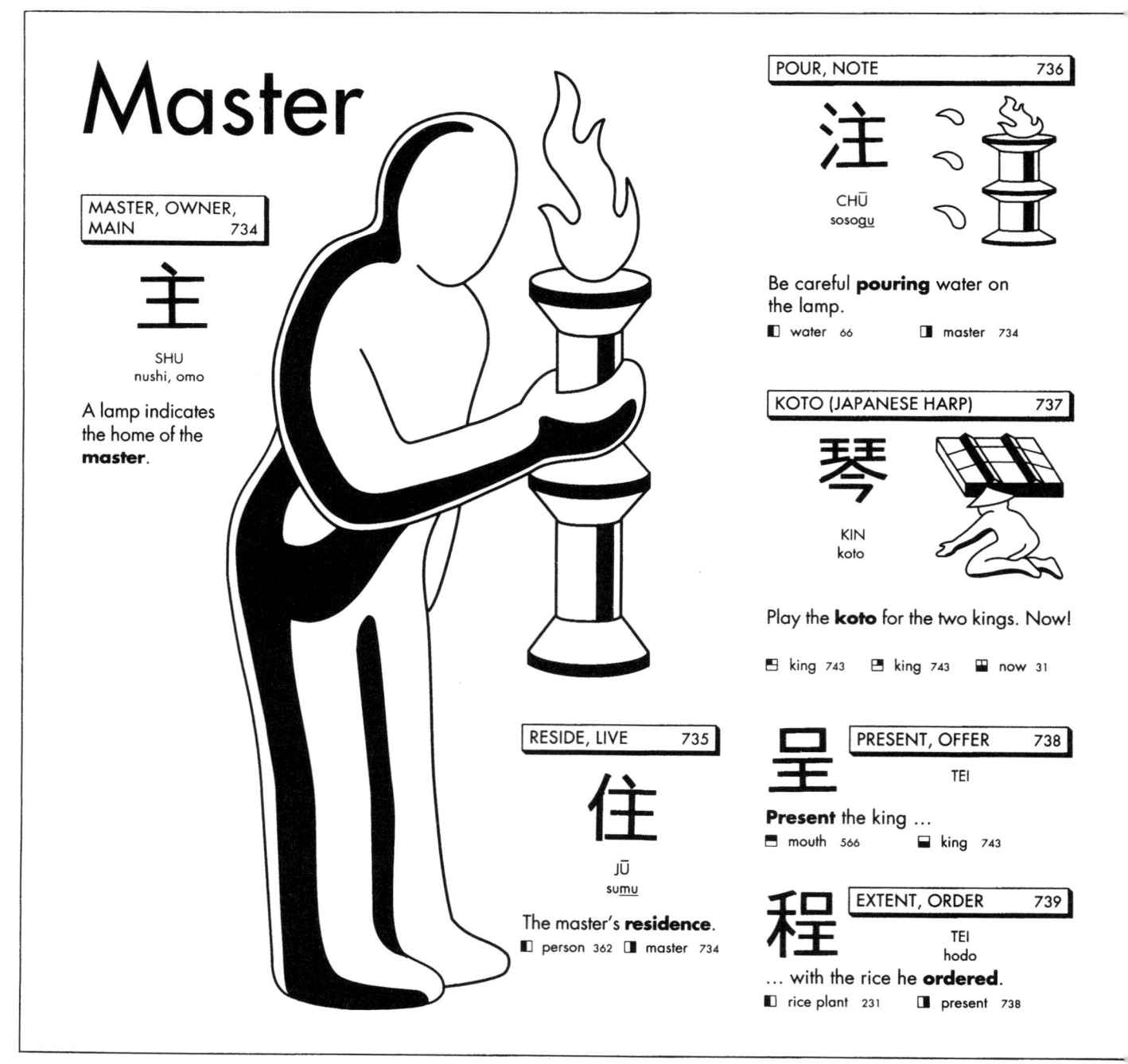

MASTER, OWNER, MAIN 734

主

SHU
nushi, omo

A lamp indicates the home of the **master**.

RESIDE, LIVE 735

住

JŪ
sumu

The master's **residence**.
- person 362
- master 734

POUR, NOTE 736

注

CHŪ
sosogu

Be careful **pouring** water on the lamp.
- water 66
- master 734

KOTO (JAPANESE HARP) 737

琴

KIN
koto

Play the **koto** for the two kings. Now!
- king 743
- king 743
- now 31

PRESENT, OFFER 738

呈

TEI

Present the king ...
- mouth 566
- king 743

EXTENT, ORDER 739

程

TEI
hodo

... with the rice he **ordered**.
- rice plant 231
- present 738

MASTER / KING

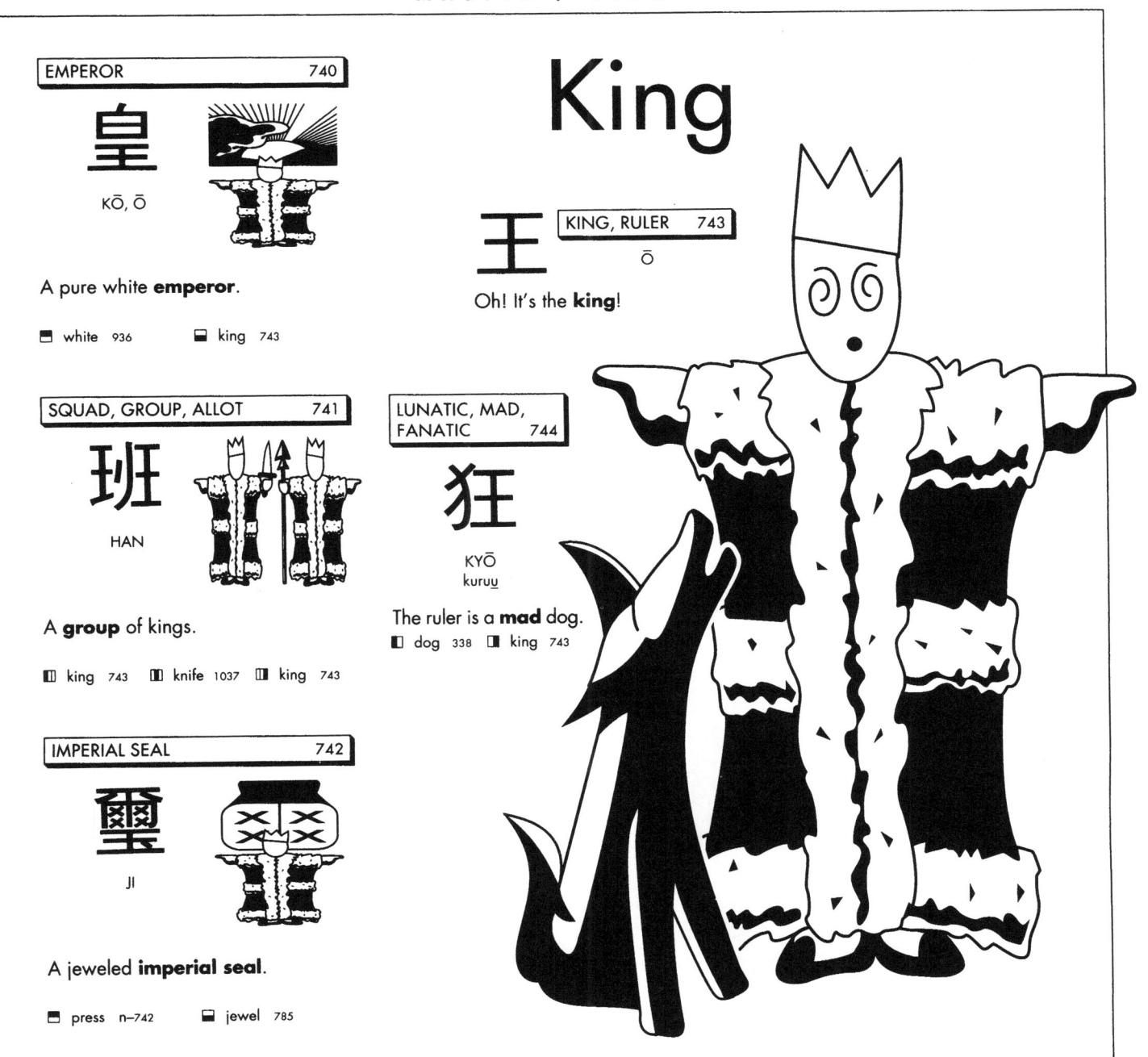

King

EMPEROR 740

皇

KŌ, Ō

A pure white **emperor**.

- white 936
- king 743

SQUAD, GROUP, ALLOT 741

班

HAN

A **group** of kings.

- king 743
- knife 1037
- king 743

IMPERIAL SEAL 742

璽

JI

A jeweled **imperial seal**.

- press n-742
- jewel 785

KING, RULER 743

王

Ō

Oh! It's the **king**!

LUNATIC, MAD, FANATIC 744

狂

KYŌ
kuru<u>u</u>

The ruler is a **mad** dog.

- dog 338
- king 743

Power

POWER, STRENGTH, EFFORT 745
力 RYOKU, RIKI
   chikara

Powerful biceps.

BRAVE, SPIRITED 746
勇 YŪ
   isamashii

A **brave** man.
- emerge n–746
- man 46

THREATEN, COERCE 747
脅 KYŌ
   odo(ka)su,
   obiyakasu

They **threatened** to beat his flesh to a pulp.
- power (x3) 745
- meat 267

COOPERATE 748
協 KYŌ

Cooperation increases power tenfold.
- ten 906
- power (x3) 745

LABOR, TOIL 749
労 RŌ

Labor and **toil** at the break of dawn.
- shine n–749
- power 745

POWER / SOLDIER

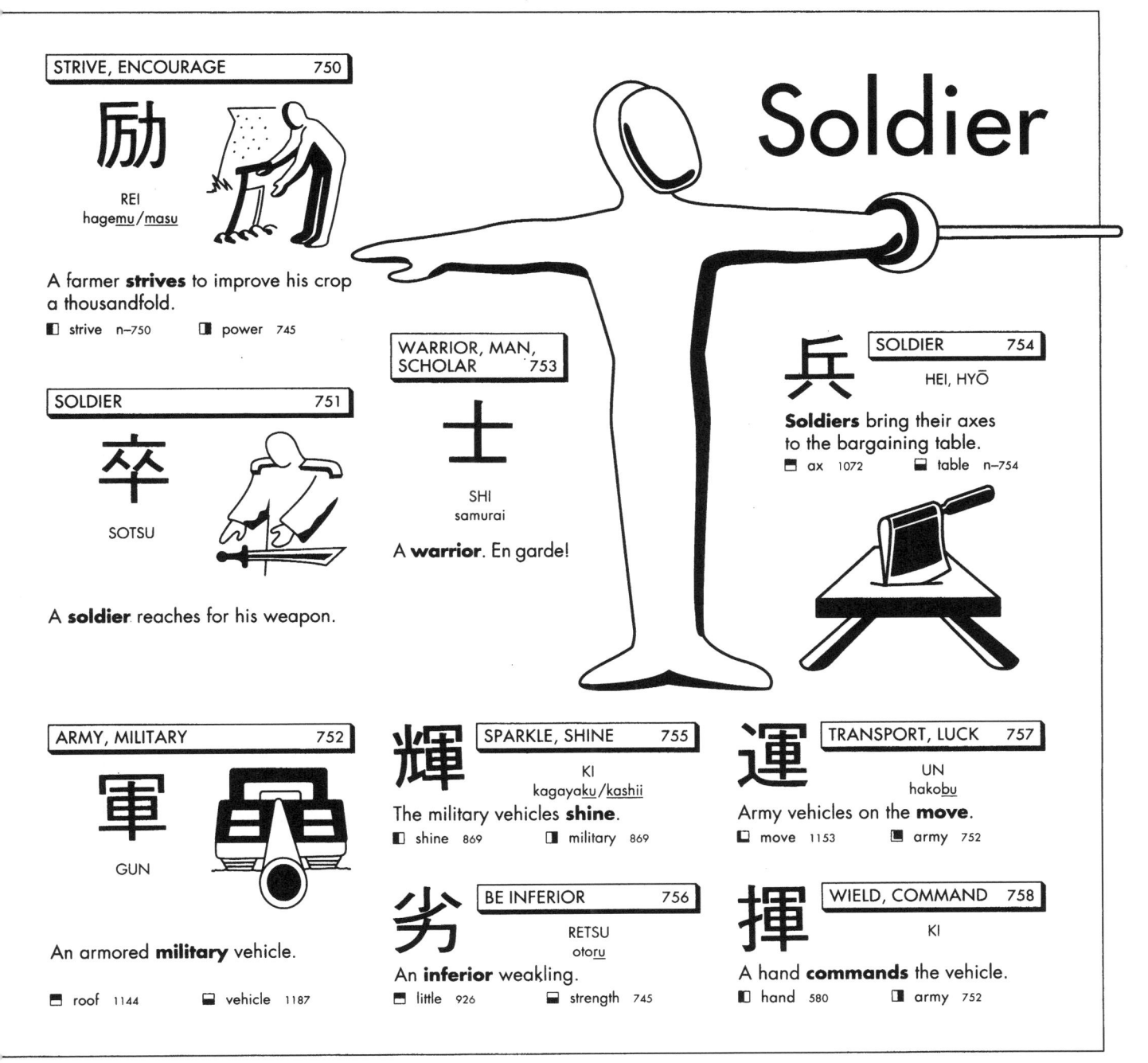

STRIVE, ENCOURAGE 750

励

REI
hage*mu*/*masu*

A farmer **strives** to improve his crop a thousandfold.

- strive n–750
- power 745

SOLDIER 751

卒

SOTSU

A **soldier** reaches for his weapon.

ARMY, MILITARY 752

軍

GUN

An armored **military** vehicle.

- roof 1144
- vehicle 1187

WARRIOR, MAN, SCHOLAR 753

士

SHI
samurai

A **warrior**. En garde!

SPARKLE, SHINE 755

輝

KI
kagaya*ku*/*kashii*

The military vehicles **shine**.

- shine 869
- military 869

BE INFERIOR 756

劣

RETSU
oto*ru*

An **inferior** weakling.

- little 926
- strength 745

Soldier

SOLDIER 754

兵

HEI, HYŌ

Soldiers bring their axes to the bargaining table.

- ax 1072
- table n–754

TRANSPORT, LUCK 757

運

UN
hako*bu*

Army vehicles on the **move**.

- move 1153
- army 752

WIELD, COMMAND 758

揮

KI

A hand **commands** the vehicle.

- hand 580
- army 752

(Never Budge an) Inch

寸 | MEASURE, INCH 759
SUN

Never budge an **inch**.

*Although this means **inch**, it is often found in characters that have violent connotations; the illustrations here reflect this.*

CLOSE OFF 760

封 FŪ, HŌ

All boarded up and **closed off**.

- soil 101
- soil 101
- inch 759

FIGHT 761

闘 TŌ / tatakau

If you **fight** outside the gate I'll knock your bean off.

- gate 1101
- bean + inch n–761

OPPOSE, AGAINST, PAIR 762

対 TAI, TSUI

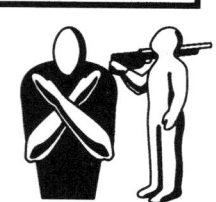

He **opposes** any violent texts.

- text 837
- inch 759

ATTACK, (TO) DEFEAT 763

討 TŌ / utsu

He verbally **attacked** me.

- word 840
- inch 759

SHOOT 764

射 SHA / iru

He will **shoot** anybody.

- body 459
- inch 759

謝 APOLOGIZE, THANKS 765
SHA / ayamaru

Apologize for shooting me.

- word 840
- shoot 765

奨 URGE, ENCOURAGE 766
SHŌ

The big commander **urges** violence.

- command 768
- big 913

(NEVER BUDGE AN) INCH

VALUE, ESTEEM, YOUR 767
尊 
SON
tatto<u>i</u>/<u>bu</u>, tōto<u>i</u>

A hired hand guards the **valuable** wine jar.

- wine 249
- inch 759

COMMAND, ABOUT TO 768
将
SHŌ
masa

I'm **about to** hand the **commander** plans.

- offer n–768
- hand 611
- inch 759

ENDURE, BEAR 769
耐
TAI
ta<u>eru</u>

Endure being behind bars.

- wet n–769
- inch 759

INSULT, HUMILIATE 770
辱
JOKU
hazuka<u>shimeru</u>

He trembles in **humiliation** at being held captive.

- tremble n-50
- inch 759

ATTACH, APPLY 771
付 
FU
tsu<u>ku</u>/<u>keru</u>

He **attaches** a medal to a person …

- person 362
- inch 759

ATTACH 772
附
FU

… **attached** to the hill regiment.

- hill 759
- attach 771

BLESSING, KINDNESS 773
恵
KEI, E
megu<u>mu</u>

He is **kind** to the captured people.

- hold n–773
- heart 499

SEIZE, CAPTURE 774
捕
HO
tora<u>eru</u>, to<u>ru</u>

Captured by hand.

- hand 580
- hold n–774

EXCLUSIVE, SOLE 775
専
SEN
moppa<u>ra</u>

I am the **sole** captive.

- hold n–775
- inch 759

BIND 776
縛 
BAKU
shiba<u>ru</u>

The prisoner's hands are **bound** with thread.

- thread 775
- sole 775

Enclosed

MAP, CHART, PLAN 777
ZU, TO
hakaru

I have a **map**.
- enclosed 778
- field n–100

| "ENCLOSED" 778 |

This box often means **enclosed**.

COUNTRY, REGION 779
KOKU
kuni

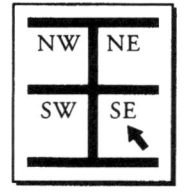

In a certain **region** of the **country** …
- enclosed 778
- jewel 785

WARD, SECTION 780
KU

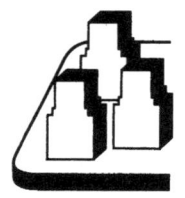

… in a **section** of town …
- enclosed 778
- enclosures n–780

GARDEN, PARK 781
EN
sono

… is a **garden** …
- enclosed 778
- spacious n–100

ENCLOSED

DEEP, INSIDE 782

奥

Ō
oku

... with a big hole that leads **deep inside** ...

JEWEL, BALL 785

玉

GYOKU
tama

... of **jewels**.

- king 743
- dot n–785

BE IN DIFFICULTY 786

困

KON
komaru

But I have **difficulty** getting it ...

- enclosed 778
- tree 126

SURROUND 783

井

I
kakomu/u

... the walls that **surround** ...

- enclosed 778
- surround n–783

PRISONER 787

囚

SHŪ

... for I am a **prisoner**.

- enclosed 778
- person 363

TREASURE 784

宝

HŌ
takara

... the king's **treasure** ...

- roof 1144
- jewel 785

POWER

STRIKE, ATTACK, FIRE — 788
撃
GEKI
ut*su*

Attack from chariots.

- cart 1187
- hand w/ax 100
- hand 579

DESTROY — 789
滅
METSU
horo*biru*/*bosu*

Destruction by fire and water.

- water 66
- fire 83
- halberd 801

COMMAND, ADMONISH — 793
戒
KAI
imashi*meru*

A **commander admonishes** ten men.

- halberd 801
- ten 906

HISTORY — 790
史
SHI

History is filled with wars.

I, SELF, MY — 794
我
GA
ware, wa*ga*

My weapon is an extension of **myself**.

- me n–794
- halberd 801

SINK, DISAPPEAR, DIE — 791
没
BOTSU

He **died** of a hatchet wound.

- water 66
- hand w/ax 792

RIGHTEOUSNESS — 795
義
GI

He is so self-**righteous**.

- fine 290
- self 794

"HAND" — 792
殳
An element showing a **hand holding an ax**.

HIT, BEAT, ASSAULT — 796
殴
Ō
nagu*ru*

Assault people throughout the ward.

- ward 780
- hand w/ax 792

Attack

REBEL, PLUNDER, INJURE 797

賊

ZOKU

The commander **plunders** for money.

- money 708
- command 793

MILITARY, WARRIOR 798

武

BU, MU

Stop the military **warriors** …

- stop 1205
- halberd 801

LEVY, TRIBUTE, ODE 799

賦

FU

… who make us pay **tribute**.

- money 708
- military 798

ATTACK, CUT DOWN 800

伐

BATSU, HATSU

People are **cut down** with halberds.

- person 362
- halberd 801

"HALBERD" 801

戈

This element means **lance** or **halberd**.

Strike with a Stick

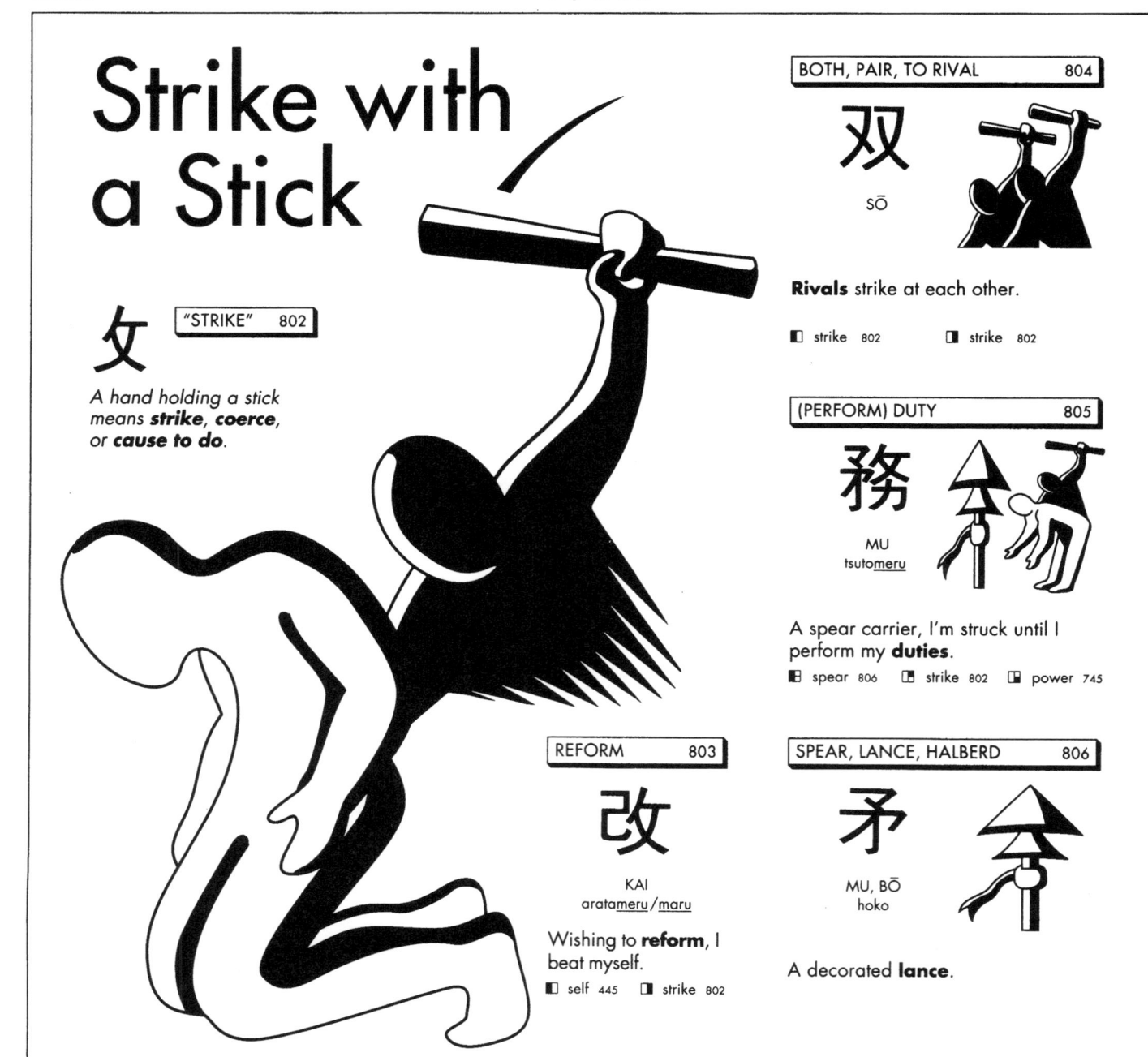

"STRIKE" 802

攴

A hand holding a stick means **strike**, **coerce**, or **cause to do**.

REFORM 803

改

KAI
arata<u>meru</u>/<u>maru</u>

Wishing to **reform**, I beat myself.

- self 445
- strike 802

BOTH, PAIR, TO RIVAL 804

双

SŌ

Rivals strike at each other.

- strike 802
- strike 802

(PERFORM) DUTY 805

務

MU
tsuto<u>meru</u>

A spear carrier, I'm struck until I perform my **duties**.

- spear 806
- strike 802
- power 745

SPEAR, LANCE, HALBERD 806

矛

MU, BŌ
hoko

A decorated **lance**.

STRIKE WITH A STICK

GO THROUGH, CLEAR, REMOVE 807
徹 TETSU

Clear the path.

- path 1192
- educate 830
- strike 802

REMOVE, WITHDRAW 808
撤 TETSU

People are forcefully **removed** by hand.

- hand 580
- educate 830
- strike 802

SCATTER, DISPERSE 809
散 SAN
chiru / rakaru / rasu

Crowds are **dispersed** by force.

- hemp n–809
- strike 802

TINY, FAINT, SECRETIVE 810
微 BI

From a **secret** path come **faint** cries of a **tiny** man being beaten.

- path 1192
- mountain 830
- strike 802

DEPEND, PROTECT 811
護 GO

Speak in **defense** of bird **protection**.

- speak 840
- bird 319
- hand 600

DEFEAT 812
敗 HAI
yabureru

Money was lost with the **defeat**.

- money 708
- strike 802

ATTACK 813
攻 KŌ
semeru

I was **attacked** by a striking construction worker.

- construction 1054
- strike 802

PRACTICE, MASTER 814
修 SHŪ, SHU
osameru / maru

I'll **master** my stroke with **practice**.

- person 362
- strike 802
- delicate 536

GOVERNMENT 815
政 SEI, SHŌ
matsurigoto

The **government** corrects problems.

- correct 826
- strike 802

DRIVE (A HERD) 816
駆 GYO

Drive a herd of horses with a stick.

- horse 291
- strike 802

Bow & Arrow

BOW, ARCHERY 817

弓 KYŪ / yumi

An **archery bow** ...

ARROW 818

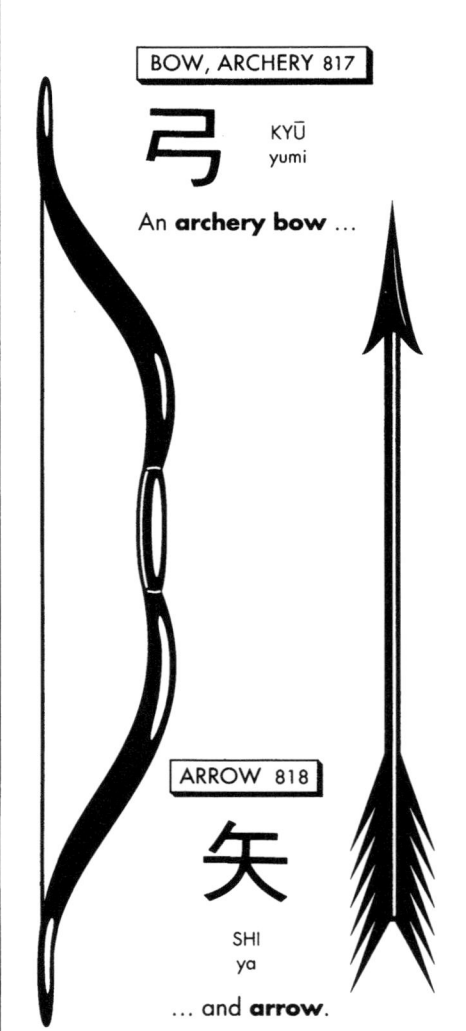

矢 SHI / ya

... and **arrow**.

WEAK 819

弱 JAKU / yowai

Two **weak** bows.

- bow 817
- bow 817

ARC, ARCH, BOW 820

弧 KO

Arc-shaped bows.

- bow 817
- rounded n–820

(BOW) STRING 821

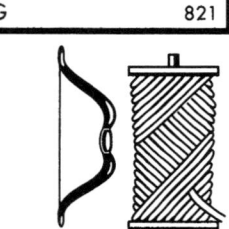

弦 GEN / tsuru

A bow is **strung** with thread.

- bow 817
- thread 964

DOUBT, SUSPECT 822

疑 GI / utagau

I doubt we'll catch the **suspects**.

- 2 persons n–822
- arrow 818
- leg 617

FIGHT, WAR 823

戦 SEN / tatakau, ikusa

Each warrior **fights** with a simple weapon.

- simple 824
- halberd 801

SIMPLE, SINGLE, UNIT 824

単 TAN

An arrow is a **simple** weapon.

BULLET, SPRING, PLAY 825

弾 DAN / hiku, hazumu, tama

Bullets beat simple bows and arrows.

- bow 824
- simple 824

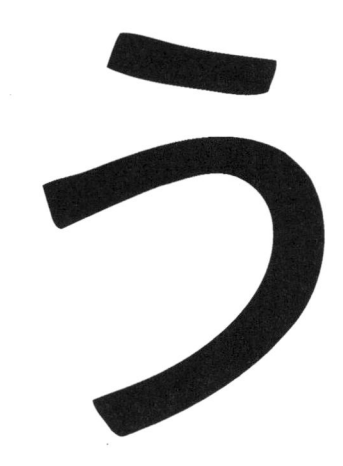

OKURIGANA

The tense and voice of Japanese verbs are indicated by "trailing kana," or *okurigana*, which are added to the kanji that represents the verb root. For example, the verb *narau*, "to learn," shown at right, uses the kanji **SHŪ** 326 for the root *nara-* and the kana *u* to create the plain, present-tense form. Other forms—past, negative, passive, etc.—are similarly indicated by kana following the root.

LEARNED
習った
nara (t) ta

IS LEARNED
習われる
nara wa re ru

MAKES LEARN
習わせる
nara wa se ru

習う

8 LEARN

Learn

CORRECT, PROPER 826
正
SEI, SHŌ
tada*shii*/*su*

Correct, **proper** posture.

CEREMONY, FORM 827
式
SHIKI

Hal is sworn in at the official **ceremony**.
- halberd 801
- construction 1054

TRIAL, TEST 828
試
SHI
kokoro*miru*, tame*su*

He speaks out at the **trial**.
- speak 840
- ceremony 827

PROOF 829
証
SHŌ
akashi

Here is **proof** that my words are correct.
- words 840
- correct 826

RAISE, EDUCATE 830
育
IKU
sodat*su*/*teru*

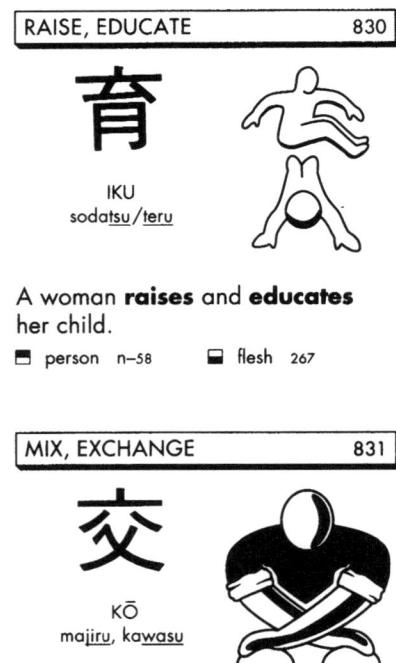

A woman **raises** and **educates** her child.
- person n–58
- flesh 267

MIX, EXCHANGE 831
交
KŌ
ma*jiru*, ka*wasu*

Mix them up.

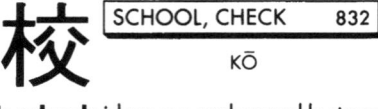

SCHOOL, CHECK 832
校
KŌ

In **schools** ideas are exchanged by trees.
- tree 126
- exchange 831

COMPARISON 833
較
KAKU, KŌ

Compare the cartloads of goods.
- vehicle 1187
- exchange 831

LEARN

GIVE 834
呉
GO
ku<u>reru</u>

The woman opens her mouth to **give** advice.

▫ mouth 566   ▫ man n–834

GIVE, CONVEY, IMPART 835
与
YO
ata<u>eru</u>

This man **gives** generously.

FINISH, COMPLETE, UNDERSTAND 836
了
RYŌ

I don't **understand**. This doesn't look **finished**.

WRITING, TEXT 837
文
BUN, MON
fumi

He's **writing** an "X" in the sand.

CREST, PATTERN 838
紋
MON

The **pattern** is "written" in thread.

▫ thread 964   ▫ writing 837

字

LEARNING 839
学
GAKU
mana<u>bu</u>

The child is **learning**.

▫ shine n–127   ▫ child 447

Speak

WORD, SAY, SPEAK 840
GEN, GON
koto, i<u>u</u>

He **spoke** four **words**.

- feelings n–840
- mouth 566

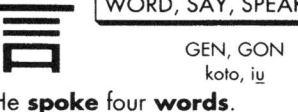

KNOWLEDGE 841
SHIKI

Every day I must stand and say something **knowledgeable**.

- word 840
- stand 627
- halberd 801

SUE, APPEAL 842
SO
utta<u>eru</u>

The lawyer's words repelled the **suit** and led to an **appeal**.

- word 840
- repel 1076

PRISON, LITIGATION 843
GOKU

A good argument at **litigation** can hound a man into **prison**.

- dog 338
- word 840
- dog 335

TRUST, BELIEVE 844
SHIN

If you **trust** me, **believe** what I say.

- person 362
- word 840

INVITE, TEMPT, LEAD 845
YŪ
saso<u>u</u>

I was **tempted**, **led on**, with an **invitation** to have …

- word 840
- rice plant 231
- reach n–567

EXCEL, EXCELLENT 846
SHŪ
hii<u>deru</u>

… **excellent** rice.

- rice plant 231
- hand n–567

SPEAK

LANGUAGE, SPEAK — 847
GO
kataru

Fifty words of **language** …

- word 840
- five 901
- mouth 566

PERCEIVE, DISCERN — 848
GO
satoru

… filled fifty hearts with new **perception**.

- heart 498
- five 901
- mouth 566

MISTAKE, MIS- — 849
GO
ayamaru

What she said was filled with **mistakes**.

- word 840
- give 834

CONVERSATION, TALK — 850
DAN

He **talks** like his tongue is aflame.

- word 840
- flame 86

LESSON, TEACH, READ — 851
KUN

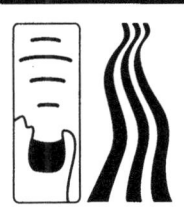

His **lessons** flow like a river.

- word 840
- river 55

ACKNOWLEDGE, RECOGNIZE — 852
NIN
mitomeru

Endure his words and you will **recognize** how true they are.

- word 840
- endure 510

WORD, PART OF SPEECH — 853
SHI
kotoba

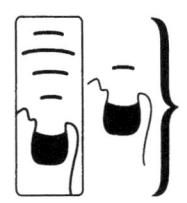

Identify the part of **speech** of each of the four words spoken.

- word 840
- administer n–853

CORRECT, REVISE — 854
TEI

He **corrected** my pronunciation of the letter "t."

- word 840
- exact 1089

NOH CHANT, SONG — 855
YŌ
utai, utau

Sing a **song** while swinging the basket.

- speak 840
- hand 609
- basket n–607

Read

READ — 856
読 DOKU, TOKU
yo*mu*

He **reads** the words from the book.

- word 840
- soil 101
- call n–856

PHRASE, CLAUSE — 857
句 KU

He wraps his tongue around a **phrase**.

- wrap 944
- mouth 566

SEIZE, ADHERE TO — 858
拘 KŌ
kakawa*ru*

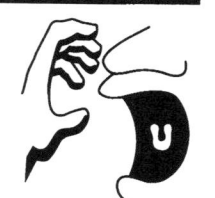

A hand **adheres** to his mouth.

- hand 580
- phrase 857

RECITE, PREACH — 859
唱 SHŌ
tona*eru*

They **recite** with clear voices.

- mouth 566
- clear 2

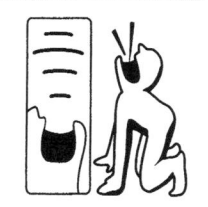

PREACH, EXPLAIN — 860
説 SETSU
to*ku*

His words **preach** brotherly love.

- word 840
- split 456
- brother 438

ANSWER — 861
答 TŌ
kota*eru*

He **answered** a question about bamboo.

- bamboo 123
- join 583

READ

SEAL, SIGN, SYMBOL 862
IN
shirushi

A "top secret" **seal**.

ONE OF A PAIR, ONE SIDE, PIECE 865
HEN
kata

The man in the chair is holding **one of a pair** of aces.

ROLL, REEL, VOLUME 863
KAN
maki, ma<u>ku</u>

This **rolled** up document speaks **volumes** about my personal life.
- hands n–863
- personal 445

PRINT, BOARD 866
HAN

Paper is pressed against a **board** to make **prints**.
- piece 865
- against 957

ARGUMENT, OPINION 864
RON

When we got into an **argument** over the book's **opinions**, he walked out.
- speak 840
- person 362
- book 868

TRANSLATION 867
YAKU
wake

Translation means carrying words from one language to another.
- word 840
- measure 884

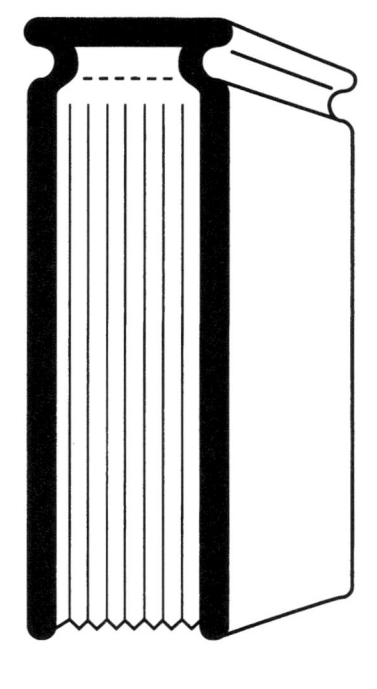

BOOK, VOLUME 868
SATSU

A bound **book**.

149

The Arts

LIGHT, SHINE, BRILLIANCE 869

光

KŌ
hikari, hikaru

The candle **light** shines **brilliantly**.

CODE, RULE, PRECEDENT 870

典

TEN
nori

A book of legal **codes** and **precedents**.

TALENT, YEAR OF AGE 871

才

SAI

He shows great theatrical **talent** for someone his **age**.

EXIST, KNOW, THINK 872

存

SON, ZON

I teach my child all that I **know** of **existence**.

☐ dam n–872   ■ child 447

DWELL, COUNTRYSIDE, BE 873

在

ZAI
aru

A farmer **dwells** in the **countryside**.

☐ dam n–872   ■ soil 101

INFER, PUSH AHEAD 874

推

SUI
osu

I **infer** that the hand is pushing the bird forward, not backward.

■ hand 580   ■ bird 319

PRESSURE 875

圧

ATSU

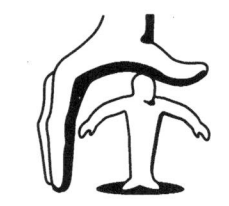

My friend Cliff is under a lot of **pressure**.

☐ cliff n–81   ■ soil 101

MATCH, ANIMAL COUNTER 876

匹

HITSU
hiki

Two wrestlers in loincloths have a sumo **match**.

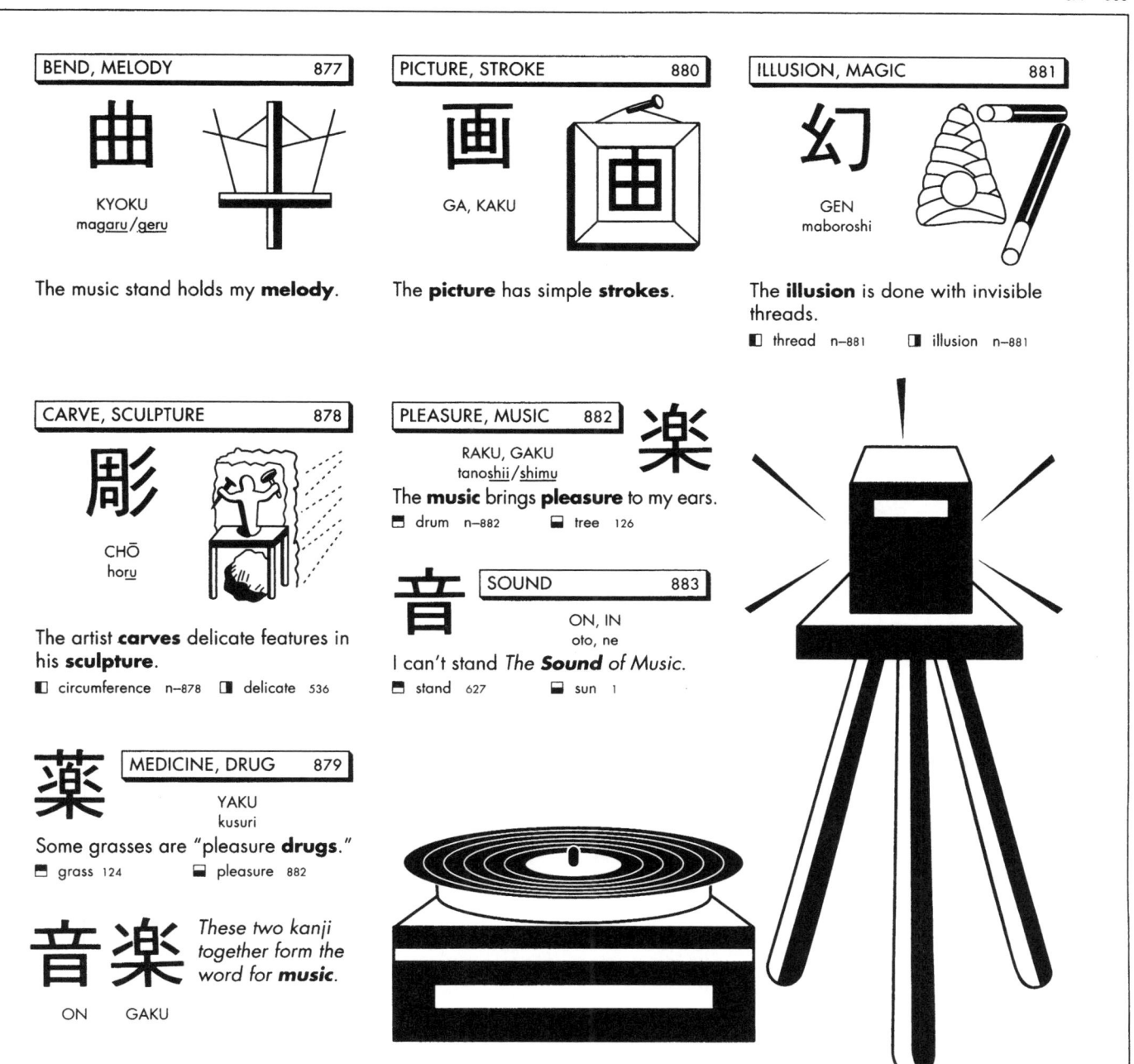

THE ARTS

BEND, MELODY — 877
曲
KYOKU
ma*garu*/*geru*

The music stand holds my **melody**.

PICTURE, STROKE — 880
画
GA, KAKU

The **picture** has simple **strokes**.

ILLUSION, MAGIC — 881
幻
GEN
maboroshi

The **illusion** is done with invisible threads.
- thread n–881
- illusion n–881

CARVE, SCULPTURE — 878
彫
CHŌ
ho*ru*

The artist **carves** delicate features in his **sculpture**.
- circumference n–878
- delicate 536

PLEASURE, MUSIC — 882
楽
RAKU, GAKU
tano*shii*/*shimu*

The **music** brings **pleasure** to my ears.
- drum n–882
- tree 126

SOUND — 883
音
ON, IN
oto, ne

I can't stand The **Sound** of Music.
- stand 627
- sun 1

MEDICINE, DRUG — 879
薬
YAKU
kusuri

Some grasses are "pleasure **drugs**."
- grass 124
- pleasure 882

音楽
ON GAKU

These two kanji together form the word for **music**.

MEASURE, FOOT 884
SHAKU, SEKI
I pace off the **measure** with my feet.

MEASURE 885
KEI
hakaru
Metric **measures** are based on ten.

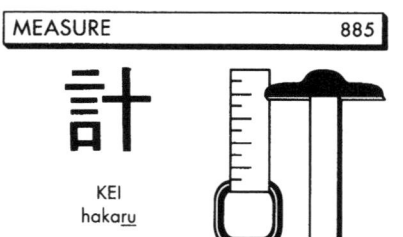

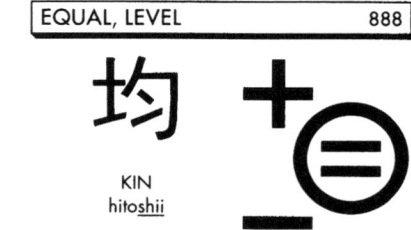

- word 840
- ten 906

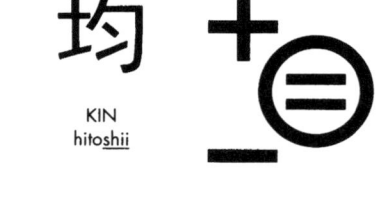

DIPPER, MEASURE 886
TO
I **measure** with calipers.

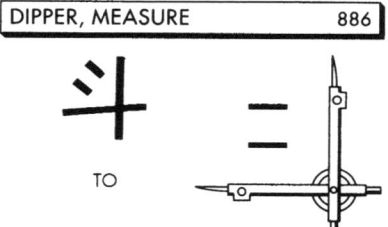

STARTING POINT, MEANS, USE 887
I
motte
This line is the **starting point**.

EQUAL, LEVEL 888
KIN
hitoshii
Positive and negative **equals** zero.

- soil 101
- flat n–888

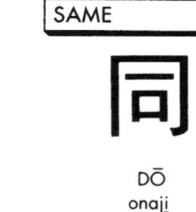

SAME 889
DŌ
onaji
The diameter of a circle is the **same** in all directions.

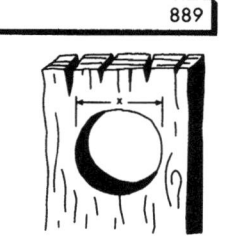

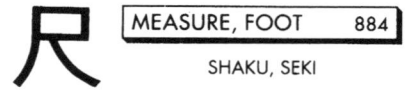

MANY 890
TA
ōi
Many moons ago—99 months to be exact.

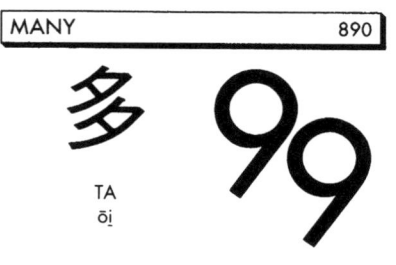

- moon 14
- moon 14

Measure

BOTH, PAIR, COIN — 891
両
RYŌ

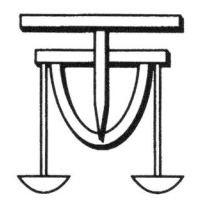

A **pair** of coins are on **both** sides of the scale.

FULL, FILL — 892
満
MAN
michiru/tasu

Both halves of the melon are **full** of water.

- water 66
- grass 124
- both 891

LENGTH, MEASURE, STATURE — 894
丈
JŌ
take

I'll measure the **length** with this rule.

INCLUDE, CONTAIN — 893
含
GAN
fukumu/meru

Now the box **contains** a puppet.

- now 31
- opening 566

OBTAIN, STORE, SUPPLY — 895
収
SHŪ
osameru/maru

Keep a **supply** of sticks on hand in the **storage** box.

- seek out n-895
- hand 600

WHAT, HOW MANY — 896
何
KA
nan, nani

What's in the box?

- person 362
- opening 566

Numbers

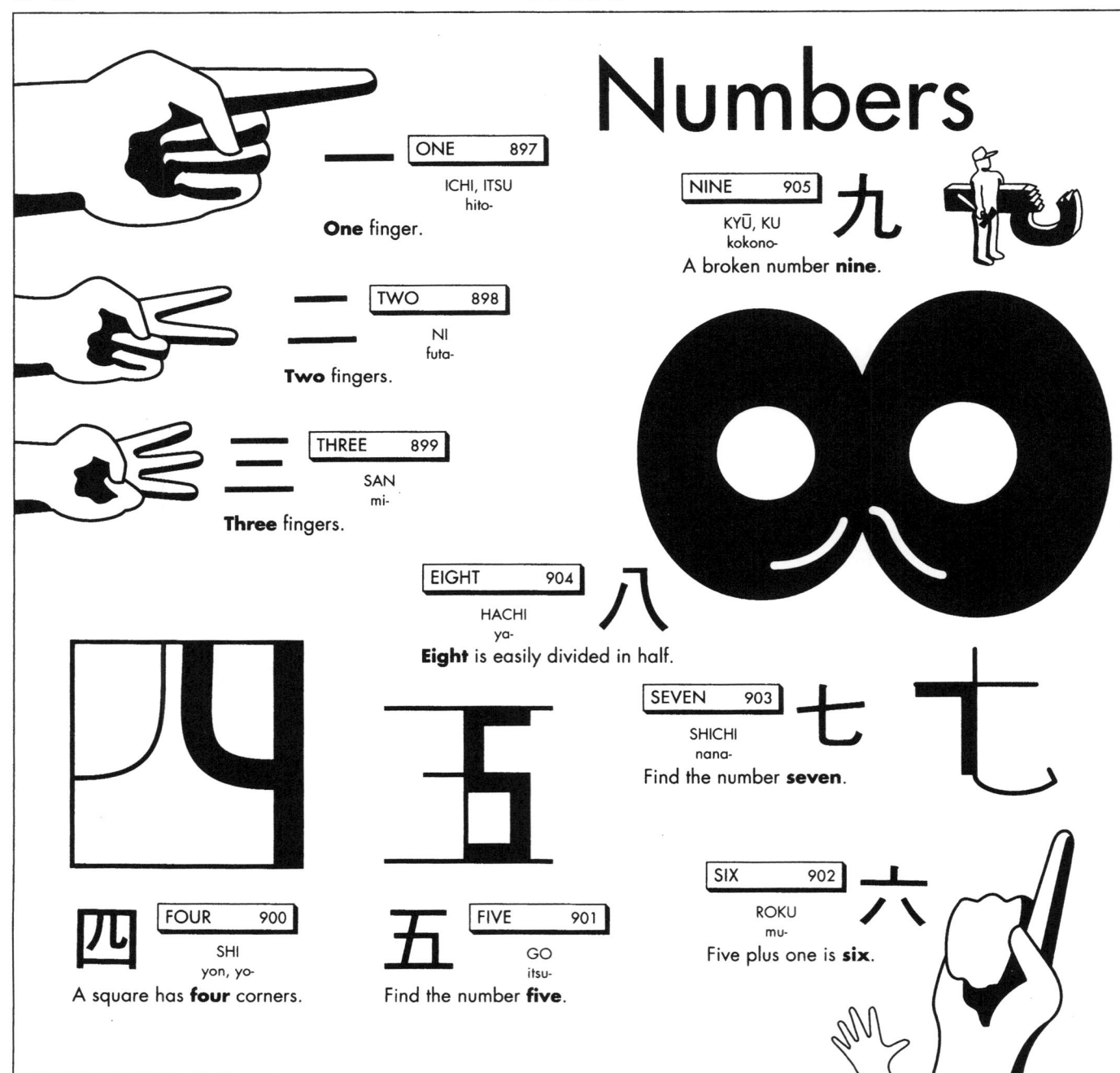

—	ONE	897

ICHI, ITSU
hito-

One finger.

二	TWO	898

NI
futa-

Two fingers.

三	THREE	899

SAN
mi-

Three fingers.

四	FOUR	900

SHI
yon, yo-

A square has **four** corners.

五	FIVE	901

GO
itsu-

Find the number **five**.

SIX	902	六

ROKU
mu-

Five plus one is **six**.

SEVEN	903	七

SHICHI
nana-

Find the number **seven**.

EIGHT	904	八

HACHI
ya-

Eight is easily divided in half.

NINE	905	九

KYŪ, KU
kokono-

A broken number **nine**.

NUMBERS

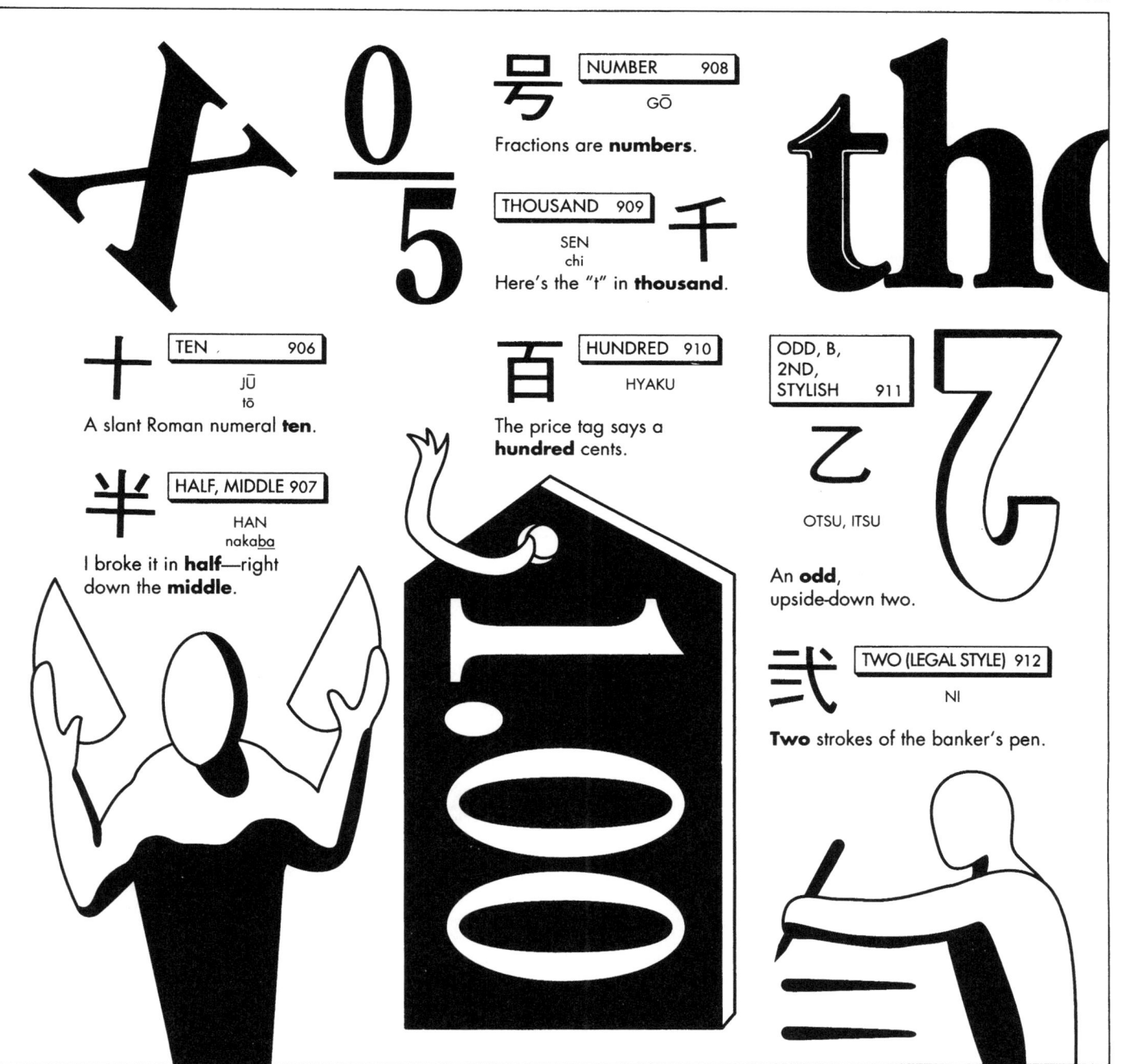

十 TEN 906
JŪ
tō

A slant Roman numeral **ten**.

半 HALF, MIDDLE 907
HAN
naka**ba**

I broke it in **half**—right down the **middle**.

号 NUMBER 908
GŌ

Fractions are **numbers**.

千 THOUSAND 909
SEN
chi

Here's the "t" in **thousand**.

百 HUNDRED 910
HYAKU

The price tag says a **hundred** cents.

乙 ODD, B, 2ND, STYLISH 911
OTSU, ITSU

An **odd**, upside-down two.

弐 TWO (LEGAL STYLE) 912
NI

Two strokes of the banker's pen.

Sizes

BIG — 913
大
TAI, DAI
ōkii

"It was this **big**!"

FAT — 914
太
TAI, TA
futoi/ru

See the **fat** man with the big belly button.
- big 100
- two n–914

LONG, SENIOR — 915
長
CHŌ
nagai

Long hair is a sign of old age.

STRETCH — 916
張
CHŌ
haru

Pulled back, his hair **stretches** a long way.
- pull 817
- long 915

HOLLOW, CONCAVE, DENT — 917
凹
Ō
kubo, boko
hekomu

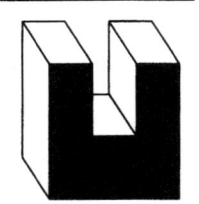

A **concave** figure.

CONVEX, PROTRUSION — 918
凸
TOTSU
deko

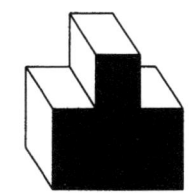

A **convex** figure.

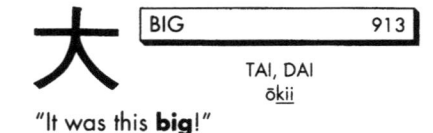

ROUND, CIRCLE, BALL, SHIP — 919
丸
GAN
maru, marui

Curl up in a **ball**.

SHAPE, PATTERN 920

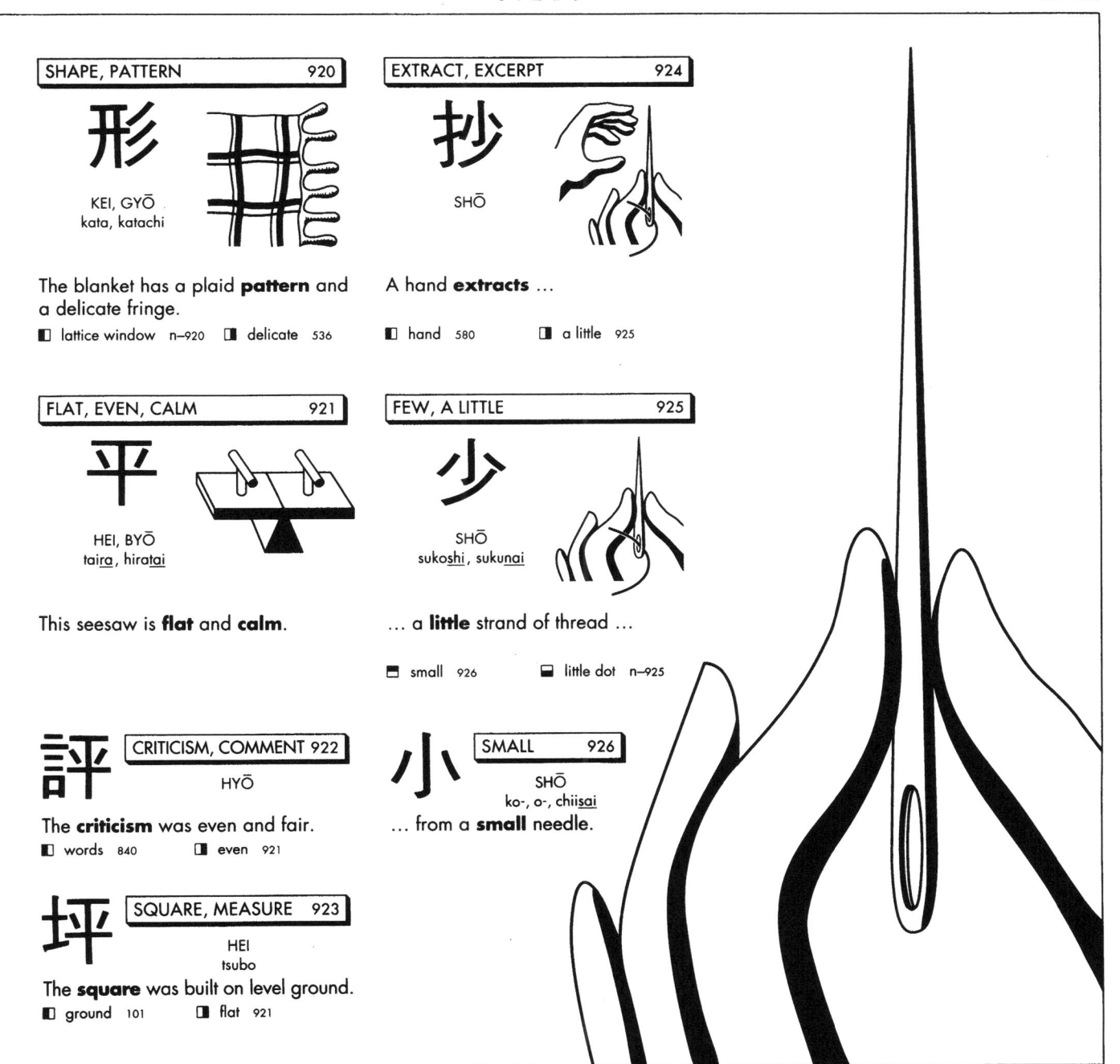

形

KEI, GYŌ
kata, katachi

The blanket has a plaid **pattern** and a delicate fringe.

- lattice window n–920
- delicate 536

FLAT, EVEN, CALM 921

平

HEI, BYŌ
tai<u>ra</u>, hira<u>tai</u>

This seesaw is **flat** and **calm**.

CRITICISM, COMMENT 922

評

HYŌ

The **criticism** was even and fair.

- words 840
- even 921

SQUARE, MEASURE 923

坪

HEI
tsubo

The **square** was built on level ground.

- ground 101
- flat 921

EXTRACT, EXCERPT 924

抄

SHŌ

A hand **extracts** …

- hand 580
- a little 925

FEW, A LITTLE 925

少

SHŌ
suko<u>shi</u>, suku<u>nai</u>

… a **little** strand of thread …

- small 926
- little dot n–925

SMALL 926

小

SHŌ
ko-, o-, chii<u>sai</u>

… from a **small** needle.

Colors

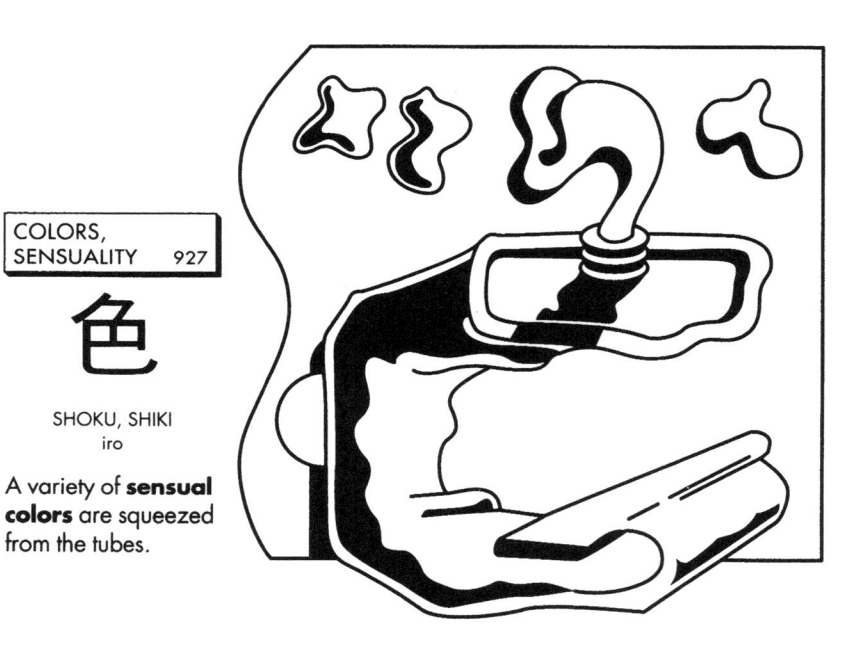

COLORS, SENSUALITY — 927
色
SHOKU, SHIKI
iro

A variety of **sensual colors** are squeezed from the tubes.

COLOR — 928
彩
SAI
irodo*ru*

Rays of light shine on the **colorful** hand-picked tree blossoms.

- hand 609
- tree 126
- delicate 536

RED — 929
赤
SEKI, SHAKU
aka*i*

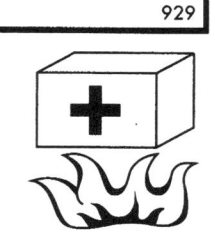

A **red** cross is on the first aid kit.

- soil 101
- fire 82

RED, CRIMSON, ROUGE — 930
紅
KŌ, KU
kurenai, beni

A **red** construction sign.

- thread 964
- constructrion 1054

BLACK — 931
黒
KOKU
kuro*i*

Black soot is on the BBQ grill.

- village 1087
- fire 82

INK, INKSTICK — 932
墨
BOKU
sumi

An **inkstick** is made of black soot.

- black 931
- soil 101

FORGIVENESS — 933
赦
SHA

I'll **forgive** you after you're beaten red.

- red 929
- strike 802

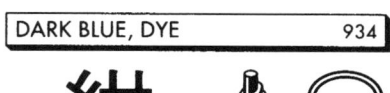

COLORS

DARK BLUE, DYE 934
紺
KON

The **blue** thread is dyed in sweet blueberries.

- thread 964
- sweet 272

GREEN 935
緑
RYOKU, ROKU
midori

Pour the **green** liquid over the thread.

- thread 964
- liquid n–935

WHITE 936
白
HAKU
shiroi

A **white** ray of sunshine.

- ray n–936
- sun 1

BLUE, YOUNG 937
青
SEI, SHŌ
aoi

A **green** plant grows on the moon.

- plant 214
- moon 14

CLEAR, BRIGHT 938
晴
SEI
hareru

Bright and sunny with **clear** blue skies.

- sun 1
- blue 937

SPIRIT, VITALITY 939
精
SEI, SHŌ

Eat blue/green rice for **vitality**.

- rice 217
- blue 937

FEELING, PITY 940
情
JŌ, SEI
nasake

Pity me, my heart **feels** blue.

- heart 498
- blue 937

PURE, CLEAN 941
清
SEI, SHŌ
kiyoi/meru

The water is a **pure**, clear blue.

- water 66
- blue 937

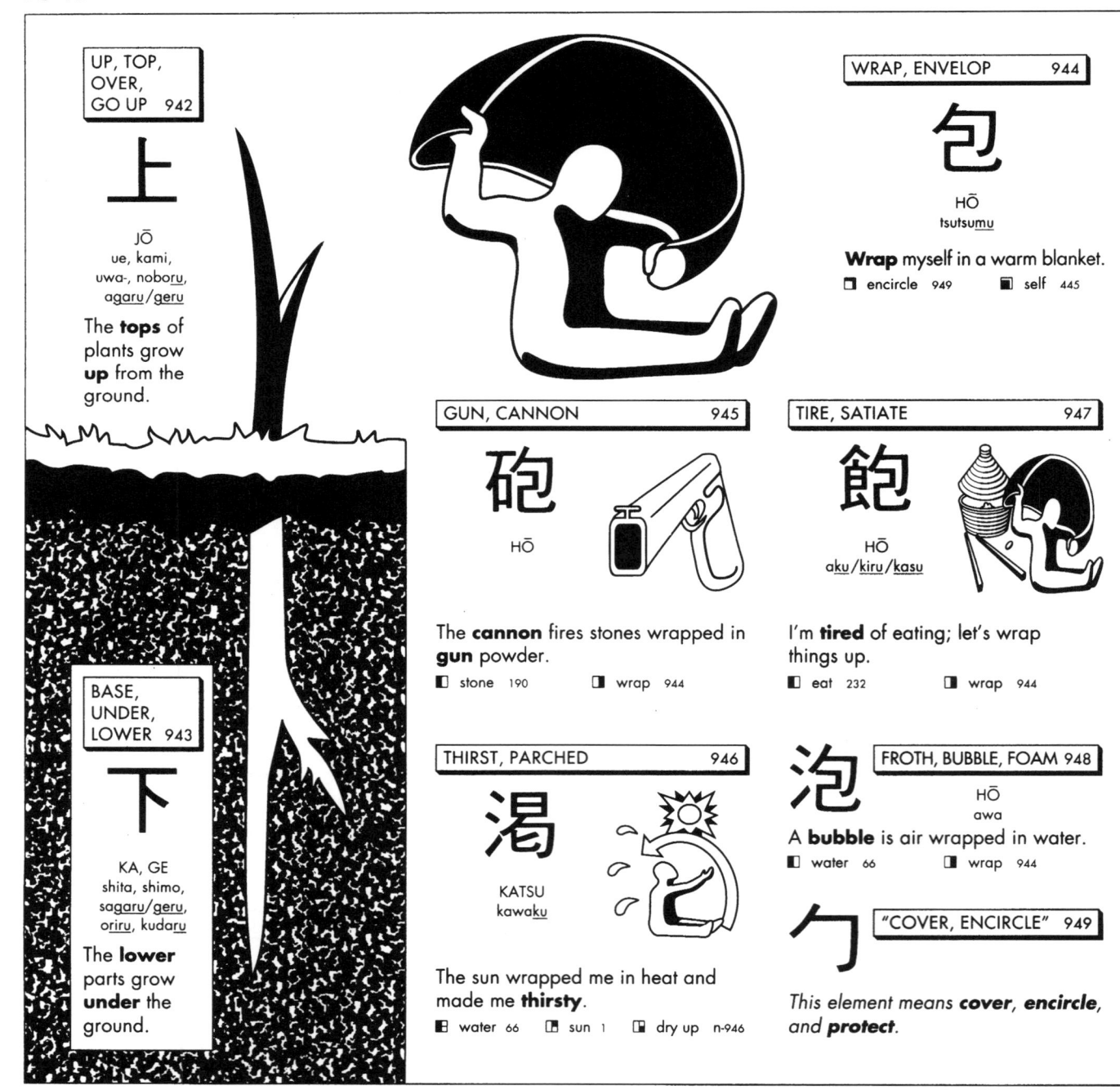

LEARN

UP, TOP, OVER, GO UP 942

上

JŌ
ue, kami, uwa-, nobo*ru*, a*garu*/*geru*

The **tops** of plants grow **up** from the ground.

BASE, UNDER, LOWER 943

下

KA, GE
shita, shimo, sa*garu*/*geru*, o*riru*, kuda*ru*

The **lower** parts grow **under** the ground.

WRAP, ENVELOP 944

包

HŌ
tsutsu*mu*

Wrap myself in a warm blanket.

- encircle 949
- self 445

GUN, CANNON 945

砲

HŌ

The **cannon** fires stones wrapped in **gun** powder.

- stone 190
- wrap 944

THIRST, PARCHED 946

渇

KATSU
kawa*ku*

The sun wrapped me in heat and made me **thirsty**.

- water 66
- sun 1
- dry up n-946

TIRE, SATIATE 947

飽

HŌ
a*ku*/*kiru*/*kasu*

I'm **tired** of eating; let's wrap things up.

- eat 232
- wrap 944

FROTH, BUBBLE, FOAM 948

泡

HŌ
awa

A **bubble** is air wrapped in water.

- water 66
- wrap 944

"COVER, ENCIRCLE" 949

勹

*This element means **cover**, **encircle**, and **protect**.*

Positions

MIDDLE, INSIDE, CHINA 950
中
CHŪ 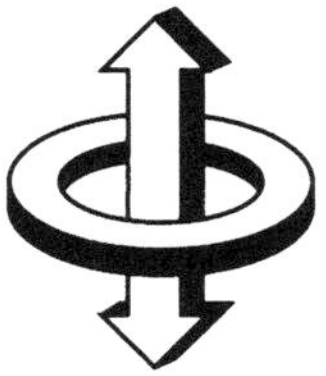
naka

A line through the **middle** of the opening.

CENTER 951
央 
Ō

Lines radiate from the **center** of the opening.

INSIDE, WITHIN 952
内 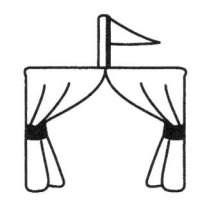
NAI, DAI
uchi

We kept things **inside** the tent.

PUT IN, CROWDED 953
込
komu/meru

He didn't enter the **crowded** tent.
- move 1153
- enter 950

EMERGE, PUT OUT 955
出
SHUTSU
deru, dasu

He **emerged** from the tent feeling **put out**.

ENTER, PUT IN 954
入
NYŪ
hairu, ireru/ru

Enter the tent.

OBTAIN, STORE, SUPPLY 956
納 
NŌ, NA,
NATSU, TŌ
osameru

Our **supply** of thread is **stored** inside the tent.
- thread 964
- inside 952

Oppose

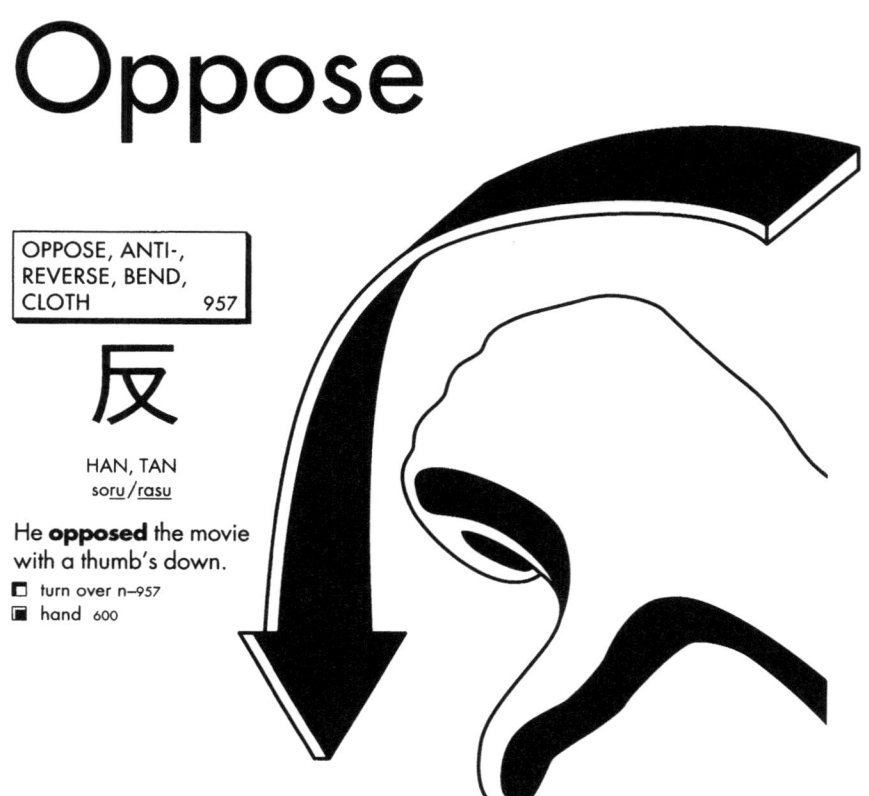

OPPOSE, ANTI-, REVERSE, BEND, CLOTH 957
反
HAN, TAN
so<u>ru</u>/<u>rasu</u>

He **opposed** the movie with a thumb's down.
- turn over n–957
- hand 600

NOT, NONE, CEASE TO BE 958
無
MU, BU
na<u>i</u>/<u>shi</u>

Burn the books til there are **none**.
- book 868
- fire 82

NOT, UN-, DIS- 959
不
FU, BU

He **dis**likes something.

NOT, UN-, FAULT 960
非
HI

The signs are **not** pointing in one direction.

REJECT, EXPEL, PUSH, ANTI- 961
排
HAI

He **rejected** the handout by covering his mouth.
- hand 580
- not 960

ACTOR 962
俳
HAI

It was not really him; he was **acting**.
- person 362
- not 960

NO, DECLINE, DENY 963
否
HI
ina, ina<u>mu</u>

He always says **no**.
- not 958
- mouth 566

STROKE ORDER

Kanji are written according to rules of stroke order established long ago by calligraphers and teachers. Generally: (1) strokes are written from top to bottom and from left to right; (2) horizontal crossing strokes precede vertical crossing strokes; (3) enclosures are drawn first, but a closing line at bottom is drawn last; (4) strokes that slant from right to left are written before strokes that slant left to right; (5) piercing vertical lines are written last. There are many exceptions, however. In the kanji **DŌ** 534 of *dōgu,* meaning "tool," shown at right, the element MOVEMENT 1153 that stretches from upper left to lower right is actually written last. In the examples here, stroke order numbers have been placed at the beginning point of each stroke.

DŌ
way 534

GU
equipment 1039

9 TOOLS

TOOLS

Thread

THREAD 964
糸
SHI
ito

A spool of **thread**.

SILK 965
絹
KEN
kinu

Silk comes from a worm.

- thread 964
- mouth 566
- flesh 267

EDIT, KNIT, BOOK 966
編
HEN
amu

Editing a book is like **knitting** words.

- thread 964
- door 1113
- book 868

SPIN (YARN) 967
紡
BŌ
tsumugu

Spin a spool of thread.
- thread 964
- direction 386

REEL, TURN 968
繰
SŌ
kuru

The wooden **reel turns** thread.
- thread 964
- goods 1038
- tree 126

164

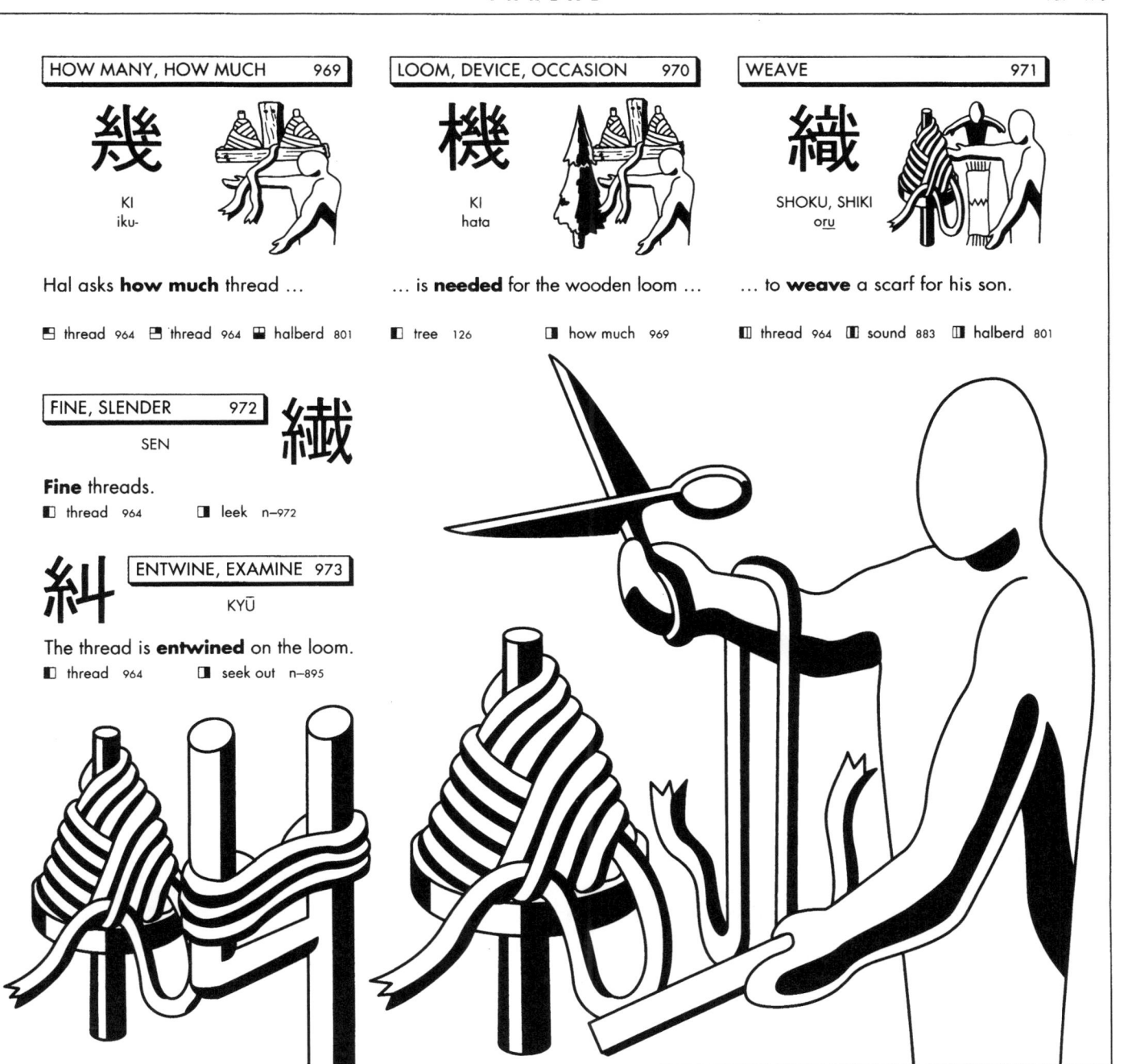

THREAD

HOW MANY, HOW MUCH 969
幾
KI
iku-

Hal asks **how much** thread …

▫ thread 964 ▫ thread 964 ▫ halberd 801

LOOM, DEVICE, OCCASION 970
機
KI
hata

… is **needed** for the wooden loom …

▫ tree 126 ▫ how much 969

WEAVE 971
織
SHOKU, SHIKI
o<u>ru</u>

… to **weave** a scarf for his son.

▫ thread 964 ▫ sound 883 ▫ halberd 801

FINE, SLENDER 972
繊
SEN

Fine threads.

▫ thread 964 ▫ leek n–972

ENTWINE, EXAMINE 973
糾
KYŪ

The thread is **entwined** on the loom.

▫ thread 964 ▫ seek out n–895

TOOLS

PAPER 974
紙
SHI
kami

This **paper** is made of stringy fibers.

- thread 964
- family 396

LINE 975
線
SEN

Thread, water, and rays of sunshine travel in a **line**.

- thread 964
- white 936
- water 57

INVOLVEMENT 976
係
KEI
kakari

This person is **involved** in finding …

- person 362
- lineage 977

LINEAGE, CONNECTION 977
系
KEI

… where one string **connects** to another.

- hand n–977
- thread 964

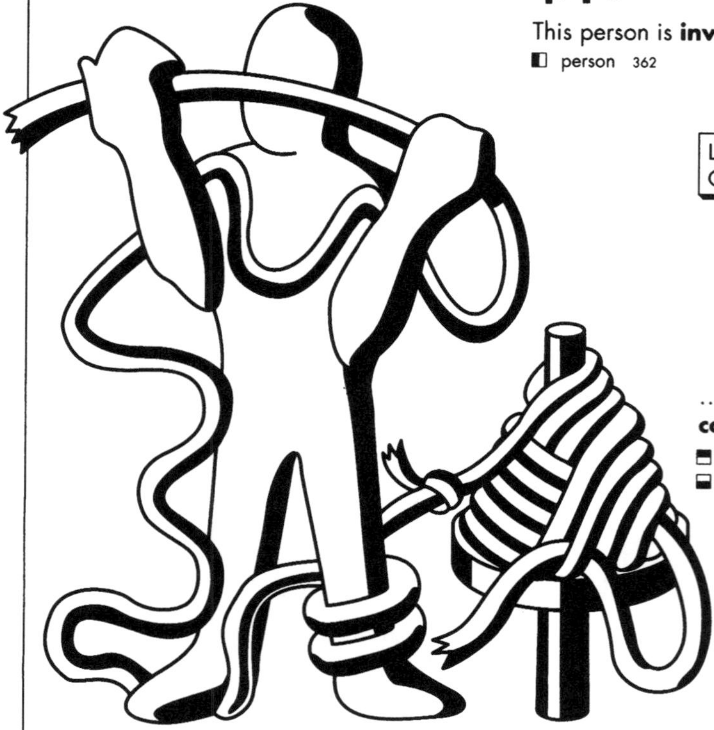

ACCUMULATE, INVOLVE 978
累
RUI

Thread has **accumulated** in the field.

- field 201
- thread 964

STRAW, CORD 979
縄
JŌ
nawa

Two knots are tied in the **straw** cord.

- thread 964
- twist n–979

FINISH 980
終
SHŪ
owaru/eru

The ends of the string are **finished** with a knot.

- thread 964
- winter 42

THREAD

STRANGLE, WRING — 981
絞
KŌ
shibo*ru*, shi*meru*

This mixed-up person **strangles** people with string.

- thread 964
- mix 831

BIND, TIGHTEN, CLOSE — 982
締
TEI
shi*maru*/*meru*

Bind the broom straws with thread.

- thread 964
- stand 627
- broom n–982

STOP, FASTEN — 983
留
RYŪ, RU
to*maru*/*meru*

Stop and help me **fasten** this package.

- family n–983
- knife 1023
- field 201

NET, NETWORK — 984
網
MŌ
ami

The dead body is entwined in a **net**.

- thread 964
- net n–984
- die 660

"NET" — 987
This element means **net**, but also looks like an eye on its side.

GAUZE, NET, INCLUDE — 988
羅
RA

A **gauze net** and a rope …

- net 987
- thread 964
- bird 319

ELEMENT, BASE, BARE — 985
素
SO, SU
moto

A plant is made of threadlike **elements**.

- plant 214
- thread 964

FINE, NARROW — 986
細
SAI
hoso*i*, koma*kai*

The field is as **narrow** as thread.

- thread 964
- field 201

FASTEN, ROPE, SUPPORT — 989
維
I

… **fastened** to its leg hold the bird.

- thread 964
- bird 319

Baskets

"BASKET" 990
西

This element means **basket**.

NECESSARY 991
要
YŌ
iru

The woman finds it **necessary** to carry the basket on her head ...
- basket 990
- woman 411

HIP, LOWER BACK, BEARING 992
腰
YŌ
koshi

... to prevent **lower back** pain.
- flesh 267
- basket 990
- woman 411

VOTE, SLIP OF PAPER 993
票
HYŌ

Votes are collected in the basket.
- basket 990
- altar 701

SIGN(POST), MARK 994
標
HYŌ
shirushi

A **sign** is **marked** with a slip of paper.
- tree 126
- vote 993

"BASKETS" 995
冓

This element means **baskets**.

PRICE, VALUE, WORTH 996
価
KA
atai

A person rings up the **price** of a basket.
- person 362
- basket 990

LECTURE 997
講
KŌ

A wordy **lecture** on baskets.
- speak 840
- baskets 995

BUY 998
購
KŌ

With inflation, you need baskets of money to **buy** anything.
- money 708
- baskets 995

BASKETS / NEEDLES

DITCH, CHANNEL 999

溝

KŌ
mizo, dobu

Baskets were used to fill the **ditch** with water.

- water 66
- baskets 995

BUILD, MIND 1000

構

KŌ
kamau/eru

Baskets are **built** from trees.

- tree 126
- baskets 995

NEW 1001

新

SHIN
atarashii, arata

A **new** ax is needle-sharp.

- needle 1006
- ax 1072

AVOID 1002

避

HI
sakeru

Move quickly to **avoid** getting a needle in your rear.

- move 1153
- needle + buttocks n-1002

HABIT, KINK 1003

癖

HEKI
kuse

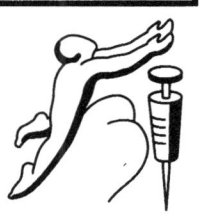

Any bad **habit** can be cured by a needle in your rear.

- illness 655
- needle + buttocks n-1002

ADMINISTER 1004

宰

SAI

Needles are **administered** in this building.

- roof 1144
- needle 1005

Needles

SHARP, BITTER 1005

辛

SHIN
karai, tsurai

A **sharp** needle.

"NEEDLE" 1006

辛

This element means **needle**.

169

Cloth

巾 "CLOTH" 1007
This element means **cloth**.

布 CLOTH, SPREAD 1008
FU
nuno

A hand spreads out the **cloth**.
- hand 598
- cloth 1007

希 DESIRE, SCANTY 1009
KI, KE

I **desire** to cut this cloth pajama top into a **scanty** negligee.
- weave n-1009
- cloth 1007

帝 EMPEROR 1010
TEI

What is an **emperor** but a man standing in fine clothes?
- stand 627
- cloth 1007

帳 REGISTER, DRAPE 1011
CHŌ

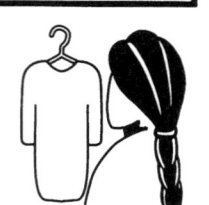

Cloth and long hair **drape** down her back.
- cloth 1007
- long 915

帆 SAIL 1012
HAN
ho

A cloth **sail**.
- cloth 1007
- wind n-1012

幕 CURTAIN, TENT, ACT 1013
MAKU, BAKU

A cloth **tent** protects you from the sun and itchy grass.
- grass 124
- sun 1
- cloth 1007

綿 COTTON 1014
MEN
wata

Cloth is made of white **cotton** thread.
- thread 964
- white 936
- cloth 1007

旅 JOURNEY 1015
RYO
tabi

Clothing fit for a **journey**.
- flag n-387
- clothing 1021

CLOTH

WEAR, CLOTHING, GEAR 1016

装

SŌ, SHŌ
yosōu

I **wear** manly **gear**.

- manly 420
- clothing 1021

REVERSE SIDE, INSIDE, LINING 1017

裏

RI
ura

The label is on the **inside lining** of the clothes.

- shelter 1147
- village 1086
- clothing 1021

NAKED, BARE 1018

裸

RA
hadaka

He hung his clothes on the fruit tree while running **naked**.

- clothing n–1015
- field 201
- tree 126

CLOTHES, YIELD, SERVE 1019

服

FUKU

I keep my **clothes** on the shelf.

- flesh 267
- hand w/tool n–1019

CLOTHING 1021

衣

I
koromo

A piece of **clothing**.

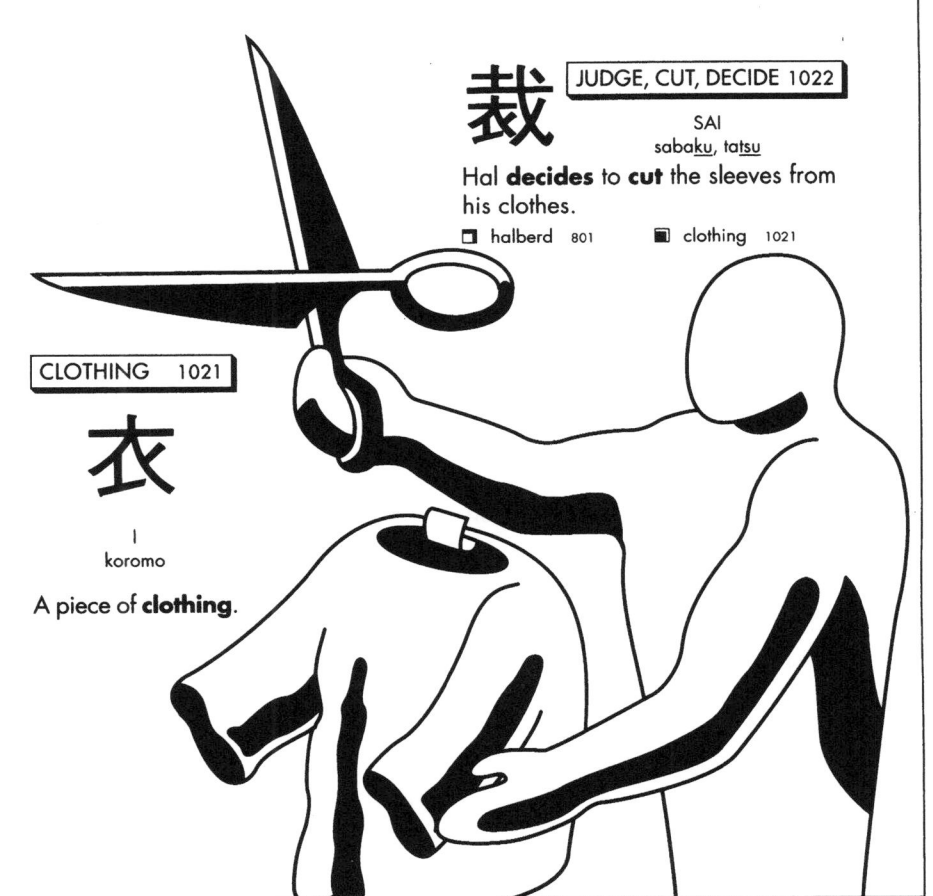

REPORT, REWARD 1020

報

HŌ
mukuiru

Reportedly, the **reward** was yen plus clothes.

- happiness 731
- seize n–1020

JUDGE, CUT, DECIDE 1022

裁

SAI
sabaku, tatsu

Hal **decides** to **cut** the sleeves from his clothes.

- halberd 801
- clothing 1021

Knife

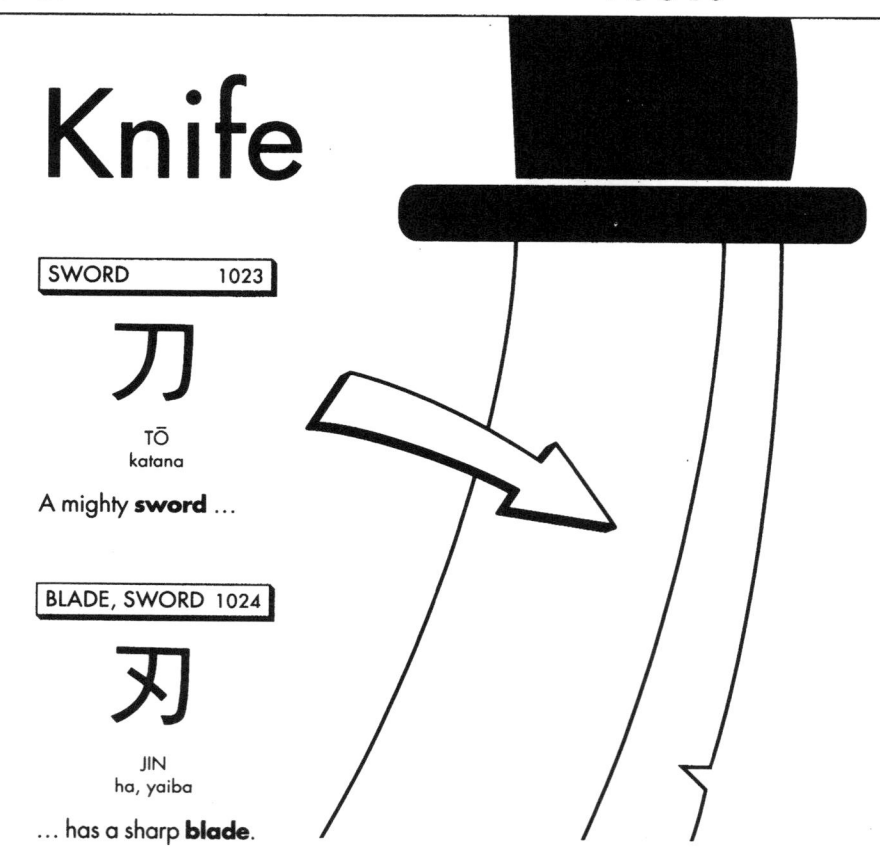

SWORD 1023
刀
TŌ
katana

A mighty **sword** …

BLADE, SWORD 1024
刃
JIN
ha, yaiba

… has a sharp **blade**.

DIVIDE, MINUTE, UNDERSTAND 1025
紛 
BUN, FUN, BU
wa<u>karu</u>/<u>keru</u>

I fell into confusion when my lifeline **divided** in two.
- split 456
- sword 1023

PUNISH 1026
刑 
KEI

Stabbing is **punished** by imprisonment.
- grill n–920
- knife 1037

PIERCE, STAB, THORN 1027
刺
SHI
sa<u>su</u>/<u>saru</u>, toge

The **thorn pierces** like a knife.
- thorn n–1027
- knife 1037

CHOP, MINCE, ENGRAVE 1028
刻
KOKU
kiza<u>mu</u>

The **chopped** wood becomes an **engraved** bedpost.
- pig n–1028
- knife 1037

CORE, NUCLEUS 1029
核
KAKU

A bedpost was made of a tree's **core**.
- tree 126
- pig n–1028

PUNISHMENT 1030
罰
BATSU, BACHI

Speaking gets the knife/net **punishment**.
- net 987
- speak 840
- knife 1037

KNIFE

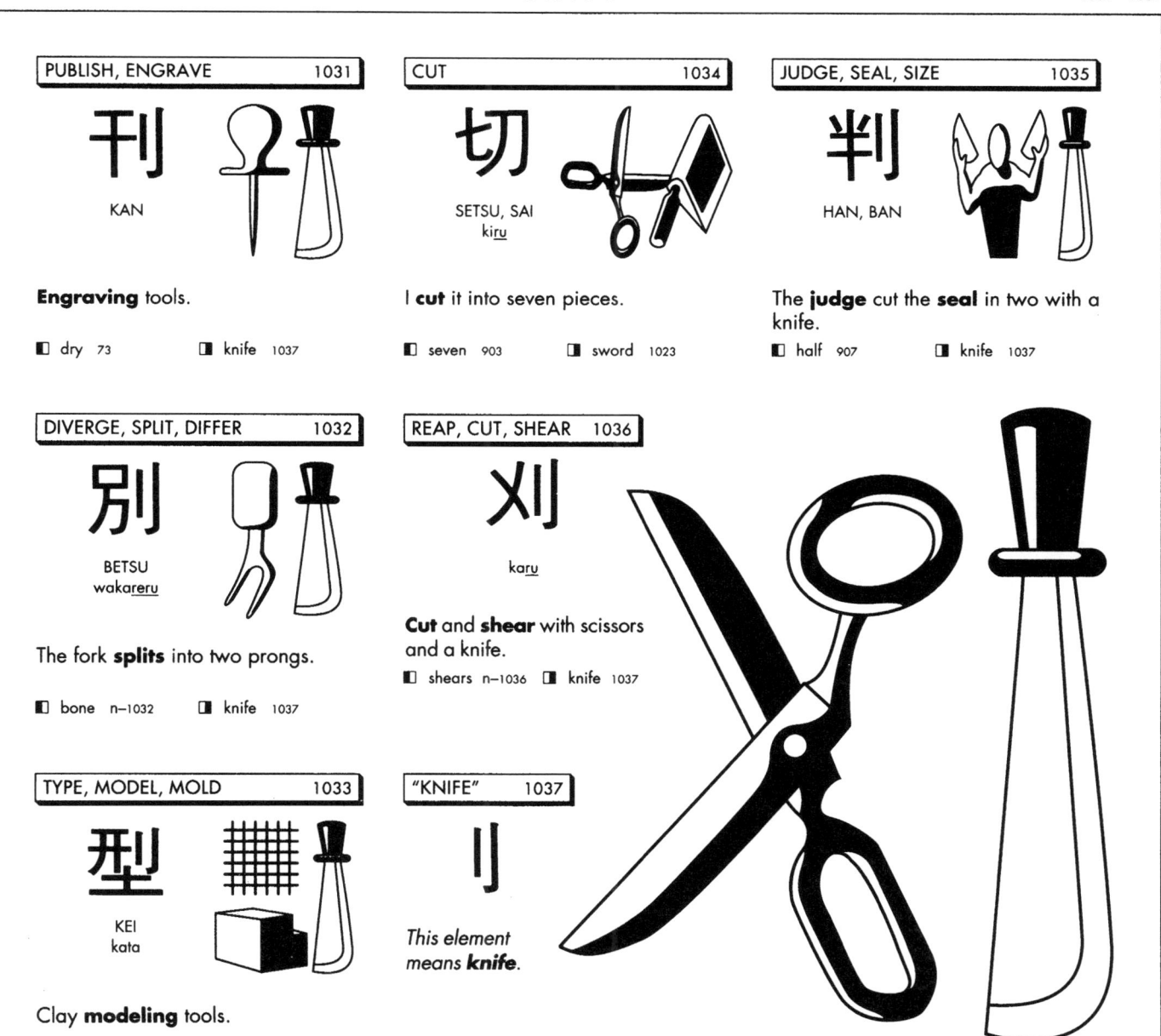

PUBLISH, ENGRAVE 1031

刊

KAN

Engraving tools.

- dry 73
- knife 1037

DIVERGE, SPLIT, DIFFER 1032

別

BETSU
waka*reru*

The fork **splits** into two prongs.

- bone n–1032
- knife 1037

TYPE, MODEL, MOLD 1033

型

KEI
kata

Clay **modeling** tools.

- grill n–920
- knife 1037
- soil 101

CUT 1034

切

SETSU, SAI
ki*ru*

I **cut** it into seven pieces.

- seven 903
- sword 1023

JUDGE, SEAL, SIZE 1035

判

HAN, BAN

The **judge** cut the **seal** in two with a knife.

- half 907
- knife 1037

REAP, CUT, SHEAR 1036

刈

ka*ru*

Cut and **shear** with scissors and a knife.

- shears n–1036
- knife 1037

"KNIFE" 1037

刂

This element means **knife**.

Equipment

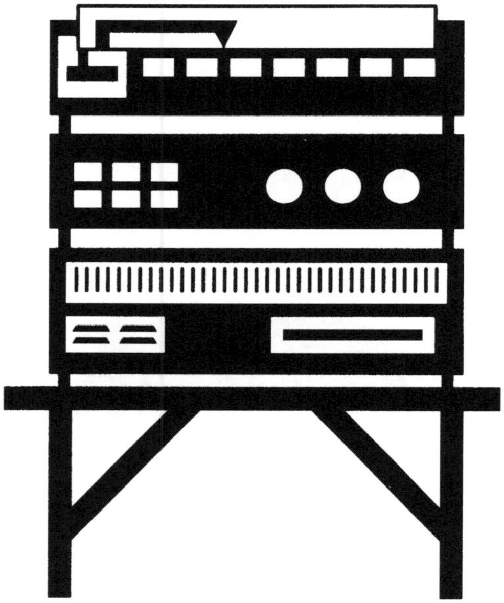

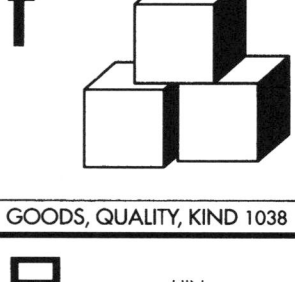

GOODS, QUALITY, KIND 1038

品 HIN
shina

Three opened boxes of **goods**.
- opening 566
- opening 566
- opening 566

EQUIPMENT, MEANS 1039

具 GU
sona*eru*

Stereo and video **equipment**.
- eye 538
- utensil n–1039

VESSEL, UTENSIL, SKILL 1040

器 KI
utsuwa

A big kitchen **utensil**.
- opening (x4) 566
- big 913

SPEECH, KNOW, VALVE, PETAL 1041

弁 BEN

I wish I could put a shut-off **valve** on his **speech**.

TURN, ROTATE 1042

回 KAI
mawa*ru*/*su*

Nuts **rotate** around bolts.
- enclose 778
- opening 566

UMBRELLA, PARASOL 1043

傘 SAN
kasa

This **umbrella** can comfortably shade four people.
- enter 950
- person (x4) 363

HIT, STRIKE 1044

打 DA
utsu

Hold a nail and **strike** it exactly on its head.
- hand 580
- exact 1089

EQUIPMENT / BROOMS

HONEST, CHEAP, ANGLE — 1045
廉
REN

Every house can buy two brooms at one **honest**, **cheap** price.

- building 1143
- combine 1051

DISLIKE — 1046
嫌
KEN, GEN
kirau/i, iya

The woman **dislikes** housework.

- woman 411
- combine 1051

ORDINARY, WORK — 1047
庸
YŌ

This building is used for **ordinary work**.

- building 1143
- hand 597
- use 385

SWEEP — 1048
掃
SŌ
haku

A hand **sweeps** the broom.

- hand 580
- hand w/broom 1052

RETURN — 1049
帰
KI
kaeru

I'm **returning** your broom.

- follow n-1049
- hand w/broom 1052

SOAK, IMMERSE — 1050
浸
SHIN
hitasu/ru

A mop **soaked** up the water.

- water 66
- hand 597
- hand 600

Brooms

COMBINE, UNABLE — 1051
兼
KEN
kaneru

Two brooms are **combined** into one.

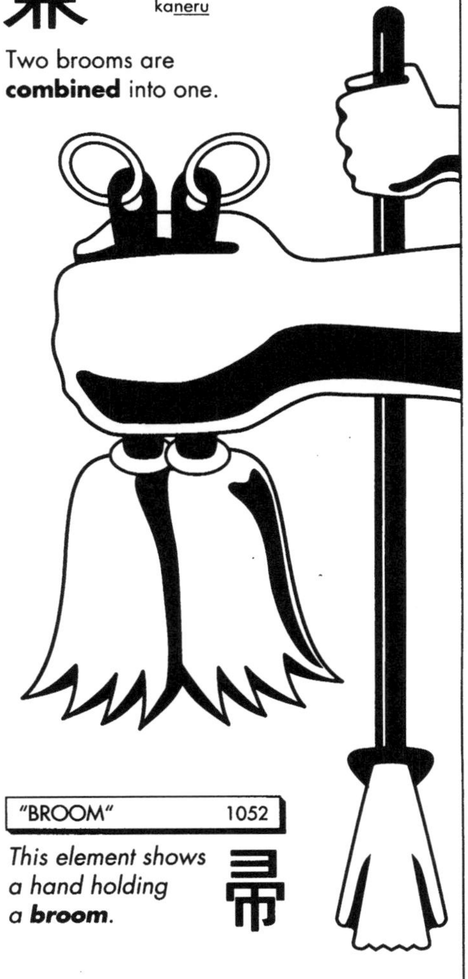

"BROOM" — 1052
帚

This element shows a hand holding a **broom**.

Build

TOOLS

MERIT, SERVICE 1053

功

KŌ, KU

He offers his construction **services**.

- construction 1054
- power 745

CONSTRUCTION, WORK 1054

工

KŌ, KU

A carpenter's square is used in **construction**.

BUILD 1055

築

CHIKU
kizu<u>ku</u>

The Japanese commonly **build** their homes of bamboo and wood.

- bamboo 123
- work 1054
- common 1056

MEDIOCRE, COMMON 1056

凡

BON, HAN
oyo<u>so</u>

This **common** person tries to hide his **mediocrity**.

BUILD

1057–1068

TRIBUTE 1057
貢 
KŌ, KU
mitsugu

The **tribute** was paid with money and construction labor.

- construction 1054
- money 708

MAKE 1058
作
SAKU, SA
tsukuru

What shall I **make** with my saw?

- person 362
- adze n–1058

VINEGAR, SOUR 1059
酢
SAKU
su, suppai

Vinegar is made from alcohol.

- alcohol 249
- adze n–1058

LIE, DECEIVE 1060
詐
SA

Lies are fabricated words.

- words 840
- adze n–1058

LARGE BEAM, FLAG POLE 1061
杠 
KŌ
chigi

A wooden **beam** is used in construction.

- tree 126
- construction 1054

SUSPEND, HANG DOWN 1062
垂
SUI
tareru/rasu

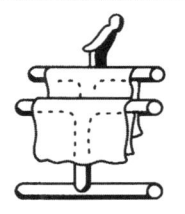

The blankets **hang** on the drying racks.

SPINDLE, SINKER 1063
錘
SUI
tsumu, omori

The metal **sinker** hangs in the water.

- metal 105
- hang down 1062

SLEEP 1064
睡
SUI
nemuru

When I'm **sleepy** my eyelids hang down.

- eye 538
- hang down 1062

BECOME, MAKE, CONSIST 1065
成 
SEI, JŌ
naru/su

Hal **becomes** a **maker** of things with his ax.

- halberd 100
- exact n–1065

CASTLE 1066
城 
JŌ
shiro

In Hal's hands, earth is piled up and becomes a **castle**.

- earth 101
- become 1065

PROSPER, HEAP, SERVE 1067
盛
SEI, JŌ
moru, sakaru/n

Hal's dish is **heaping** with rice.

- become 1065
- dish 261

SINCERITY 1068
誠
SEI
makoto

Hal's **sincere**. His words become true.

- word 840
- become 1065

TOOLS

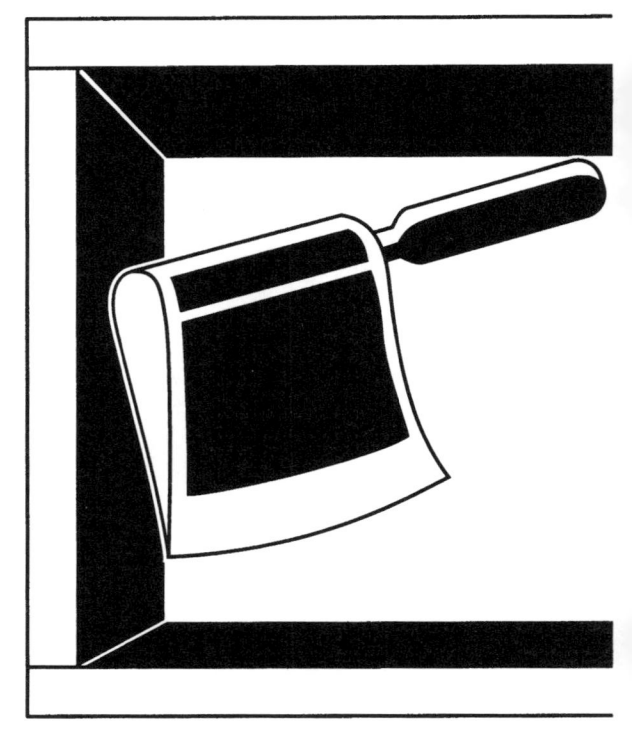

CUT, DECLINE, WARN, JUDGE 1069

断

DAN
kotowa<u>ru</u>, tat<u>su</u>

Cut up the rice.

- rice 217
- ax 1072

QUALITY, PAWN 1070

質

SHITSU,
SHICHI, CHI

Pawn two **quality** axes for some money.

- ax (x2) 1072
- money 708

BEND, BREAK, OCCASION 1071

折

SETSU
ori, o<u>ru</u>/<u>reru</u>

Grab the **bent** and **broken** ax.

- hand 580
- ax 1072

Ax

AX, WEIGHT 1072

斤

KIN

A **weighty ax**.

CRAFTSMAN 1073

匠

SHŌ

A **craftsman** keeps his tools in a box.

- enclosed 778
- ax 1072

PLEDGE, VOW, OATH 1074

誓

SEI
chika<u>u</u>

I **pledge** never to break my word.

- break 1071
- word 840

DIE, PASS ON, DEATH 1075

逝

SEI
yu<u>ku</u>

Death breaks life's motion.

- movement 1153
- break 1071

REPEL, REJECT 1076

斥

SEKI
shirizo<u>keru</u>

I **repelled** it with an ax.

RADICALS

Thousands of kanji are built from a few hundred basic elements. Of these basic elements, roughly eighty of the most frequently used elements are known as radicals. Radicals often indicate the "topic" of a character. Kanji with the radical SOIL 101 often have meanings associated with soil or ground, such as **BA** 28, PLACE, in *basho*, "location," shown at right. Below are a handful of frequently used radicals.

WATER 66	FIRE 82	SOIL 101
氵	灬	土

GRASS 124	HEART 498	HAND 580
艹	忄	扌

WORD 840	KNIFE 1037	MOVE 1153
言	刂	辶

場所

10 PLACES

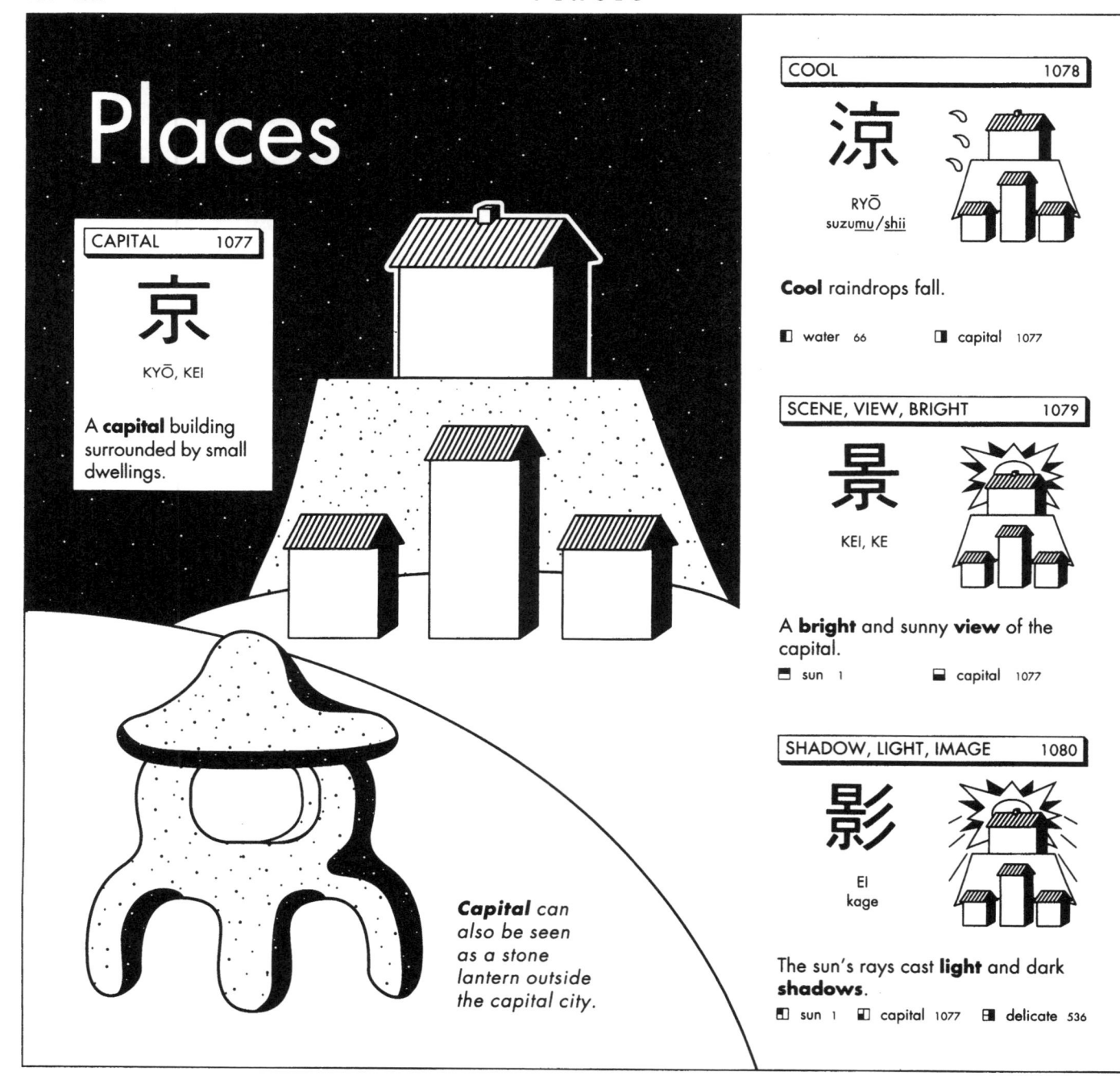

Places

CAPITAL 1077

京

KYŌ, KEI

A **capital** building surrounded by small dwellings.

Capital can also be seen as a stone lantern outside the capital city.

COOL 1078

涼

RYŌ
suzu<u>mu</u>/<u>shii</u>

Cool raindrops fall.

- water 66
- capital 1077

SCENE, VIEW, BRIGHT 1079

景

KEI, KE

A **bright** and sunny **view** of the capital.

- sun 1
- capital 1077

SHADOW, LIGHT, IMAGE 1080

影

EI
kage

The sun's rays cast **light** and dark **shadows**.

- sun 1
- capital 1077
- delicate 536

PLACES 1081–1089

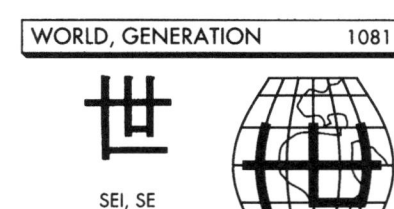

WORLD, GENERATION 1081
世
SEI, SE
yo

Longitude and latitude lines on a **world** map.

CITY, MARKET 1084
市
SHI
ichi

I buy clothes in the **city market**.

VILLAGE 1087
里
RI
sato

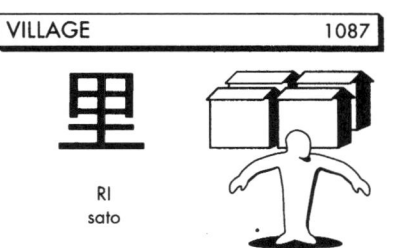

A samurai stands in a field before the **village**.

▫ field 201   ▫ soil 101

NEXT, SUB-, ASIA 1082
亜
A

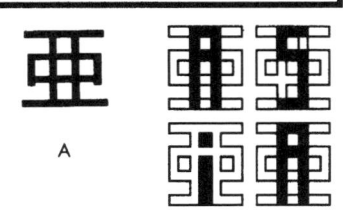

Lattice and design motifs from **Asia**.

RISE, RAISE, INTEREST 1085
興
KYŌ, KŌ
oko<u>su</u>/<u>ru</u>

High-**rise** apartments all look the same—of no **interest**.

TOWN, BLOCK 1088
町
CHŌ
machi

This sign shows what **town** you're in …

▫ field 201   ▫ soil 101

(T'ANG) CHINA 1083
唐 
TŌ
kara

In a building in **China**, a hand practices k'ung fu chops.

▫ building 1143   ▫ hand 597   ▫ opening 566

VILLAGE 1086
村 
SON
mura

A sentry protects every inch of our **village**.

▫ tree 126   ▫ inch 759

BLOCK, EXACT 1089
丁 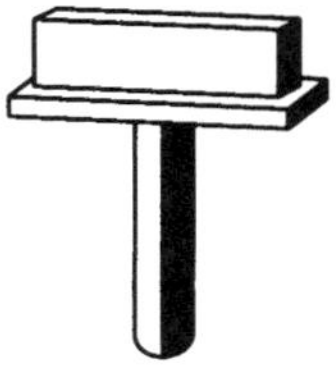
CHŌ, TEI

… but this sign tells you **exactly** what **block** you're in.

181

Village

PLACES

都 CAPITAL, METROPOLIS 1090
TO, TSU
miyako

People flock to the **metropolis** to sell their wares.

- person 408
- village 1094

郊 SUBURBS 1091
KŌ

The **suburbs** are beyond the village.

- mix 831
- village 1094

郡 COUNTY, DISTRICT 1092
GUN
kōri

Lord of the **county**.

- lord 417
- village 1094

郵 MAIL, RELAY STATION 1093
YŪ

A **mail** bag waits at the **relay station**.

- hand down 1062
- village 1094

阝 "VILLAGE/HILL" 1094

This element means **village** when on the right side of a character and **hill** when on the left. Picture a flag placed on a hill to mark a village.

VILLAGE / HILL

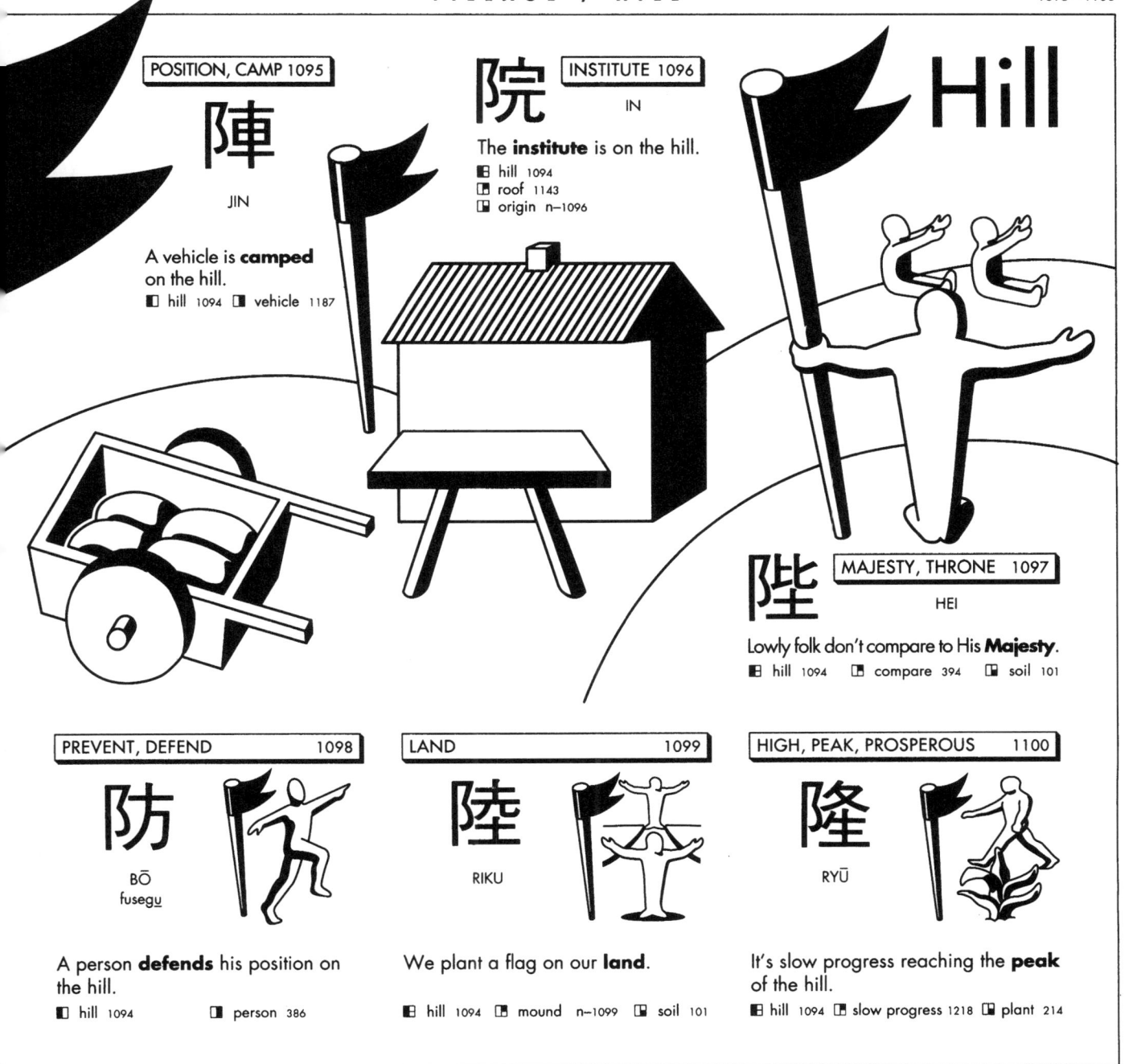

1095 – 1100

POSITION, CAMP 1095
陣
JIN

A vehicle is **camped** on the hill.
- hill 1094
- vehicle 1187

INSTITUTE 1096
院
IN

The **institute** is on the hill.
- hill 1094
- roof 1143
- origin n–1096

Hill

MAJESTY, THRONE 1097
陛
HEI

Lowly folk don't compare to His **Majesty**.
- hill 1094
- compare 394
- soil 101

PREVENT, DEFEND 1098
防
BŌ
fusegu

A person **defends** his position on the hill.
- hill 1094
- person 386

LAND 1099
陸
RIKU

We plant a flag on our **land**.
- hill 1094
- mound n–1099
- soil 101

HIGH, PEAK, PROSPEROUS 1100
隆
RYŪ

It's slow progress reaching the **peak** of the hill.
- hill 1094
- slow progress 1218
- plant 214

PLACES

Gate

門 GATE, DOOR 1101
MON
kado

Two **doors** form a **gate**.

閑 LEISURE, QUIET 1102
KAN

There's a **quiet**, peaceful scene of trees outside my gate.

　gate 1101　　　tree 126

GATE

CLOSE, SHUT — 1103
閉 
HEI
to*jiru*, shi*maru*/*meru*

A post holds the gate **shut**.

- gate 1101
- talent 871

OPEN — 1104
開
KAI
hira*ku*, a*keru*

Two hands **open** the gate.

- gate 1101
- hands n-1104

SPACE, GAP — 1105
間
KAN, KEN
aida, ma

Sunshine pours through the **gap** in the gate.

- gate 1101
- sun 1

FACTION, CLAN LINEAGE — 1106
閥 
BATSU

One **faction** attacks outside the gate.

- gate 1101
- attack 800

DARKNESS, GLOOM — 1107
闇 
AN
yami

Gloom stood at the gate, shrouded in **darkness**, making no sound.

- gate 1101
- sound 883

BE OBSTRUCTED — 1108
閊
tsuka*eru*

The gate **obstructs** my view of the mountain.

- gate 1101
- mountain 167

SUDDEN ENTRY, INQUIRE — 1109
闖
CHIN

Suddenly, a horse **entered** the gate.

- gate 1101
- horse 291

BARRIER, CONNECTION — 1110
関 
KAN
seki

A **barrier** prevents me from leaving the gate.

- gate 1101
- bar n-1110

ASK — 1111
問
MON
to*u*

Ask by putting your mouth to the gate.

- gate 1101
- ear 551

HEAR, ASK, LISTEN — 1112
聞
BUN, MON
ki*ku*/*koeru*

Hear more with your ear to the gate.

- gate 1101
- mouth 566

PLACES

Door

戸 DOOR 1113
KO
to

Half of a saloon **door**.

尸 "DOOR" 1114

This **door** is really the element BODY 460.

TEAR 1115
涙
RUI
namida

Big John shed **tears** when his wife walked out the door.
- water 66
- door 1113
- big 913

PLACE, SITUATION 1116
所
SHO
tokoro

The **place** to chop wood is by the door.
- door 1113
- ax 1072

FURNACE 1117
炉
RO

A **furnace** has fire behind its door.
- fire 83
- door 1113

ROOM, WIFE, TUFT 1118
房
BŌ
fusa

My **wife** is in the **room** on the other side of the door.
- door 1113
- person 1113

FAN 1119
扇
SEN
ōgi, aogu

A **fan** is like a flapping door.
- door 1113
- wings 330

STORE, BUILDING 1120
屋
OKU
ya

Go through a door to reach the **store**.
- door 1113
- reach 1135

DOOR

DOOR, FRONT PAGE — 1121
扉 
HI
tobira

Automatic doors slide open in **opposite** directions.

- door 1113
- opposite 960

PALACE, LORD, MR. — 1122
殿 
DEN, TEN
tono, -dono

The **lord** of the **palace** shakes an ax at all who come to his door.

- door 1113
- together 383
- hand/ax 1113

WEAR, WALK, FOOTWEAR — 1123
履 
RI
ha<u>ku</u>

Wear shoes when **walking** outdoors.

- door 1114
- walk n–1123

DELIVER, REPORT — 1124
届
todo<u>ku</u>/<u>keru</u>

Deliver the pizza to my door.

- door 1114
- cause 76

SUBMIT, CROUCH — 1125
屈 
KUTSU

You must **crouch** to leave through this strange door.

- door 1114
- leave 956

LEAK — 1126
漏 
RŌ
mo<u>ru</u>/<u>reru</u>/<u>rasu</u>

Drops of rain **leak** through the door.

- water 66
- door 1114
- rain 45

MOAT, DITCH CANAL — 1127
堀 
hori

A drawbridge door covers the **moat**, but people still have trouble leaving.

- soil 101
- submit 1125

FENCE, WALL — 1128
塀 
HEI

We built this **fence** to keep people out.

- soil 101
- fence n–1128

DIG — 1129
掘 
KUTSU
ho<u>ru</u>

I often have to **dig** them out by hand.

- hand 580
- submit 1125

PLACES

HALL, TEMPLE — 1130
堂 DŌ

A chalice is used in **temples** and **halls**.
- roof 1144
- opening 566
- soil 101

PALACE, SHRINE, PRINCE — 1131
宮 KYŪ, GŪ, KU; miya

The prince lives in a two-storied **palace**.
- roof 1144
- joined blocks n–1131

LODGE, SHELTER, HOUSE — 1132
宿 SHUKU; yado, yado*ru*

The **lodge** holds a hundred people.
- roof 1144
- person 362
- hundred 909

HOUSE, HOME — 1133
宅 TAKU

Home is a roof over your head.
- roof 1144
- open up n–1133

ROOM, HOUSE — 1134
室 SHITSU; muro

Reach for some flowers to decorate the **house**.
- roof 1144
- reach 1135

REACH, GO, PEAK — 1135
至 SHI; ita*ri*/*ru*

Reach for the plant in the soil.
- arrow n–1135
- soil 101

SPREAD — 1136
拡 KAKU

Spread your hand wide.
- hand 580
- wide 1139

GOV'T OFFICE, PREFECTURE — 1137
府 FU

Government office workers give themselves medals.
- building 1143
- attach 771

GOV'T OFFICE, AGENCY — 1138
庁 CHŌ

The sign marks the **government agency**.
- building 1143
- exact 1089

WIDE, SPACIOUS — 1139
広 KŌ; hiro*i*/*geru*

I have a wide and **spacious** building for myself.
- building 1143
- private 450

BUILDING & ROOF 1140–1146

Building & Roof

STOREHOUSE 1140

庫
KO

Store the cart in the garage.

- building 100
- vehicle 100

广 "BUILDING" 1143

*This element means **building**.*

冖 "ROOF" 1144

*This element means **roof**.*

SEAT, PLACE 1141

席
SEKI

This **place seats** one person.

- building 1143
- cloth 1007

STORE, PREMISES 1145

店
TEN
mise, tana

The **store** is …
- building 1143
- occupy 1146

BED, FLOOR, ALCOVE 1142

床
SHŌ
toko, yuka

In the **alcove** is a bonsai tree.

- building 1143
- tree 126

DIVINE, OCCUPY 1146

占
SEN
uranau, shimeru

… **occupied** by a green grocer.

189

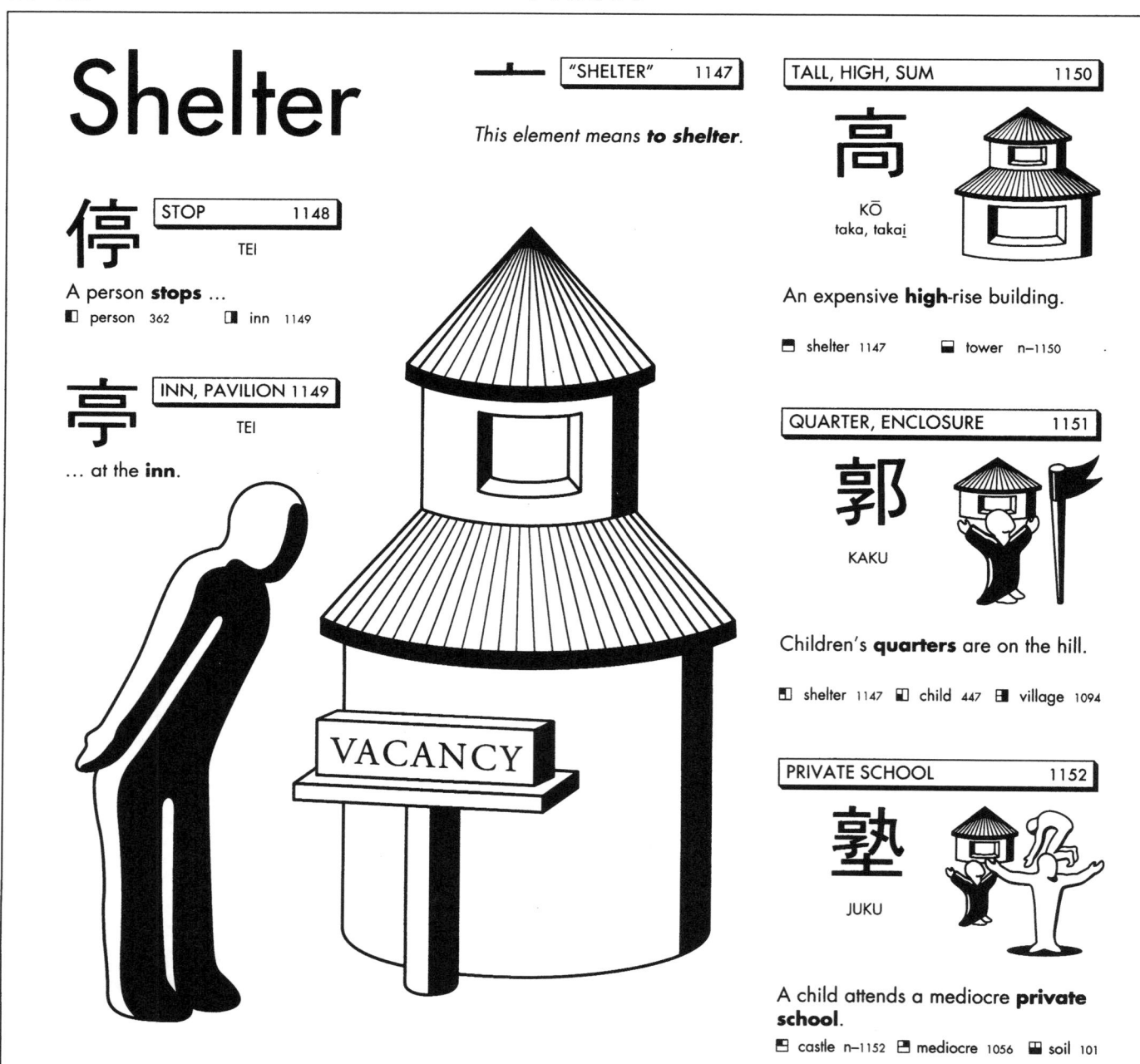

PLACES

Shelter

"SHELTER" 1147

⊥

This element means **to shelter**.

STOP 1148

停 TEI

A person **stops** ...

■ person 362   ■ inn 1149

INN, PAVILION 1149

亭 TEI

... at the **inn**.

TALL, HIGH, SUM 1150

高 KŌ
taka, taka<u>i</u>

An expensive **high**-rise building.

■ shelter 1147   ■ tower n–1150

QUARTER, ENCLOSURE 1151

郭 KAKU

Children's **quarters** are on the hill.

■ shelter 1147   ■ child 447   ■ village 1094

PRIVATE SCHOOL 1152

塾 JUKU

A child attends a mediocre **private school**.

■ castle n–1152   ■ mediocre 1056   ■ soil 101

READINGS

Kanji in dictionaries can be found by three methods: radical search, stroke counting, and pronunciation. Each method is laborious and uncertain. Which element is the defining radical? Which is the correct reading of several possibilities? Even after you identify the reading/meaning of an individual character, you may then have to search in a separate compound dictionary to find the definition of a word like *ryokō*, at right, which means "trip," "travel," or "journey." Kanji dictionaries are usually arranged by radical and stroke count. Word dictionaries are arranged in the order of the syllabaries—*a, i, u, e, o, ka, ki, ku, ke, ko,* etc.

TRIP 1015

旅

radical: 方
stroke count: 10
readings: RYO, tabi
other meanings: TRAVEL, JOURNEY

GO 1192

行

radical: 彳
stroke count: 6
readings: KŌ, AN, GYŌ, ik*u*, okona*u*, -yuki
other meanings: CONDUCT, COLUMN

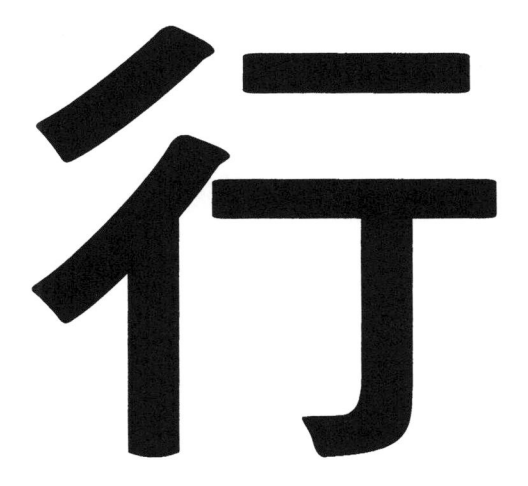

旅行

11 JOURNEY

JOURNEY

Move

"MOVEMENT" 1153
This element means **movement**.

LOST, PERPLEXED 1154
迷
MEI
mayo<u>u</u>

I got **lost** searching for rice.

◻ move 1153　◼ rice 217

A CROSSING 1155
辻
tsuji

I **cross** ten intersections ...

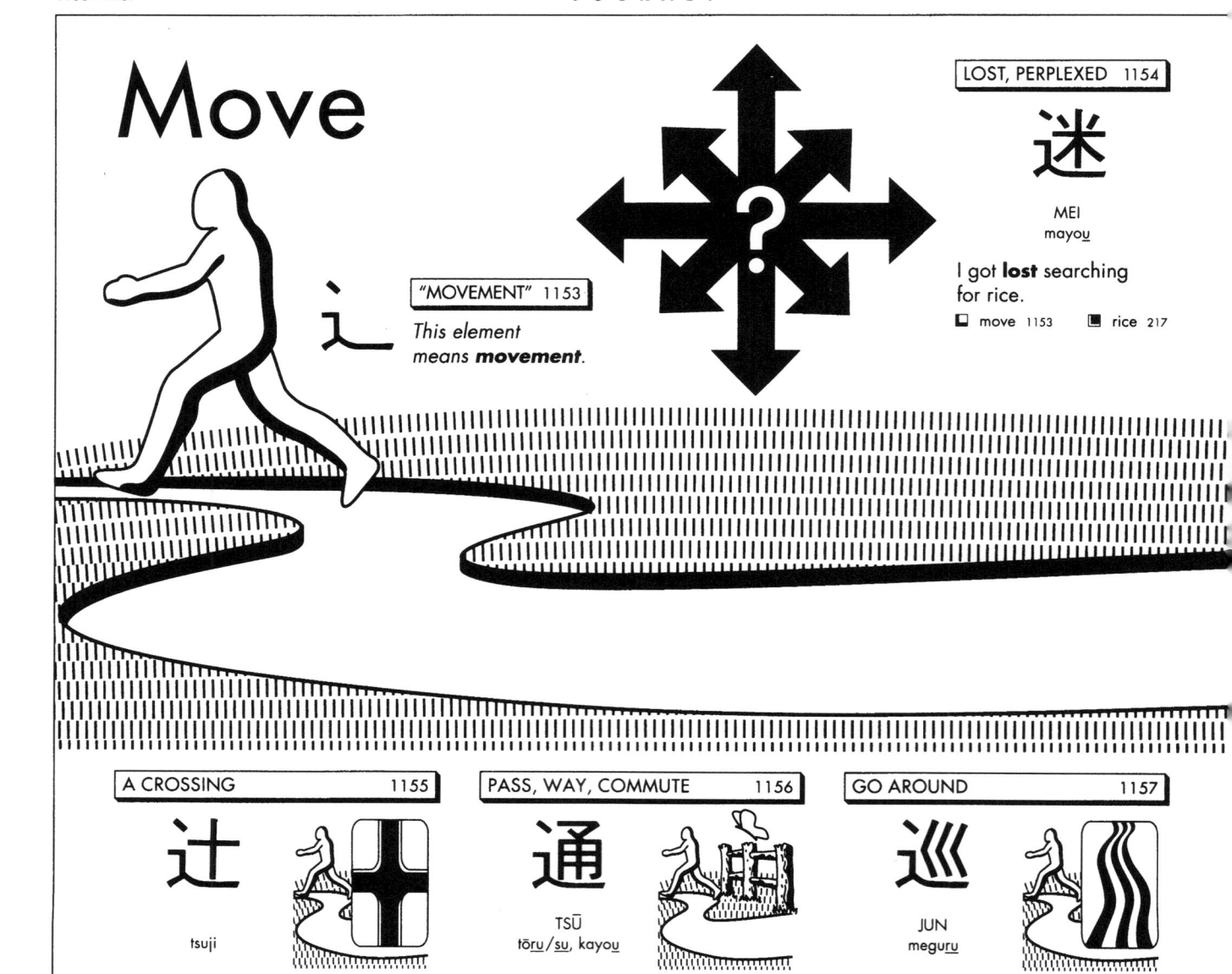

◻ move 1153　◼ ten 906

PASS, WAY, COMMUTE 1156
通
TSŪ
tō<u>ru</u>/<u>su</u>, kayo<u>u</u>

... and **pass** many things as I **commute** to work.

◻ move 1153　◼ use 385

GO AROUND 1157
巡
JUN
megu<u>ru</u>

Go around the river.

◻ move 1153　◼ river 55

MOVE

FAST, INTENSE — 1158

迅
JIN
haya*i*

Move **fast**!

- move 1153
- fast n–1158

SPEED, FAST — 1159

速
SOKU
haya*i*, sumi*yaka*

A **speedy** delivery of a bundle of branches.

- move 1153
- bundle 153

PRESS, DRAW NEAR — 1160

迫
HAKU
sema*ru*

Press on, for dawn is **drawing near**.

- move 1153
- white 936

EXCESS, AMPLE — 1161

余
YO
ama*ri*/*ru*/*su*

There was an **excess** of material for building the road.

ROAD, WAY — 1162

途
TO

The **road** was built with excess materials.

- move 1153
- excess 1161

RETURN — 1163

返
HEN
kae*ru*/*su*

It **returns** in the opposite direction.

- move 1153
- oppose 957

FOLLOW, OBEY — 1164

遵
JUN

I **follow** out of respect.

- move 1153
- respect 767

EXCLUDE, REMOVE — 1165

除
JO, JI
nozo*ku*

Remove the excess materials from the road.

- hill 1094
- excess 1161

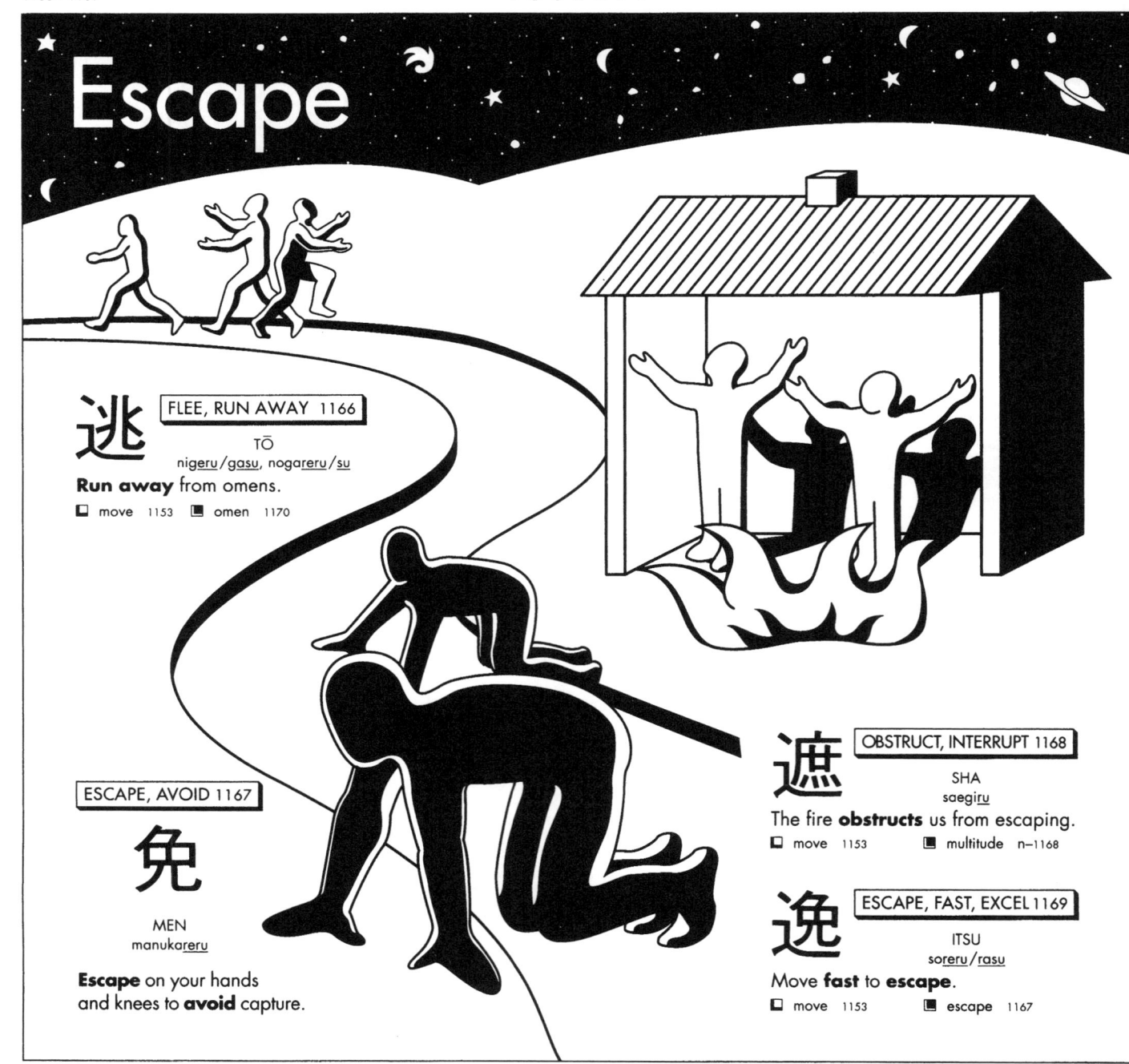

Escape

逃 FLEE, RUN AWAY 1166
TŌ
nige<u>ru</u>/<u>gasu</u>, noga<u>reru</u>/<u>su</u>
Run away from omens.
- move 1153
- omen 1170

免 ESCAPE, AVOID 1167
MEN
manuka<u>reru</u>
Escape on your hands and knees to **avoid** capture.

遮 OBSTRUCT, INTERRUPT 1168
SHA
saegi<u>ru</u>
The fire **obstructs** us from escaping.
- move 1153
- multitude n–1168

逸 ESCAPE, FAST, EXCEL 1169
ITSU
sore<u>ru</u>/<u>rasu</u>
Move **fast** to **escape**.
- move 1153
- escape 1167

ESCAPE 1170–1179

SIGN, OMEN, TRILLION 1170
兆 
CHŌ
kiza*shi*/*su*

A **trillion** people were frightened by the **omen**.

FLEE, EVADE 1171
逋 
HO

Flee from the prison.

- move 1153
- capture n–773

CHASE, PURSUE 1172
追
TSUI
o*u*

Move your butt in hot **pursuit**.

- move 1153
- buttocks 466

VICINITY, BOUNDARY 1173
辺
HEN
ata*ri*, be

Men with swords guard the **boundary**.

- move 1153
- sword 1023

NEAR 1174
近 
KIN
chika*i*

This way "chopped" time off our journey. We are **near**.

- move 100
- ax 100

CONTRARY, UPSIDE DOWN 1175
逆 
GYAKU
saka*sa*, saka*rau*

She's walking **upside down** just to be **contrary**.

- move 1153
- big n–1175

RETREAT, WITHDRAWAL 1176
退
TAI
shirizo*ku*/*keru*

Retreat from the scary sight.

- move 1153
- stop/stare 1178

RESENT, REGRET 1177
恨
KON
ura*mu*

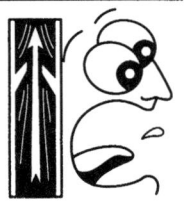

I **resent** people staring at me.

- heart 498
- stop/stare 1178

"STOP AND STARE" 1178
艮

As an element this can mean **stop and stare** *with bulging eyes and gaping mouth.*

ALTERNATE, ROTATE 1179
迭
TETSU

I took an **alternate** path and got lost.

- move 1153
- lose 577

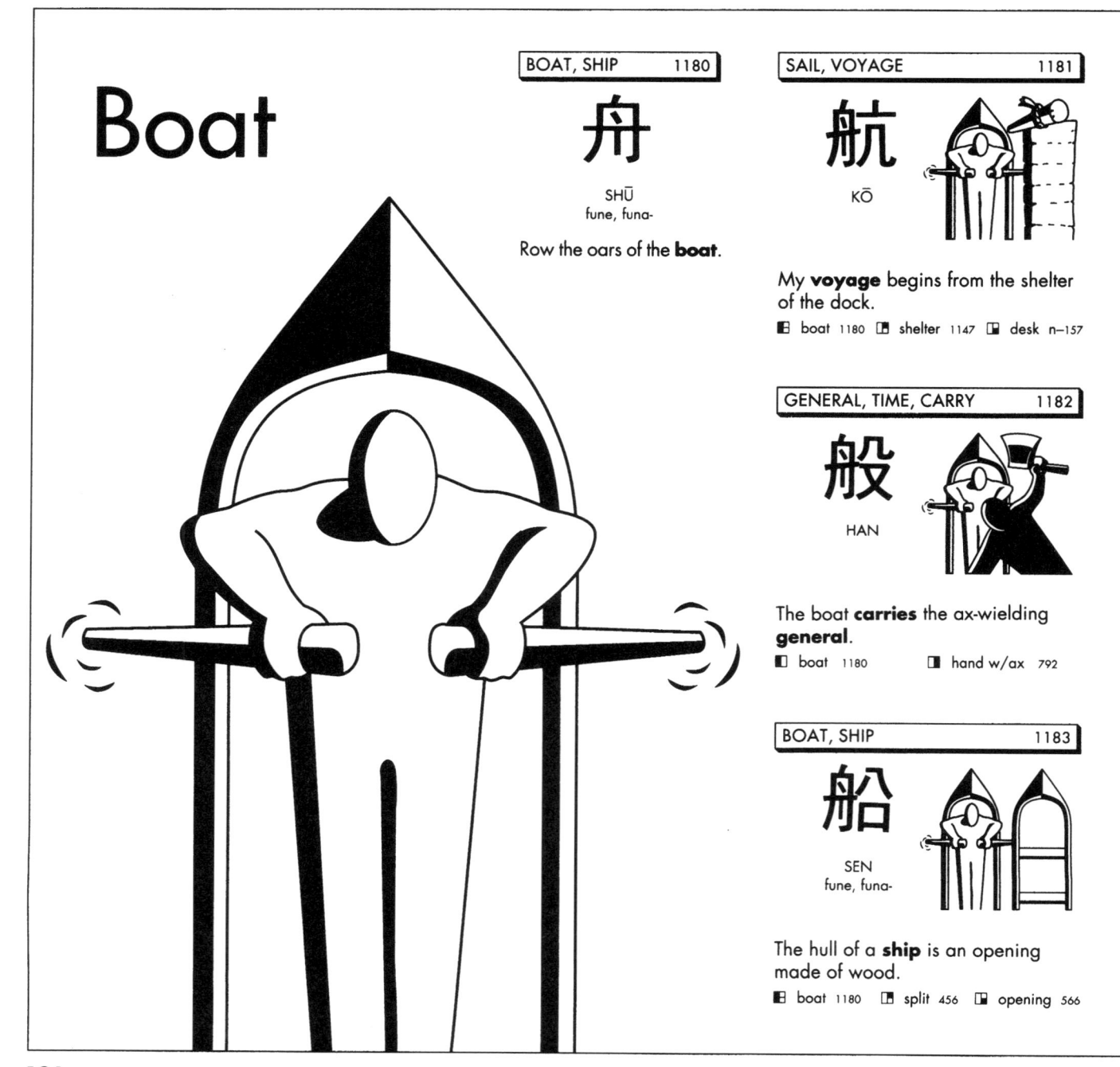

JOURNEY

Boat

BOAT, SHIP 1180
舟

SHŪ
fune, funa-

Row the oars of the **boat**.

SAIL, VOYAGE 1181
航

KŌ

My **voyage** begins from the shelter of the dock.

- boat 1180
- shelter 1147
- desk n–157

GENERAL, TIME, CARRY 1182
般

HAN

The boat **carries** the ax-wielding **general**.

- boat 1180
- hand w/ax 792

BOAT, SHIP 1183
船

SEN
fune, funa-

The hull of a **ship** is an opening made of wood.

- boat 1180
- split 456
- opening 566

BOAT / CART 1184–1190

Cart

LOAD, CARRY 1184
載 
SAI
no<u>ru</u>/<u>seru</u>

Hal **loads** the cart with soil.

■ soil 101   ■ cart 1187   ■ halberd 801

VEHICLE, CHARIOT, CART 1187
車
SHA
kuruma

This **cart** carries things from the field.

TRACK, RUT, WAY 1188
軌
KI

Nine times the cart got stuck in the **rut**.

■ cart 1187   ■ nine 905

RICKSHAW 1185
俥
kuruma

A person pulls the **rickshaw**.

■ person 362   ■ cart 1187

ACCOMPANY
連
REN 
tsu<u>reru</u>, tsura<u>neru</u>

Ride in the cart and **accompany** me on my trip.

■ move 1153   ■ cart 1187

WHEEL, HOOP 1189
輪 
RIN
wa

The **wheel** fell off my cart.

■ cart 1187   ■ person 363   ■ book 868

AXLE, SHAFT, SCROLL 1190
軸 
JIKU

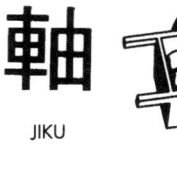

The **axle** was the cause of my problem.

■ cart 1187   ■ cause 76

JOURNEY

Road

ROAD, AREA 1191
街
GAI, KAI
machi

I'm new to this **area**. Which **road** …

- path 1192
- soil (x2) 101

GO, CONDUCT, COLUMN 1192
行
KŌ, GYŌ, AN
iku, yuku, okonau

… **goes** into town?

PATH, DIRECT 1193
径
KEI

Cut a **direct path** through the jungle.

- path 1192
- hand 600
- soil 101

GO, GONE, PAST 1194
往
Ō

My master has **gone** down this path.

- path 1192
- master 743

WANDER ABOUT 1195
彷
HŌ

That person **wandered** about in all directions.

- path 1192
- direction 386

ROLE, SERVICE, DUTY 1196
役
YAKU, EKI

Ax-wielding sentries do their **duty**.

- path 1192
- hand w/ax 792

SUBJUGATE, TRAVEL 1197
征
SEI

You must only **travel** the correct path.

- path 1192
- correct 826

ROAD / CRASH!

Crash!

ROAR, THUNDER, REVERBERATE 1198

轟

GŌ
todoroku

Three **Thunder**birds **roar** down the road.

- car 1187
- car 1187
- car 1187

ROTATE, ROLL, TUMBLE 1199

転

TEN
korobu/garu
/geru/gasu

The car **rolls** and **tumbles** in a cloud of smoke.

- car 1187
- cloud 54

COLLIDE, ROAD 1201

衝

SHŌ

A **collision** in the **road** ...

- path 1192
- heavy 1202

HEAVY, PILE, FOLD 1202

重

JŪ, CHŌ
kasaneru/naru,
omoi, e

... left a **heavy pile** of **folded** metal.

MOVE 1200

動

DŌ
ugoku/kasu

A man tries to **move** the heavy car with all his power.

- heavy 1202
- power 745

MERIT 1203

勲

KUN

Gain **merit** by trying to move the heavy, burning car.

- move 1200
- fire 82

WORK 1204

働

DŌ
hataraku

We **worked** to get the car to move on its own power.

- person 362
- move 1200

JOURNEY

Stop...

STOP 1205
止
SHI
to<u>maru</u>/<u>meru</u>

Stop.

PLAN, UNDERTAKE 1206
企
KI
kuwada<u>teru</u>

We **plan** to stop that person.

- person 363
- stop 1205

WALK 1207
歩
HO
aru<u>ku</u>, ayu<u>mu</u>

We **walk** a little then stop a while.

- stop 1205
- little 924

CROSS OVER, LIAISE 1208
渉
SHŌ

Walk across the river.

- water 66
- walk 1207

EACH 1209
各
KAKU
ono-ono

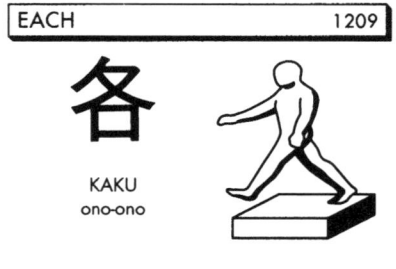

Step in **each** box.

- slow progress 1218
- opening 566

DEAL WITH, PLACE 1210
処
SHO

I do business **deals** at my desk.

- slow progress 1218
- desk n–157

BASE, BASIS 1211
拠
KYO, KO
yo<u>ru</u>

The deals are **based** on handshakes.

- hand 580
- deal with 1210

STOP... & START AGAIN

ENTWINE, CONNECT 1212

絡

RAKU
kara<u>mu</u>/<u>maru</u>

He became **entwined** in the thread.

- thread 964
- each 1209

CABINET, CHAMBER 1213

閣

KAKU

Each official retreated to his **chamber**.

- gate 1101
- each 1209

ROAD, ROUTE 1214

路

RO
ji

We leg it down each and every **road**.

- leg 617
- each 1209

FALL, DROP 1215

落

RAKU
o<u>chiru</u>/<u>tosu</u>

Each person **falls** on the wet grass.

- grass 124
- water 66
- each 1209

GUEST, VISITOR 1216

客

KYAKU, KAKU

Each man is a **guest** at this house.

- roof 1144
- each 1209

FALL, ALIGHT, DESCEND 1217

降

KŌ
fur<u>u</u>, or<u>iru</u>/<u>rosu</u>

It's slow work **descending** these steps.

- hill 1094
- slow progress 1094

"FOLLOW, SLOW PROGRESS" 1218

夂

This element suggests **slow progress**, or stops and starts.

...& Start Again

Come

来 COME 1219
RAI
ku*ru*

Come follow me.

遭 ENCOUNTER, MEET 1220
SŌ
a*u*

I will **meet**...

- move 1153
- companion 1220

曹 OFFICIAL, COMPANION 1221
SŌ, ZŌ

... my **companion** ...

- east n-1220
- sun 1

槽 TANK, TUB, VAT 1222
SŌ

... for our Hot **Tub** Encounter Group.

- wood 100
- companion 1221

迎 GREET, WELCOME 1223
GEI
muka*eru*

He went to **greet** his friend at the turnstile.

- move 1153
- bending person n-1223

仰 LOOK UP, STATE, RESPECT 1224
GYŌ, KŌ
aog*u*, ō*se*

This person **respectfully looks up** at his friend by the turnstile.

- person 362
- bending person n-1223

抑 RESTRAIN, PRESS DOWN 1225
YOKU
osa*eru*

The turnstile **restrains** visitors.

- hand 580
- bending person n-1223

NOTES

These brief notes give information about elements not covered in the main text. The evolution of phonetic, symbolic, and graphic connotations over centuries makes it difficult to fully describe the meaning of each element. See Kenneth Henshall's *A Guide to Remembering Japanese Characters*, from which much of this information is derived.

n-6 **wet** Part of a phonetic element meaning "wet."

n-9 **rise** The sun rising through the grass. Compare with EARLY 19.

n-13 **crack** Phonetic meaning.

n-18 **winged bird** See WING 330 and BIRD 319.

n-19 **grass** Variant of GRASS 124.

n-20 **clear/high** Entry 20 refers to the element's phonetic meaning of "clear." Entry 85 refers to a Chinese character meaning "high."

n-21 **high** Phonetic meaning.

n-22 **kneeling** From a pictograph of a person kneeling.

n-23 **big-eyed lizard** May refer to the chameleon which can change colors.

n-26 **rays** From a pictograph of rays of sunlight. Distinguish from EASY 23.

n-40 **mask** From a pictograph of a summer festival mask.

n-43 **branches** From a pictograph of branches.

n-49 **lightning** From a pictograph of lightning.

n-50 **tremble** Phonetic meaning.

n-58 **person** From a pictograph of an upside-down child. Compare with CHILD 447.

n-62 **planks** From a pictograph of a tree cut in half.

n-65 **red** Variant of RED 929.

n-68 **previous** As a stand-alone character, this element has the readings SEN, saki.

n-69 **steam** From a pictograph of swirling vapors.

n-70 **stagnant** From a pictograph of a waterweed.

n-78 **emerge** Refers to a geyser; can also mean "boil."

n-81 **cliff** From a pictograph of a cliff.

n-89 **offer** From a pictograph of two hands holding an offering.

n-93 **plants** Picture a variant of LIFE 214 doubled.

n-94 **crack** Represents a crack in the ice.

n-102 **creature** From a pictograph of a scorpion.

n-106 **scene** Picture it as a standing mirror. Distinguish from LOOK 543.

n-111 **path** May derive from MOVEMENT 1153.

n-117 **speak** As a stand-alone character, this has the readings UN, i<u>u</u>, and is sometimes used to mean "speak." It can also mean "cloud." See entry 54.

n-118 **flower** From a pictograph of a flower.

n-122 **hands** From a pictograph of two hands. Graphically identical to GRASS 124.

n-125 **roots** Think of the line as representing the roots of a tree. Distinguish from TREE 126.

n-127 **shine** Picture rays of light radiating outward.

n-128 **flow** Looks graphically similar to a bent willow.

n-130 **basket** From a pictograph of a basket.

n-133 **extreme** Phonetic meaning.

n-137 **upright** As a stand-alone character, this has the readings CHOKU, JIKI, nao<u>ru</u>, su<u>gu</u>.

n-157 **desk** From a pictograph of a table or desk.

n-170 **clothes** This is the radical form for CLOTHING 1021. Distinguish from the radical RELIGION 695.

n-172 **thread (x2)** A variant of THREAD 964.

n-175 **slow progress** Actually a combination of SLOW PROGRESS 1218 and a variant of COW 275.

n-176 **insert** From a pictograph of a person being squeezed by a person on either side.

NOTES

n-177 plant From a pictograph of a plant.

n-187 uniformity From a pictograph of uniform gridwork, such as a lattice window or a grill.

n-202 person Picture PERSON 362 and its mirror image.

n-212 well As a stand-alone character, this has the reading I.

n-219 quantity As a stand-alone character, this has the readings RYŌ, haka<u>ru</u>.

n-220 stop A variant of SLOW PROGRESS 1218.

n-256 pair Convoluted etymology, acc. to Henshall.

n-256 vessel From a pictograph of a vessel.

n-257 water A variant of WATER 57.

n-295 humility From a pictograph of a bent-over body.

n-297 all Convoluted etymology, acc. to Henshall, meaning "all" in the sense of "bringing together," with the extension "examine."

n-336 protect Phonetic meaning. See also BASKET 130.

n-341 leap Phonetic meaning.

n-344 group Phonetic meaning.

n-347 hand Variant of HOLDING 597.

n-350 play Phonetic meaning.

n-351 stomach As a stand-alone character, this has the reading I.

n-359 dragon Old style of DRAGON 358.

n-366 tower A variant of TALL 1150, which comes from a pictograph of a tower.

n-371 what? As a stand-alone character, this has the readings KA, nani, nan.

n-373 hand A variant of HAND 600.

n-374 fallen person From a pictograph of a fallen or seated person.

n-375 order Phonetic meaning of "put in order."

n-384 use Possibly a variant of USE 385. Convoluted etymology acc. to Henshall.

n-387 flag From a pictograph of a flag fluttering.

n-387 device Obscure. Acc. to Henshall, it is from a picture of a winnowing mechanism for cleaning grain.

n-417 hand w/stick A variant of HOLDING 597.

n-418 elbow From a pictograph of an elbow.

n-420 big Henshall has an interesting discussion about whether the element here means "big" or "bed."

n-422 depend From a Chinese meaning of "depend on." Note similarity to BE IN DIFFICULTY 786.

n-449 breast This element's shape suggests a woman's breast. See n-692, "kneeling figure."

n-478 lungs Symbolizes a lung, with the element at right for "flesh" supporting the meaning.

n-483 north As a stand-alone character, this has the readings HOKU, kita.

n-494 order As a stand-alone character, this has the readings REI, RYŌ.

n-497 necessarily As a stand-alone character, this has the readings HITSU, kanara<u>zu</u>.

n-500 pull apart From a pictograph of an archer's hand pulling on a bow.

n-502 crouch From a pictograph of a crouching person.

n-514 pierce Depicts two objects pierced by a stake.

n-516 progress The element SLOW PROGRESS 1218.

n-542 nose Entire character comes from a pictograph of a nose.

n-546 subject As a stand-alone character, this has the readings SHIN, JIN.

n-546 person Acc. to Henshall, this represents a person bending over to stare at water in a bowl.

n-552 singing Phonetic meaning.

n-558 sudden Phonetic meaning.

n-562 exhale Symbolic meaning.

n-567 hand Think of this as REACH 373.

NOTES

n–575 **squeeze** Think of this as two men back to back being squeezed from top and bottom.

n–589 **hand grasping** From a pictograph of a hand grasping an animal's tail.

n–596 **writing** From a pictograph of a hand holding a brush.

n–603 **hands w/rope** Comprises HAND REACHING DOWN 609, HAND REACHING UP 600, and a knotted rope.

n–607 **basket** From a pictograph of a basket.

n–621 **follow** From a pictograph of PERSON 363 doubled.

n–626 **announce** Phonetic meaning.

n–630 **prostitution** Graphically similar to a character meaning "sell."

n–649 **brain** From a pictograph of a brain. Imagine the X marking the brain enclosed in a skull topped with hair.

n–650 **vapors** From a pictograph. See STEAM 69.

n–650 **rice** A simplification of RICE 217.

n–652 **enclosed** A simplification of ENCLOSED 778.

n–664 **man on cliff** From a pictograph of a bent figure on a cliff.

n–677 **appropriate** Phonetic meaning.

n–692 **kneeling figure** From a pictograph of a kneeling person.

n–716 **bent figure** From a pictograph of a bent figure.

n–717 **official** As a stand-alone character, this has the reading IN.

n–718 **pierce** From a pictograph of money threaded on a string.

n–720 **burden** Phonetic meaning. It looks like WARRIOR 753 carrying a load.

n–725 **exchange** Acc. to Henshall, this is from a picture of a horse's bit, suggesting "change of direction."

n–731 **person** Of convoluted etymology.

n–733 **give** Phonetic meaning.

n–742 **press** Phonetic meaning.

n–749 **shine** From a pictograph of FIRE 83 doubled.

n–750 **strive** Phonetic meaning.

n–754 **hands** From a pictograph of two hands wielding an ax, as a soldier does in battle.

n–761 **bean + inch** Convoluted etymology. Derives from a character meaning "hit."

n–768 **offer** Phonetic meaning.

n–769 **wet** Phonetic meaning. Obscure relation to endure.

n–773 **hold** Acc. to Henshall, from a pictograph of a child holding a toy.

n–780 **enclosures** The enclosed X is a simplification of what was originally three enclosed squares.

n–783 **surround** Phonetic meaning.

n–785 **dot** Acc. to Henshall, the dot was used to distinguish a pictograph of a string of beads from the similarly shaped character KING 743.

n–794 **me** Phonetic meaning.

n–809 **hemp** Acc. to Henshall, a simplification of plants.

n–820 **rounded** Phonetic meaning

n–822 **2 persons** Two persons, one fallen, the other crouched.

n–834 **man** From a pictograph of a man opening his mouth to brag. Evolved into meaning of "give."

n–840 **feelings** Phonetic meaning.

n–853 **administer** As a stand-alone character, this has the readings SHI, tsukasado*ru*.

n–863 **hands** From a pictograph of hands rolling rice. This is the kanji used in *temaki sushi*.

n–872 **dam** From a pictograph of a dam; borrowed meanings lead to "exist."

n–878 **circumference** As a stand-alone character, this has the readings SHŪ, mawa*ri*.

NOTES

n–881 thread Borrowed meaning from graphically similar character meaning occult.

n–881 illusion Unclear origin and meaning.

n–882 drum From a pictograph of a tasseled drum.

n–888 flat Phonetic meaning.

n–895 seek out Phonetic meaning.

n–914 two A simplification of TWO 898 to suggest twice as big and fat.

n–925 little dot Whole character was once written as four little dots.

n–935 liquid A variant of WATER 57.

n–936 ray Acc. to Henshall, the entire character derived from a picture of a pointed thumbnail. It is easier to think of this top element as a "ray."

n–946 dry up Phonetic meaning.

n–957 turn over Phonetic meaning.

n–972 leek Convoluted etymology acc. to Henshall.

n–979 twist Phonetic meaning.

n–982 broom From a pictograph of a broom. Often shown with a hand as in BROOM 1052.

n–1002 needle + buttocks A combination of SHARP 1005 and BUTTOCKS 466.

n–1009 weave From a pictograph of interwoven sticks.

n–1012 wind Actually a stand-alone character (BON, HAN, oyo*so*) meaning "mediocre," but used here as a simplification of WIND 44.

n–1019 hand w/tool From a pictograph of a hand with a tool.

n–1020 seize Graphically identical to entry n-1019, but this element comes from a pictograph of a hand seizing a bent-over figure.

n–1027 thorn This combines a tree with a pointed element to suggest "thorn."

n–1028 pig A variant of PIG 279.

n–1032 bone A variant of VERTEBRA 474.

n–1036 shears From a pictograph of shears.

n–1039 utensil From a pictograph of a pair of hands holding up a kettle; came to mean "equipment."

n–1049 follow A very simplified variant of CHASE 1172.

n–1058 adze From a pictograph of an adze.

n–1065 exact A variant of BLOCK 1089.

n–1096 origin As a stand-alone character, this has the readings GEN, GAN, *moto*.

n–1099 mound From a pictograph of mounds of earth.

n–1104 hands From a pictograph of two hands reaching to open the gate.

n–1110 bar Phonetic meaning.

n–1123 walk From an old character meaning "walk." Includes SLOW PROGRESS 1218.

n–1128 fence Phonetic meaning.

n–1131 joined blocks Symbolic meaning suggesting, acc. to Henshall, "connected rooms."

n–1133 open up Phonetic meaning.

n–1135 arrow The whole character comes from a pictograph of an arrow reaching its destination.

n–1150 tower From a pictograph of a tower.

n–1152 castle From a pictograph of a castle.

n–1158 fast Phonetic meaning.

n–1169 multitude As a stand-alone character, this has the reading SHO.

n–1175 big An inversion of BIG 913.

n–1220 east From a doubling of EAST 91.

n–1223 bending person From a pictograph of a person bending to greet someone.

INDEX

亞	A 1082	扇	aogu......1119	謝	ayamaru.....765	母	BO 446	知	CHI.............560	柱	CHŪ............161
暴	abareru/ku...89	仰	aogu......1224	誤	ayamaru.....849	墓	BO 681	痴	CHI.............656	駐	CHŪ............292
浴	abiru 71	青	aoi 937	怪	ayashii	暴	BO 89	質	CHI...........1070	虫	CHŪ............304
危	abunai........664	荒	arai 661		/shimu.....503	棒	BO 162	乳	chi 449	仲	CHŪ............379
油	abura 77	争	arasou 593	操	ayatsuru 570	剖	BO 248	血	chi 506	忠	CHŪ............515
脂	abura 271	新	arata........1001	危	ayaui 664	肪	BO 274	千	chi 910	抽	CHŪ............587
徒	ada 624	改	aratameru	歩	ayumu.......1207	乏	BO 365	父	chichi 437	注	CHŪ............736
崇	agameru 705		/maru......803	鮮	azayaka.....283	傍	BO 390	乳	chichi 449	中	CHŪ............950
上	agaru	洗	arau 68	畔	aze 207	亡	BO 660	契	chigi 1061	駄	DA.............303
	/geru 942	荒	areru	馬	BA 291	忙	BO 662	小	chiisai 926	蛇	DA.............312
挙	ageru 612		/rasu......661	場	ba 28	忘	BO 663	近	chikai 1174	妥	DA.............431
揚	ageru	在	aru 873	罰	BACHI......1030	妄	BO 669	力	chikara 745	打	DA...........1044
	/garu 26	歩	aruku 1207	培	BAI 246	坊	BO 702	警	chikau......1074	代	DAI.............376
顎	ago 530	朝	asa 9	賠	BAI 247	貿	BO 725	竹	CHIKU 123	弟	DAI.............439
愛	AI 516	浅	asai 72	倍	BAI 631	矛	BO 806	逐	CHIKU 289	台	DAI.............455
間	aida 1105	汗	ase 74	陪	BAI 632	紡	BO 967	築	CHIKU 1055	大	DAI.............913
赤	akai 929	汗	asebamu 74	賈	BAI 707	防	BO 1098	賃	CHIN 721	内	DAI.............952
明	akarui............8	焦	aseru 320	化	bakeru 374	房	BO 1118	閑	CHIN 1109	濁	DAKU 309
証	akashi 829	足	ashi 617	暴	BAKU 89	凹	boko 917	散	chiru/rakaru	男	DAN 419
暁	akatsuki 20	与	ataeru 835	爆	BAKU 90	木	BOKU 126		/rasu 809	暖	DAN 605
明	akeru 8	価	atai 996	麦	BAKU 211	牧	BOKU 276	秩	CHITSU 227	弾	DAN 825
開	akeru 1104	頭	atama 529	縛	BAKU 776	目	BOKU 538	頂	CHŌ 528	談	DAN 850
秋	aki 41	新	atarashii...1001	幕	BAKU 1013	墨	BOKU 932	貯	CHO 727	断	DAN 1069
商	akinau 630	辺	atari 1173	晩	BAN 17	盆	BON 258	朝	CHŌ 9	出	dasu 955
悪	AKU 522	当	ataru/teru ...595	板	BAN 156	煩	BON 526	釣	CHŌ 108	奪	DATSU 322
空	aku. 196	暖	atatakai/maru	盤	BAN 260	凡	BON 1056	鳥	CHŌ 314	弟	DE..............439
飽	aku/kiru/kasu...		/meru 605	蛮	BAN 308	没	BOTSU 791	腸	CHŌ 476	凸	deko 918
	947	温	atatakai	判	BAN 1035	奉	BU 703	脹	CHŌ 481	電	DEN 49
雨	ama 45		/meru 7	末	BATSU 145	武	BU 798	聴	CHŌ 549	伝	DEN 52
天	ama 688	跡	ato 618	抜	BATSU 606	無	BU 958	挑	CHŌ 573	田	DEN 201
甘	amai/eru	圧	ATSU 875	伐	BATSU 800	不	BU 959	跳	CHŌ 619	殿	DEN 1122
	/yakasu..272	暑	atsui 405	罰	BATSU 1030	分	BU 1025	提	CHŌ 623	出	deru 955
余	amari/ru/su ...	集	atsumeru	閥	BATSU 1106	文	BUN 837	忌	CHŌ 682	土	DO 101
	1161		/maru......129	辺	be 1173	分	BUN 1025	彫	CHŌ 878	怒	DO 519
雨	ame 45	会	au 364	弁	BEN 1041	聞	BUN 1112	長	CHŌ 915	奴	DO 520
網	ami 984	逢	au 1220	紅	beni 930	豚	buta 285	張	CHŌ 916	洞	DŌ 63
編	amu 966	合	au	別	BETSU 1032	物	BUTSU 277	帳	CHŌ 1011	胴	DŌ 475
暗	AN 10		/waseru 583	美	BI 287	仏	BUTSU 684	町	CHŌ 1088	道	DŌ 534
安	AN 429	泡	awa 948	備	BI 384	苗	BYŌ 208	丁	CHŌ 1089	導	DŌ 535
闇	AN 1107	淡	awai 87	鼻	BI 470	平	BYŌ 921	庁	CHŌ 1138	同	DŌ 889
行	AN 1192	慌	awateru	尾	BI 533	着	CHAKU 288	兆	CHŌ 1170	堂	DŌ 1130
穴	ana 195		/tadashii..668	微	BI 810	嫡	CHAKU 680	重	CHŌ 1202	動	DŌ 1200
姉	ane 440	肖	ayakaru 268	瓶	BIN 256	地	CHI 102	昼	CHŪ 16	働	DŌ 1204
兄	ani 438	過	ayamachi ...694	貧	BIN 710	恥	CHI 548	沖	CHŪ 61	溝	dobu 999

207

INDEX

毒	DOKU......210
読	DOKU......856
曇	DON......47
殿	-dono......1122
枝	e......150
重	e......1202
会	E......364
恵	E......773
枝	eda......150
映	EI......5
栄	EI......127
影	EI......1080
易	EKI......23
益	EKI......257
駅	EKI......301
疫	EKI......658
役	EKI......1196
笑	emu......471
淵	EN......62
炎	EN......86
塩	EN......244
宴	EN......430
援	EN......604
円	EN......712
園	EN......781
択	erabu......568
獲	eru......342
悦	ETSU......518
越	ETSU......622
浮	FU......75
富	FU......204
膚	FU......351
婦	FU......423
夫	FU......434
扶	FU......435
父	FU......437
怖	FU......505
赴	FU......626
負	FU......716
付	FU......771
附	FU......772
賦	FU......799
不	FU......959
布	FU......1008
府	FU......1137
風	FŪ......44
富	FŪ......204
夫	FŪ......434
封	FŪ......760
淵	fuchi......62
筆	fude......592
伏	FUKU......369
服	FUKU......1019
吹	fuku......556
含	fukumu
	/meru......893
膨	fukuramu
	/reru......481
文	fumi......837
雰	FUN......53
粉	FUN......222
奮	FUN......321
憤	FUN......523
分	FUN......1025
舟	funa-......1180
船	funa-......1183
舟	fune......1180
船	fune......1183
触	fureru......310
降	furu......1217
古	furui......671
奮	furuu......321
震	furuu/eru......50
房	fusa......1118
防	fusegu......1098
伏	fusu/seru......369
二	futa-......898
太	futoi/ru......914
沸	FUTSU......78
彿	FUTSU......524
払	FUTSU......574
仏	FUTSU......684
冬	fuyu......42
餓	GA......234
雅	GA......495
我	GA......794
画	GA......880
外	GAI......13
街	GAI......1191
顎	GAKU......530
学	GAKU......839
楽	GAKU......882
岩	GAN......189
含	GAN......893
丸	GAN......919
月	GATSU......14
外	GE......13
夏	GE......40
華	GE......118
解	GE......278
下	GE......943
芸	GEI......117
鯨	GEI......361
迎	GEI......1223
劇	GEKI......346
撃	GEKI......788
源	GEN......79
原	GEN......81
弦	GEN......821
言	GEN......840
幻	GEN......881
嫌	GEN......1046
月	GETSU......14
戯	GI......350
議	GI......452
義	GI......795
疑	GI......822
吟	GIN......34
午	GO......32
娯	GO......413
互	GO......578
護	GO......811
呉	GO......834
語	GO......847
悟	GO......848
誤	GO......849
五	GO......901
強	GŌ......313
拷	GŌ......407
合	GŌ......583
号	GŌ......908
轟	GŌ......1198
極	GOKU......133
獄	GOKU......843
権	GON......131
言	GON......840
毎	-goto......443
灰	hai......192
入	hairu......954
恥	haji......548
始	hajimeru
	/maru......414
恥	hajiru
	/zukashii...548
墓	haka......681
図	hakaru......777
計	hakaru......885
箱	hako......163
運	hakobu......757
拍	HAKU......576
白	HAKU......936
迫	HAKU......1160
吐	haku......559
掃	haku......1048
履	haku......1123
坂	HAN......99
板	HAN......156
畔	HAN......207
飯	HAN......237
煩	HAN......526
犯	HAN......666
販	HAN......726
班	HAN......741
版	HAN......866
半	HAN......907
反	HAN......957
帆	HAN......1012
判	HAN......1035
凡	HAN......1056
般	HAN......1182
花	hana......116
華	hana......118
鼻	hana......470
離	hanareru
	/su......318
放	hanasu
	/tsu......389
背	HAI......483
敗	HAI......812
排	HAI......961
俳	HAI......962
拝	HAI.........
配	HAI......254
羽	hane......330
跳	haneru......619
原	hara......81
払	harau......574
腸	harawata......476
晴	hareru......938
針	hari......109
春	haru......43
張	haru......916
挟	hasamaru
	/mu......575
端	hashi......177
橋	hashi......367
柱	hashira......161
走	hashiru......625
端	hata......177
畑	hata......206
旗	hata......387
機	hata......970
働	hataraku......1204
果	hatasu......240
果	hate......240
髪	HATSU......537
伐	HATSU......800
早	hayai......19
迅	hayai......1158
速	hayai......1159
林	hayashi......142
辱	hazukashimeru
	770
弾	hazumu......825
外	hazusu......13
蛇	hebi......312
並	HEI......633
兵	HEI......754
平	HEI......921
坪	HEI......923
陛	HEI......1097
閉	HEI......1103
塀	HEI......1128
癖	HEKI......1003
凹	hekomu......917
片	HEN......865

208

INDEX

編	HEN...966	久	hisashii...33	干	hosu...73	因	IN...653	自	JI...542	塾	JUKU...1152
返	HEN...1163	浸	hitasu/ru...1050	彫	horu...878	員	IN...730	耳	JI...551	旬	JUN...37
辺	HEN...1173	人	hito...363	掘	horu...1129	印	IN...862	次	JI...555	順	JUN...527
日	hi...1	一	hito-...897	星	hoshi...216	音	IN...883	事	JI...590	巡	JUN...1157
陽	hi...27	均	hitoshii...888	欲	hoshii...171	院	IN...1096	寺	JI...685	遵	JUN...1164
火	hi...83	泌	HITSU...497	細	hosoi...986	否	ina...963	持	JI...690	日	-ka...1
灯	hi...84	筆	HITSU...592	蛍	hotaru...305	否	inamu...963	時	JI...691	蚊	ka...306
飛	HI...327	匹	HITSU...876	仏	hotoke...684	犬	inu...335	示	JI...701	夏	KA...40
比	HI...394	羊	hitsuji...290	百	HYAKU...909	入	ireru/ru...954	璽	JI...742	火	KA...83
批	HI...399	帆	ho...1012	氷	HYŌ...94	色	iro...927	除	JI...1165	花	KA...116
肥	HI...465	捕	HO...774	拍	HYŌ...576	彩	irodoru...928	路	ji...1214	華	KA...118
皮	HI...486	逋	HO...1171	兵	HYŌ...754	射	iru...764	軸	JIKU...1190	嫁	KA...223
披	HI...487	歩	HO...1207	評	HYŌ...922	要	iru...991	人	JIN...363	香	KA...224
疲	HI...490	芳	HŌ...119	票	HYŌ...993	勇	isamashii...746	仁	JIN...368	科	KA...229
泌	HI...497	崩	HŌ...174	標	HYŌ...994	石	ishi...190	神	JIN...697	課	KA...239
悲	HI...504	峰	HŌ...175	易	I...23	忙	isogashii...662	刃	JIN...1024	果	KA...240
卑	HI...644	方	HŌ...386	位	I...370	急	isogu...502	陣	JIN...1095	家	KA...281
碑	HI...646	放	HŌ...389	威	I...432	板	ita...156	迅	JIN...1158	荷	KA...371
費	HI...709	訪	HŌ...391	医	I...652	頂	itadaki...528	焦	jireru...320	化	KA...374
非	HI...960	胞	HŌ...479	遺	I...729	頂	itadaku...528	日	JITSU...1	嫁	KA...428
否	HI...963	抱	HŌ...581	以	I...887	痛	itai/mu	助	JO...181	靴	KA...488
避	HI...1002	奉	HŌ...703	維	I...989		/meru...654	女	JO...411	歌	KA...552
扉	HI...1121	封	HŌ...760	衣	I...1021	悼	itamu...507	除	JO...1165	禍	KA...693
左	hidari...601	宝	HŌ...784	一	ICHI...897	至	itari/ru...1135	場	jō...28	過	KA...694
東	higashi...91	包	HŌ...944	市	ichi...1084	徒	itazura...624	量	JŌ...209	貨	KA...723
秀	hiideru...846	砲	HŌ...945	抱	(i)daku...581	終	ito...964	剰	JŌ...416	何	KA...896
肱	hiji...468	飽	HŌ...947	挑	idomu...573	一	ITSU...897	浄	JŌ...594	下	KA...943
聖	hijiri...550	泡	HŌ...948	家	ie...281	乙	ITSU...911	丈	JŌ...894	価	KA...996
光	hikari...869	報	HŌ...1020	怒	ikaru...519	逸	ITSU...1169	情	JŌ...940	角	kado...280
光	hikaru...869	彷	HŌ...1195	城	IKI...98	五	itsu-...901	上	JŌ...942	門	kado...1101
匹	hiki...876	程	hodo...739	憤	ikidōru...523	言	iu...840	縄	JŌ...979	省	kaerimiru...541
弾	hiku...825	施	hodokosu...388	生	ikiru...214	岩	iwa...189	成	JŌ...1065	帰	kaeru...1049
低	hikui...392	外	hoka...13	育	IKU...830	嫌	iya...1046	城	JŌ...1066	返	kaeru
貧	HIN...710	矛	hoko...806	幾	iku...969	卑	iyashii	盛	JŌ...1067		/su...1163
品	HIN...1038	誉	homare...613	行	iku...1192		/shimu...645	辱	JOKU...770	鏡	kagami...106
開	hiraku...1104	葬	hōmuru...636	戦	ikusa...823	医	iyasu...652	授	JU...608	輝	kagayaku/kashii
平	hiratai...921	本	HON...125	今	ima...31	泉	izumi...80	受	JU...610		...755
広	hiroi	翻	HON...329	戒	imashimeru	蛇	JA...312	汁	JŪ...243	影	kage...1080
	/geru...1139	骨	hone...472		...793	弱	JAKU...819	獣	JŪ...336	海	KAI...67
拾	hirou...584	炎	honō...86	妹	imōto...441	児	JI...22	拾	JŪ...584	械	KAI...155
昼	hiru...16	洞	hora...63	忌	imu/mawashii	地	JI...102	従	JŪ...621	灰	KAI...192
干	hiru...73	堀	hori...1127		...683	磁	JI...188	住	JŪ...735	介	KAI...202
翻	hirugaeru	滅	horobiru	飲	IN...236	仕	JI...372	十	JŪ...906	界	KAI...203
	/su...329		/bosu...789	姻	IN...422	侍	JI...381	重	JŪ...1202	解	KAI...278

INDEX

会	KAI..........364	館	KAN..........233	方	kata..........386	係	KEI..........976	鬼	KI..........645	極	kiwamaru...133
快	KAI..........500	甘	KAN..........272	肩	kata..........484	系	KEI..........977	気	KI..........650	清	kiyoi
怪	KAI..........503	観	KAN..........332	片	kata..........865	刑	KEI..........1026	危	KI..........664		/meru..........941
貝	KAI..........708	勧	KAN..........333	形	kata..........920	型	KEI..........1033	忌	KI..........683	刻	kizamu.....1028
戒	KAI..........793	歓	KAN..........334	型	kata..........1033	京	KEI..........1077	貴	KI..........728	兆	kizashi
改	KAI..........803	甲	KAN..........357	形	katachi..........920	景	KEI..........1079	輝	KI..........755		/su..........1170
回	KAI..........1042	姦	KAN..........412	敵	kataki..........678	径	KEI..........1193	揮	KI..........758	築	kizuku.....1055
開	KAI..........1104	官	KAN..........467	刀	katana..........1023	権	KEN..........131	幾	KI..........969	児	ko..........22
街	KAI..........1191	患	KAN..........514	語	kataru..........847	研	KEN..........187	機	KI..........970	粉	ko..........222
抱	kakaeru.....581	看	KAN..........539	傍	katawara....390	験	KEN..........297	希	KI..........1009	子	ko..........447
係	kakari..........976	緩	KAN..........603	糧	kate..........219	剣	KEN..........298	器	KI..........1040	鼓	KO..........147
拘	kakawaru.....858	貫	KAN..........718	滑	KATSU..........477	検	KEN..........299	帰	KI..........1049	虎	KO..........352
囲	kakomu/u...783	巻	KAN..........863	渇	KATSU..........946	険	KEN..........300	軌	KI..........1188	己	KO..........445
嚇	KAKU..........88	刊	KAN..........1031	且	katsu..........182	繭	KEN..........307	企	KI..........1206	呼	KO..........562
種	KAKU..........230	閑	KAN..........1102	買	kau..........707	犬	KEN..........335	木	ki..........126	口	KO..........566
角	KAKU..........280	間	KAN..........1105	川	kawa..........55	肩	KEN..........484	吉	KICHI..........557	古	KO..........671
鶴	KAKU..........317	関	KAN..........1110	革	kawa..........485	見	KEN..........543	消	kieru..........270	枯	KO..........672
獲	KAKU..........342	金	kana..........105	皮	kawa..........486	絹	KEN..........965	菊	KIKU..........113	故	KO..........673
革	KAKU..........485	悲	kanashii	渇	kawaku..........946	嫌	KEN..........1046	利	kiku..........226	弧	KO..........820
覚	KAKU..........545		/shimu......504	代	kawaru	兼	KEN..........1051	聴	kiku..........549	戸	KO..........1113
較	KAKU..........833	芳	kanbashii...119		/eru..........376	間	KEN..........1105	聞	kiku/koeru	庫	KO..........1140
画	KAKU..........880	金	kane..........105	交	kawasu..........831	消	kesu..........270		1112	拠	KO..........1211
核	KAKU..........1029	兼	kaneru.....1051	通	kayou..........1156	穴	KETSU..........195	決	kimaru	晃	KŌ..........4
拡	KAKU..........1136	考	kangaeru..409	風	kaze..........44	決	KETSU..........501		/meru..........501	港	KŌ..........64
郭	KAKU..........1151	香	kaoru/ri..224	家	KE..........281	血	KETSU..........506	君	kimi..........417	坑	KŌ..........103
各	KAKU..........1209	空	kara..........196	化	KE..........374	頁	KETSU..........525	今	KIN..........31	抗	KŌ..........104
閣	KAKU..........1213	唐	kara..........1083	怪	KE..........503	欠	KETSU..........553	金	KIN..........105	耕	KŌ..........212
客	KAKU..........1216	体	karada..........134	気	KE..........650	険	kewashii..........300	勤	KIN..........114	香	KŌ..........224
書	kaku..........596	辛	karai..........1005	希	KE..........1009	削	kezuru..........269	筋	KIN..........480	酵	KŌ..........252
欠	kaku/keru...553	絡	karamu	景	KE..........1079	季	KI..........36	琴	KIN..........737	甲	KŌ..........357
窯	kama..........197		/maru..1212	毛	ke..........532	汽	KI..........69	均	KIN..........888	孝	KŌ..........403
構	kamau	枯	kareru·	獣	ke(da)mono..336	岐	KI..........151	斤	KIN..........1072	考	KŌ..........409
	/eru..........1000		/rasu..........672	汚	kegareru/su	機	KI..........157	近	KIN..........1174	好	KŌ..........448
瓶	kame..........256	狩	kari/ru..........340		/rawashii..70	崎	KI..........178	絹	kinu..........965	公	KŌ..........457
亀	kame..........356	刈	karu..........1036	茎	KEI..........112	奇	KI..........179	嫌	kirau/i..........1046	肱	KŌ..........468
髪	kami..........537	傘	kasa..........1043	敬	KEI..........295	寄	KI..........180	着	kiru..........288	荒	KŌ..........661
神	kami..........697	重	kasaneru	警	KEI..........296	飢	KI..........235	切	kiru..........1034	慌	KŌ..........668
上	kami..........942		/naru..1202	蛍	KEI..........305	騎	KI..........302	競	kisou	幸	KŌ..........731
紙	kami..........974	稼	kasegu..........223	兄	KEI..........438	亀	KI..........356		/seru..........628	皇	KŌ..........740
雷	kaminari..........48	森	kashimashii	携	KEI..........567	旗	KI..........387	汚	kitanai..........70	攻	KŌ..........813
干	KAN..........73		412	鏡	KEI..........628	規	KI..........436	吉	KITSU..........557	交	KŌ..........831
汗	KAN..........74	頭	kashira..........529	恵	KEI..........773	己	KI..........445	際	kiwa..........706	校	KŌ..........832
寒	KAN..........93	貸	kasu..........724	計	KEI..........885	肌	KI..........473	窮	kiwamaru	較	KŌ..........833
管	KAN..........121	幽	kasuka..........172	形	KEI..........920	起	KI..........620		/meru..........200	拘	KŌ..........858

210

INDEX

光	KŌ......869	穀	KOKU......225	九	KU......905	企	kuwadateru...... 1206	宮	KYŪ......1131	待	matsu......686
紅	KŌ......930	酷	KOKU......255	紅	KU......930	詳	kuwashii......284	魔	MA......641	祭	matsuri......700
絞	KŌ......981	克	KOKU......675	功	KU......1053	崩	kuzureru	馬	ma......291	政	matsurigoto...... 815
講	KŌ......997	国	KOKU......779	工	KU......1054		/su......174	間	ma......1105	祭	matsuru......700
購	KŌ......998	黒	KOKU......931	貢	KU......1057	客	KYAKU......1216	目	ma-......538	回	mawaru/
溝	KŌ......999	刻	KOKU......1028	宮	KU......1131	許	KYO......38	幻	maboroshi...... 881		/su......1042
構	KŌ......1000	細	komakai......986	空	KŪ......196	共	KYŌ......383	町	machi......1088	迷	mayou......1154
功	KŌ......1053	困	komaru......786	配	kubaru......254	胸	KYŌ......478	街	machi......1191	繭	mayu......307
工	KŌ......1054	米	kome......217	首	kubi......531	挙	KYŌ......612	未	mada......144	拙	mazui......571
貢	KŌ......1057	込	komu/meru......953	凹	kubo......917	拠	KYŌ......1211	曲	magaru/geru.... 877	貧	mazushii......710
杠	KŌ......1061	今	KON......31	口	kuchi......566	鏡	KYŌ......106	孫	mago......444	女	me......411
興	KŌ......1085	金	KON......105	管	kuda......121	峡	KYŌ......176	枚	MAI......141	目	me......538
郊	KŌ......1091	昆	KON......397	下	kudaru......943	驚	KYŌ......294	米	MAI......217	恵	megumu......773
広	KŌ......1139	婚	KON......433	鯨	kujira......361	強	KYŌ......313	妹	MAI......441	巡	meguru......1157
高	KŌ......1150	魂	KON......643	茎	kuki......112	僑	KYŌ......366	毎	MAI......443	明	MEI......8
航	KŌ......1181	困	KON......786	組	kumi......183	橋	KYŌ......367	埋	MAI......676	鳴	MEI......315
行	KŌ......1192	紺	KON......934	雲	kumo......46	供	KYŌ......382	交	majiru......831	銘	MEI......563
降	KŌ......1217	恨	KON......1177	曇	kumoru......47	教	KYŌ......404	賄	makanau......732	名	MEI......565
仰	KŌ......1224	粉	kona......222	酌	kumu......264	兄	KYŌ......438	任	makaseru......720	迷	MEI......1154
甲	kōra......357	好	konomu	組	kumi......183	叫	KYŌ......558	負	makeru	妾	mekake......426
氷	kōri......94		/mashii......448	君	KUN......417	挟	KYŌ......575		/kasu......716	盲	mekura......670
郡	kōri......1092	転	korobu/garu	訓	KUN......851	競	KYŌ......628	薪	maki......140	面	MEN......469
凍	kōru......92		/geru	勲	KUN......1203	凶	KYŌ......647	牧	maki......276	綿	MEN......1014
木	ko-......126		/gasu......1199	国	kuni......779	兇	KYŌ......648	巻	maki......863	免	MEN......1167
小	ko-......926	衣	koromo......1021	比	kuraberu......394	狂	KYŌ......744	誠	makoto......1068	飯	meshi......237
越	koeru	殺	korosu......149	暗	kurai......10	脅	KYŌ......747	幕	MAKU......1013	滅	METSU......789
	/su......622	腰	koshi......992	位	kurai......370	協	KYŌ......748	巻	maku......863	未	MI......144
肥	koeru/	答	kotaeru......861	呉	kureru......834	京	KYŌ......1077	豆	mame......245	魅	MI......642
	yasu......465	事	koto......590	紅	kurenai......930	興	KYŌ......1085	守	mamoru......339	身	mi......459
焦	kogeru	琴	koto......737	黒	kuroi......931	極	KYOKU......133	満	MAN......892	三	mi-......899
	/gasu......320	言	koto......840	繰	kuru......968	曲	KYOKU......877	学	manabu......839	道	michi......534
凍	kogoeru......92	詞	kotoba......853	来	kuru......1219	旧	KYŪ......21	免	manukareru	導	michibiku......535
恋	koi......513	異	kotonaru......325	俥	kuruma......1185	久	KYŪ......33		1167	満	michiru
恋	koishii......513	断	kotowaru	車	kuruma......1187	休	KYŪ......138	丸	maru......919		/tasu......892
九	kokono-......905		1069	苦	kurushii	究	KYŪ......194	円	marui......712	妄	midari......669
心	kokoro......499	骨	KOTSU......472		/shimu......674	窮	KYŪ......200	丸	marui......919	緑	midori......935
試	kokoromiru	怖	kowai......505	狂	kuruu......744	及	KYŪ......373	将	masa......768	右	migi......602
	828	挙	kozotte......612	鎖	kusari......107	急	KYŪ......502	益	masu......257	耳	mimi......551
快	kokoroyoi...500	久	KU......33	癖	kuse......1003	吸	KYŪ......561	升	masu......263	民	MIN......395
志	kokorozashi	供	KU......382	薬	kusuri......879	泣	KYŪ......629	末	MATSU......145	眼	MIN......540
	511	口	KU......566	屈	KUTSU......1125	弓	KYŪ......817	抹	MATSU......586	源	minamoto......79
志	kokorozasu	苦	KU......674	掘	KUTSU......1129	九	KYŪ......905	松	matsu......458	港	minato......64
	511	区	KU......780	靴	kutsu......488	糾	KYŪ......973			峰	mine......175
谷	KOKU......168	句	KU......857	食	kuu......232						

211

INDEX

醜	minikui 640	務	MU 805	何	nan 896	残	nokoru/su ... 637	踊	odoru 615		/maru 814
看	miru 539	矛	MU 806	七	nana- 903	飲	nomu 236	躍	odoru 616	収	osameru
視	miru 544	無	MU 958	何	nani 896	則	nori 711	威	odosu 432		/maru 895
見	miru/seru	六	mu- 902	並	narabi	典	nori 870	嚇	odosu	教	oshieru 404
	/eru 543	麦	mugi 211		/bu 633	載	noru/seru .1184		/kasu 88	虞	osore 349
操	misao 570	迎	mukaeru ...1223	習	narau 326	則	nottoru 711	老	oi 410	襲	osou 359
店	mise 1145	報	mukuiru 1020	成	naru/su 1065	除	nozoku 1165	老	oiru 410	雄	osu 418
認	mitomeru .. 852	胸	muna 478	情	nasake 940	抽	nuku 587	犯	okasu 666	押	osu 588
貢	mitsugu ... 1057	旨	mune 273	納	NATSU 956	抜	nuku/karu/keru	沖	oki 61	推	osu 874
宮	miya 1131	胸	mune 478	夏	natsu 40		/kasu 606	起	okiru/koru	音	oto 883
都	miyako 1090	群	mura 282	苗	nawa 208	布	nuno 1008		/kosu 620	弟	otōto 439
溝	mizo 999	村	mura 1087	縄	nawa 979	主	nushi 734	行	okonau 1192	男	otoko 419
水	mizu 57	群	mure/reru .. 282	悩	nayamashii	盗	nusumu 262	怒	okoru 519	劣	otoru 756
自	mizukara .. 542	室	muro 1134		/mu	女	NYO 411	興	okosu	訪	otozureru ... 391
茂	MO 115	虫	mushi 304		/masu 649	女	NYŌ 411		/ru 1085	乙	OTSU 911
猛	MŌ 337	脈	MYAKU 482	音	ne 883	尿	NYŌ 461	屋	OKU 1120	夫	otto 434
毛	MŌ 532	名	MYŌ 565	眠	nemui/ri/	乳	NYŪ 449	奥	oku 782	遂	ou 289
亡	MŌ 660	明	MYŌ 8		ru 540	入	NYŪ 954	贈	okuru 733	負	ou 716
妄	MŌ 669	苗	MYŌ 208	眠	nemuru 1064	尾	o 533	面	omo 469	追	ou 1172
盲	MŌ 670	妙	MYŌ 427	年	NEN 30	汚	o 70	主	omo 734	終	owaru
網	MŌ 984	納	NA 956	念	NEN 35	悪	O 522	重	omoi 1202		/eru 980
申	mōsu 698	菜	na 241	児	NI 22	和	O 564	赴	omomuku ... 626	親	oya 547
用	mochiiru .. 385	名	na 565	仁	NI 368	押	Ō 588	錘	omori 1063	及	oyobi/bu
木	MOKU 126	嬲	naburu 416	二	NI 898	皇	Ō 740	面	omote 469		/bosu 373
目	MOKU 538	苗	nae 208	弐	NI 912	王	Ō 743	思	omou 517	凡	oyoso 1056
文	MON 837	長	nagai 915	荷	ni 371	奥	Ō 782	温	ON 7	頁	pēji 525
紋	MON 838	流	nagareru	日	NICHI 1	殴	Ō 796	恩	ON 657	羅	RA 988
門	MON 1101		/su 58	苦	nigai 674	凹	Ō 917	音	ON 883	裸	RA 1018
問	MON 1111	投	nageru 572	逃	nigeru	央	Ō 951	同	onaji 889	雷	RAI 48
聞	MON 1112	和	nagoyaka ... 564	濁	nigoru/su ... 309	往	Ō 1194	鬼	oni 645	来	RAI 1219
物	mono 277	殴	naguru 796	肉	NIKU 266	扇	ōgi 1119	女	onna 411	酪	RAKU 253
者	mono 408	内	NAI 952	人	NIN 363	多	ōi 890	各	ono-ono ... 1209	楽	RAKU 882
専	moppara ... 775	無	nai/shi 958	忍	NIN 510	大	ōkii 913	己	onore 445	絡	RAKU 1212
森	mori 143	仲	naka 379	任	NIN 720	仰	ōse 1224	折	ori 1071	落	RAKU 1215
盛	moru 1067	中	naka 950	認	NIN 852	公	ōyake 457	下	oriru 943	卵	RAN 242
漏	moru/reru	半	nakaba 907	煮	niru/eru	雄	o- 418	降	oriru	覧	RAN 546
	/rasu 1126	泣	naku 629		/yasu 406	小	o- 926		/rosu 1217	麗	REI 344
許	moto 38	鳴	naku/ru 315	脳	NO 462	脅	obiyakasu ... 747	織	oru 971	齢	REI 494
本	moto 125	亡	nakunaru .. 660	悩	NŌ 649	覚	oboeru 545	折	oru	霊	REI 634
素	moto 985	生	nama 214	納	NŌ 956	落	ochiru		/reru 1071	礼	REI 692
物	MOTSU ... 277	滑	nameraka ... 477	上	noboru 942		/tosu 1215	押	osaeru 588	励	REI 750
持	motsu 690	並	nami 633	逃	nogareru	脅	odo(ka)su ... 747	抑	osaeru 1225	恋	REN 513
以	motte 887	涙	namida 1115		/su 1166	驚	odoroku	納	osameru 956	廉	REN 1045
武	MU 798	男	NAN 419				/kasu 294	修	osameru	連	REN 1186

INDEX

裂	RETSU	638
烈	RETSU	639
劣	RETSU	756
利	RI	226
離	RI	318
裏	RI	1017
里	RI	1087
履	RI	1123
律	RICHI	591
力	RIKI	745
陸	RIKU	1099
林	RIN	142
隣	RIN	220
倫	RIN	375
輪	RIN	1189
律	RITSU	591
立	RITSU	627
露	RO	51
炉	RO	1117
路	RO	1214
露	RŌ	51
糧	RŌ	219
老	RŌ	410
労	RŌ	749
漏	RŌ	1126
鹿	ROKU	343
六	ROKU	902
緑	ROKU	935
論	RON	864
流	RU	58
留	RU	983
累	RUI	978
涙	RUI	1115
略	RYAKU	205
虜	RYO	348
旅	RYO	1015
糧	RYŌ	219
料	RYŌ	221
猟	RYŌ	341
漁	RYŌ	355
竜	RYŌ	358
霊	RYŌ	634
了	RYŌ	836
両	RYŌ	891
涼	RYŌ	1078
力	RYOKU	745
緑	RYOKU	935
流	RYŪ	58
柳	RYŪ	128
粒	RYŪ	218
竜	RYŪ	358
立	RYŪ	627
留	RYŪ	983
隆	RYŪ	1100
鎖	SA	107
砂	SA	193
佐	SA	380
左	SA	601
詐	SA	1058
欺	SA	1060
裁	sabaku	1022
幸	sachi	731
遮	saegiru	1168
性	saga	509
下	sagaru/geru	943
捜	sagasu	569
探	sagasu	198
提	sageru	623
探	saguru	198
災	SAI	60
採	SAI	132
裁	SAI	136
財	SAI	154
菜	SAI	241
妻	SAI	424
祭	SAI	700
際	SAI	706
債	SAI	719
才	SAI	871
彩	SAI	928
細	SAI	986
宰	SAI	1004
裁	SAI	1022
切	SAI	1034
載	SAI	1184
遮	saigiru	1168
幸	saiwai	731
坂	saka	99
酒	saka	250
栄	sakaeru	127
魚	sakana	354
逆	sakarau	1175
盛	sakaru/n	1067
逆	sakasa	1175
酒	saké	250
叫	sakebu	558
避	sakeru	1002
崎	saki	178
柵	SAKU	160
削	SAKU	269
作	SAKU	1058
酢	SAKU	1059
裂	saku/keru	638
覚	sameru/masu	545
寒	samui	93
侍	samurai	381
士	samurai	753
算	SAN	122
山	SAN	167
産	SAN	213
散	SAN	809
三	SAN	899
傘	SAN	1043
皿	sara	261
支	sasaeru	148
誘	sasou	845
刺	sasu/saru	1027
里	sato	1087
悟	satoru	848
殺	SATSU	149
冊	SATSU	868
騒	sawagu/gashii	293
触	sawaru	310
授	sazukeru	608
施	SE	388
世	SE	1081
背	se	483
整	SEI	165
生	SEI	214
性	SEI	215
星	SEI	216
米	SEI	217
性	SEI	509
省	SEI	541
聖	SEI	550
政	SEI	815
正	SEI	826
青	SEI	937
晴	SEI	938
精	SEI	939
情	SEI	940
清	SEI	941
成	SEI	1065
盛	SEI	1067
誠	SEI	1068
誓	SEI	1074
逝	SEI	1075
世	SEI	1081
征	SEI	1197
背	sei	483
夕	SEKI	11
析	SEKI	139
石	SEKI	190
積	SEKI	228
跡	SEKI	618
尺	SEKI	884
赤	SEKI	929
斥	SEKI	1076
席	SEKI	1141
関	seki	1110
急	seku	502
迫	semaru	1160
攻	semeru	813
川	SEN	55
洗	SEN	68
浅	SEN	72
泉	SEN	80
銭	SEN	110
鮮	SEN	283
仙	SEN	377
専	SEN	775
戦	SEN	823
千	SEN	910
繊	SEN	972
線	SEN	975
扇	SEN	1119
占	SEN	1146
船	SEN	1183
雪	SETSU	96
殺	SETSU	149
接	SETSU	425
拙	SETSU	571
説	SETSU	860
切	SETSU	1034
折	SETSU	1071
砂	SHA	193
煮	SHA	406
者	SHA	408
社	SHA	696
射	SHA	764
謝	SHA	765
赦	SHA	933
遮	SHA	1168
車	SHA	1187
石	SHAKU	190
勺	SHAKU	264
酌	SHAKU	265
尺	SHAKU	884
赤	SHAKU	929
芝	SHI	111
肢	SHI	146
支	SHI	148
枝	SHI	151
脂	SHI	271
旨	SHI	273
仕	SHI	372
施	SHI	388
氏	SHI	396
孜	SHI	400
始	SHI	414
姿	SHI	415
姉	SHI	440
子	SHI	447
私	SHI	454
歯	SHI	491
志	SHI	511
誌	SHI	512
思	SHI	517
自	SHI	542
視	SHI	544
次	SHI	555
死	SHI	635
祉	SHI	699
示	SHI	701
賜	SHI	715
士	SHI	753
史	SHI	790
矢	SHI	818
試	SHI	828
詞	SHI	853
四	SHI	900
糸	SHI	964
紙	SHI	974
刺	SHI	1027
市	SHI	1084
至	SHI	1135
止	SHI	1205
幸	shiawase	731
芝	shiba	111
縛	shibaru	776
絞	shiboru	981
七	SHICHI	903
質	SHICHI	1070
柵	shigarami	160
茂	shigeru	115
虐	shiitageru	347
鹿	shika	343
式	SHIKI	827
識	SHIKI	841
色	SHIKI	927
織	SHIKI	971
島	shima	316
締	shimaru/meru	982
閉	shimaru/meru	1103
絞	shimeru	981
占	shimeru	1146
湿	shimeru/su	6
示	shimesu	701

INDEX

霜	shimo	97
下	shimo	943
震	SHIN	50
針	SHIN	109
薪	SHIN	140
森	SHIN	143
身	SHIN	459
心	SHIN	499
親	SHIN	547
神	SHIN	697
申	SHIN	698
信	SHIN	844
新	SHIN	1001
辛	SHIN	1005
浸	SHIN	1050
品	shina	1038
忍	shinobu	510
死	shinu	635
塩	shio	244
斥	shirizokeru	1076
退	shirizoku/keru	1176
城	shiro	1066
白	shiroi	936
汁	shiru	243
知	shiru	560
印	shirushi	862
標	shirushi	994
下	shita	943
従	shitagau	621
親	shitashii/shimu	547
滴	shitataru	679
湿	SHITSU	6
漆	SHITSU	164
失	SHITSU	577
疾	SHITSU	651
質	SHITSU	1070
室	SHITSU	1134
滴	shizuku	679
且	SHO	182
署	SHO	401
暑	SHO	405
書	SHO	596
所	SHO	1116
処	SHO	1210
昌	SHŌ	2
晶	SHŌ	3
昭	SHŌ	24
照	SHŌ	25
焼	SHŌ	85
生	SHŌ	214
星	SHŌ	216
升	SHŌ	263
肖	SHŌ	268
消	SHŌ	270
詳	SHŌ	284
祥	SHŌ	286
焦	SHŌ	320
象	SHŌ	345
荘	SHŌ	421
妾	SHŌ	426
訟	SHŌ	453
松	SHŌ	458
笑	SHŌ	509
性	SHŌ	471
省	SHŌ	541
掌	SHŌ	582
商	SHŌ	630
症	SHŌ	659
償	SHŌ	713
賞	SHŌ	714
奨	SHŌ	766
将	SHŌ	768
政	SHŌ	815
正	SHŌ	826
証	SHŌ	829
唱	SHŌ	859
抄	SHŌ	924
少	SHŌ	925
小	SHŌ	926
青	SHŌ	937
精	SHŌ	939
清	SHŌ	941
装	SHŌ	1016
匠	SHŌ	1073
床	SHŌ	1142
衝	SHŌ	1201
渉	SHŌ	1208
植	SHOKU	137
食	SHOKU	232
触	SHOKU	310
色	SHOKU	927
織	SHOKU	971
酒	SHU	250
守	SHU	339
狩	SHU	340
首	SHU	531
手	SHU	579
主	SHU	734
修	SHU	814
愁	SHŪ	39
秋	SHŪ	41
州	SHŪ	56
集	SHŪ	129
酬	SHŪ	259
習	SHŪ	326
襲	SHŪ	359
拾	SHŪ	584
醜	SHŪ	640
宗	SHŪ	704
囚	SHŪ	787
修	SHŪ	814
秀	SHŪ	846
収	SHŪ	895
終	SHŪ	980
舟	SHŪ	1180
宿	SHUKU	1132
春	SHUN	43
出	SHUTSU	955
且	SO	182
組	SO	183
阻	SO	184
祖	SO	185
抓	SO	496
訴	SO	842
素	SO	985
早	SŌ	19
霜	SŌ	97
巣	SŌ	130
騒	SŌ	293
壮	SŌ	420
荘	SŌ	421
抓	SŌ	496
捜	SŌ	569
操	SŌ	570
争	SŌ	593
走	SŌ	625
葬	SŌ	636
宗	SŌ	704
贈	SŌ	733
双	SŌ	804
繰	SŌ	968
装	SŌ	1016
掃	SŌ	1048
曹	SŌ	1221
槽	SŌ	1222
遭	SŌ	1220
育	sodatsu/teru	830
損	sokonau	717
束	SOKU	153
促	SOKU	614
足	SOKU	617
則	SOKU	711
速	SOKU	1159
背	somuku/keru	483
孫	SON	444
損	SON	717
尊	SON	767
存	SON	872
村	SON	1086
供	sonaeru	382
備	sonaeru	1039
供	sonaeru/waru	384
園	sono	781
空	sora	196
逸	soreru/rasu	1169
反	soru/rasu	957
注	sosogu	736
外	soto	13
卒	SOTSU	751
守	SU	339
子	SU	447
素	SU	985
州	su	56
巣	su	130
酢	su	1059
崇	SŪ	705
滑	suberu	477
末	sue	145
姿	sugata	415
過	sugiru/gosu	694
水	SUI	57
酔	SUI	251
炊	SUI	554
吹	SUI	556
推	SUI	874
垂	SUI	1062
錘	SUI	1063
睡	SUI	1064
筋	suji	480
少	sukoshi	925
好	suku	448
少	sukunai	925
炭	sumi	191
墨	sumi	932
速	sumiyaka	1159
住	sumu	735
寸	SUN	759
砂	suna	193
酢	suppai	1059
勧	susumeru	333
吸	suu	561
座	suwaru	378
涼	suzumu/shii	1078
多	TA	890
太	TA	914
田	ta	201
束	taba(neru)	153
食	taberu	232
旅	tabi	1015
正	tadashii/su	826
耐	taeru	769
互	tagai	578
耕	tagayasu	212
体	TAI	134
代	TAI	376
胎	TAI	451
台	TAI	455
逮	TAI	589
待	TAI	686
貸	TAI	724
対	TAI	762
耐	TAI	769
大	TAI	913
太	TAI	914
退	TAI	1176
平	taira	921
高	taka	1150
高	takai	1150
宝	takara	784
竹	take	123
丈	take	894
滝	taki	360
薪	takigi	140
拓	TAKU	186
濯	TAKU	323
卓	TAKU	508
択	TAKU	568
宅	TAKU	1133
炊	taku	554
貯	takuwaeru	727
霊	tama	634
魂	tama	643
玉	tama	785
弾	tama	825
卵	tamago	242
魂	tamashii	643
賜	tamawaru	715
試	tamesu	828
民	tami	395
旦	TAN	15
淡	TAN	87
端	TAN	177
炭	TAN	191
探	TAN	198
単	TAN	824